THE WADSWORTH CONTEMPORARY ISSUES IN CRIME AND JUSTICE SERIES

Todd Clear, Series Editor

Murder American Style

ALEX ALVAREZ
Northern Arizona University

RONET BACHMAN
University of Delaware

THOMSON
WADSWORTH

Australia • Canada • Mexico • Singapore • Spain
United Kingdom • United States

To Donna Mae Engleson
You have immeasurably enriched my life.
Thank you for your unconditional support.
A. A.

To Raymond Paternoster
For being the perfect safety net for a frequent faller! I love you.
R. B.

Acquisitions Editor: Sabra Horne
Assistant Editor: Dawn Mesa
Editorial Assistant: Lee McCracken
Marketing Manager: Dory Schaeffer
Marketing Associate: Neena Chandra
Project Manager, Editorial Production:
  Belinda Krohmer
Print/Media Buyer: Nancy Panziera

Permissions Editor: Elizabeth Zuber
Production Service: Gretchen Otto, G&S
  Typesetters, Inc.
Copy Editor: Jan Six
Cover Designer: Yvo Riezebos
Cover Printer: Webcom, Ltd.
Compositor: G&S Typesetters, Inc.
Printer: Webcom, Ltd.

Printed in Canada
2 3 4 5 6 7 06 05 04 03

For more information
about our products, contact us at:
**Thomson Learning Academic
Resource Center
1-800-423-0563**

For permission to use material from this text,
contact us by: **Phone:** 1-800-730-2214
Fax: 1-800-730-2215
Web: http://www.thomsonrights.com

Library of Congress Control Number:
2002106792
ISBN 0-534-53470-8

**Wadsworth / Thomson Learning
10 Davis Drive
Belmont, CA 94002-3098
USA**

Asia
Thomson Learning
5 Shenton Way #01-01
UIC Building
Singapore 068808

Australia
Nelson Thomson Learning
102 Dodds Street
South Melbourne, Victoria 3205
Australia

Canada
Nelson Thomson Learning
1120 Birchmount Road
Toronto, Ontario M1K 5G4
Canada

Europe/Middle East/Africa
Thomson Learning
High Holborn House
50/51 Bedford Row
London WC1R 4LR
United Kingdom

Contents

Foreword

Murder is the most troubling of crimes.

Some crimes cost the victims enormously, in financial and emotional ways, and we despise those crimes. Some crimes have many victims and make us catch our breath because of their cruelty. Offenses against children baffle and enrage us, and impersonal victimizations haunt us. But, because life is precious and the criminal taking of a life is almost unfathomable, there can be no doubt that murder is the most troubling offense that we encounter.

Yet murder is not unusual—especially in America. Other countries have rates of property crime that match or exceed ours, and there are places where kidnapping is frequent or where it is unwise to leave a car overnight. There are even a few countries where murder is more common than in America. But few countries have as rich or long-standing a tradition of murder as the United States. Our history of murder sets us apart from other Western, industrialized societies. The high rate at which we kill each other is a particular hallmark of American life. In years when some Western democracies have murders that number in the dozens, we have murders numbering in the tens of thousands. For some age and ethnic groups in the United States, murder is among the most common causes of death—more common than "natural causes."

And these murders are concentrated in other ways: being a resident in a poverty-stricken, marginalized neighborhood can mean being exposed to murder everyday. The large base rate of murder may define, in a nefarious way, something fundamental about America, but the way murder is concentrated among some groups and in some places also says something important about American society. Alex Kotlowitz, in his stunning ethnography of Chicago projects, *There Are No Children Here,* points out that the kids he spoke to did not say "When I grow up," but instead, "If I grow up."

Murder is committed in every culture and every society, but in America there is something especially significant about murder. We cannot fully understand American life and culture without confronting the reality of murder as a particularly American phenomenon.

That is why I am delighted to introduce *Murder American Style,* a superb, seminal text that considers in-depth the subject of murder in America. This book is a new addition to the Wadsworth Contemporary Issues in Crime and Justice Series. The series gives detailed attention to important topics and controversies in crime and justice that are not usually covered in detail in traditional textbooks. As editor of the series, I am pleased to welcome *Murder American Style* as an excellent illustration of the role this series plays in giving students of crime and justice in-depth analyses of important topics.

Professors Alvarez and Bachman investigate murder in its many manifestations. They begin with an overview of the prevalence and historical importance of murder and define its place among other crimes. They discuss legal types of murder and help us understand the important differences between what we often think when we hear the word *murder* and what we think when we hear other common terms for killing, such as *manslaughter* and *involuntary homicide*. Then they take us through a profound list of topics, such as who killers are and who they kill. They answer the questions of how murderers and their victims are related and what this relationship suggests about social interactions in American society. They also compare the phenomenon here to other societies and discuss what the results of this comparison say about us.

Of course, not all murders are alike, and so Alvarez and Bachman provide the reader with insights into certain types of killing. Which criminological theories explain murder at the individual level and which explain it at the societal level? What happens between intimates that leads to murder? How can we understand different kinds of murders as interactional processes gone awry? What distinguishes someone who murders a spouse or young family member from someone who murders a stranger? someone who murders once from someone who murders serially?

Then there are the questions of social policy. How do we understand American murder in terms of gun laws? How do alcohol and drugs relate to the propensity for murder? What about gangs and juvenile violence? Do racial and social inequality contribute to high rates of homicide? What can be done about the distressing problem of serial killing? Does our penchant for violence in the media contribute to our penchant for violence in the streets? Does capital punishment prevent murder? And perhaps equally significant, what can and should be done for the families of murder victims?

Professors Alvarez and Bachman have given us a very important and stunning book. Its penetrating coverage of the broad and complicated story of murder in America will change your thinking. It will arm you with new facts that clash with conventional views of this serious problem in our culture and legal system. It will challenge your beliefs about victims, offenders, and policies of criminal justice.

By far, murder is not the most common crime in America. But it is in many respects the most gripping public safety problem we face.

Todd R. Clear
New York City

Acknowledgments

Any project such as this book requires the assistance and support of many individuals. I would therefore like to begin by thanking my co-author and close friend Ronet Bachman. It truly has been a privilege to work with her and an even greater gift to have her as a close personal friend. I value her friendship more than I can express. I also want to thank Sabra Horne, the editor at Wadsworth Group/Thomson Learning for all her hard work on our behalf, as well as the rest of the Wadsworth Group/Thomson Learning team for helping to make this project a reality. Thanks also to the anonymous reviewers who helped develop the manuscript. Their comments and suggestions were incredibly helpful. My thanks also to Jan Six for exceptional copyediting work on the manuscript and to Gretchen Otto, Alison Rainey, and all the folks at G&S Typesetters.

I spent one month with relatives in Germany working on the manuscript, and I wish to extend my gratitude to them as well. To Hermann and Lisa Graber, thanks so much for your hospitality, great conversation, and incredible food. Thanks to Iris for coffee and great schnitzel and to Christoph and Tobias for being such great company on our walks home from school. Special thanks also to Philipp Ufholz for his graciousness and steadfast friendship. He is truly not a poser. I especially want to extend my appreciation to Bettina, who is the greatest cousin anybody could have. Her generosity and friendship are marvelous, and my time with her is always very special.

Closer to home, many friends and colleagues helped out with suggestions and support, and I wish to acknowledge their assistance. To Neil Websdale, whose humor and insight keep me sane and who always inspires me to continue writing. My gratitude also to Ingrid Davis and Cathy Spitzer, whose daily administrative support and good cheer keep the department running.

As I get older, I increasingly recognize the importance of family, and accordingly I wish to recognize my father Leroy C. Alvarez. I could not wish for a more loving and supportive dad. He is always there when I need him. He always tells me that he is proud of me and my accomplishments, but it is I who feel pride in having him as a father. My mother Marianne Alvarez has taught me that if I set my mind on something, I will always be able to achieve it. My sister Renee and my brother Leroy Jr. never fail to offer encouragement and love. To Chuck and Adrienne Engleson, my wife's parents, and to Uncle Ken and Joan, I wish to express my profound thanks for their unceasing support and encouragement. I will forever be in the debt of my wife Donna, whose strength, love, and compassion are a never-ending source of wonder and emotional sustenance. Finally, I wish to thank my children Ingrid, Joseph, and Astrid for their unconditional and absolute love. My life is meaningless without them.

A. A.

In my mind, this book has been years in the making, but it would never have begun without the learned guidance through the homicide literature by mentors such as Kirk Williams, Robert Nash Parker, and Colin Loftin. Of course, this book would never have been finished without the greatest friend and co-author in the world! Alex, you are a true scholar, and I am continually amazed at the historic breadth of your knowledge. It has been an adventure learning from you. And to Sabra Horne, our editor, for taking this book on with enthusiasm; Gretchen Otto for diligently guiding the manuscript through production; and Jan Six for careful copyediting.

Alex and I started this book with the hopes of providing students with an empirical assessment of homicide that was both accurate and accessible. There are several students I wish to acknowledge for the invaluable reciprocal learning experiences I have had, including Kathleen Curry, Carol Gregory, Christine Eith, Amy Farrell, Heather Dillaway, Lisa Gilman, Erika Harrel, Matthew Lee, Michelle Meloy, Nicole Mott, Daniel O'Connel, and Robert Peralta. Students like these inspire me to become a better teacher.

I am very fortunate to work in a department filled with first-rate scholars who are also extremely supportive, including my chair Joel Best. Other department members who have touched this work with their support include Margaret Andersen, Anne Bowler, Valerie Hans, Susan Miller, Eric Rise, Andre Rosay, and my past colleague at U.D., Ramiro Martinez Jr.

I am also extremely indebted to the support of a group known as the Fab 5 who get together for a retreat one weekend of the year for guidance, support, and laughter: Dianne Carmody, Gerri King, Peggy Plass, and Barbara Wauchope. You are the most amazing women in the world, and I am so blessed to have you in my life! To another woman who remains my inspiration, my mother Janet Vermilyea, for her courage and strength and positive outlook on life. I also want to thank my father, Ronald Bachman, for his careful review of earlier versions of this book—and for his constant reminders about the rewards of hard work. I have no tougher critic!

And finally, to my son John Phillip Bachman-Paternoster, who has brought me joy beyond my wildest dreams. I hope that my work will somehow leave your generation with a world less violent and more tolerant. I also hope you can forgive your father and me for strapping you with such a long name! And to my husband and co-conspirator, Raymond Paternoster, I want to thank you for being my fortress in this storm called life and for bringing laughter and a clear head to bear on my hysterical tendencies!

R. B.

We would also like to thank the reviewers for this book: Steven Egger, University of Illinois, Springfield; Marge Faulstich, West Valley Community College; David Forde, University of Memphis; Eric Jensen, University of Idaho; Paul Leighton, Eastern Michigan University; Joseph Pascarella, Queens College, City University of New York; Michael Palmiotto, Wichita State University; Marc Riedel, Southern Illinois University; and Cecil Willis, University of North Carolina, Wilmington.

1

Through the Looking Glass

What We Know and What We Think We Know

We sell papers to exist (or exist to sell papers). That means attracting readers by writing what they are interested in, and a "good" murder is a far surer bet than almost anything else.

STEPHEN CAIN[1]

Talk about progress is unfashionable. Instead, we characterize our world as beset by random violence, as one in which new crimes flourish, one that callously tolerates the sufferings of new victims. . . . Such talk is consequential. It scares us and it threatens to paralyze us.

JOEL BEST[2]

REPORTING ON MURDER IN THE MEDIA

By now, the scenario is familiar—on April 20, 1999, Eric Harris and Dylan Klebold turned Columbine High School, a suburban school in Colorado, into the scene of the deadliest school shooting in American history. After killing 12 students and a teacher, the teens apparently shot themselves in the head. In the end, 15 people died and 28 were injured. After the slaughter, police found the school littered with bombs and other booby traps. These two boys were not your typical terrorists. They were apparently bright young men who had become social outcasts at school, in part because of their affiliation with a group known as the Trenchcoat Mafia, whose members wore dark trenchcoats, dark sunglasses, and berets and were considered part of a larger group described by many as Goths. With hindsight, many signs of trouble were evident before the killings. Harris's Web pages were filled with images of fire, skulls, devils, and weapons, and the site included recipes for and sketches of pipe bombs. The two students also wrote poetry about death for an English assignment and made a video about guns for a video class.

The Columbine shooting in Littleton, Colorado, was not the only mass school shooting in the 1998–1999 school year. On March 23, 1998, in Jonesboro, Arkansas, a 13-year-old boy warned a friend that "he had a lot of killing to do" after he was jilted by a girl. A day later, he and his 11-year-old cousin lured classmates out of the school with a false fire alarm and sat in the trees awaiting their targets. When the students filed out of the school, the two opened fire and managed to kill four girls and a teacher who shielded another student from the attack. Eleven others were wounded. Authorities later said that as many as 27 shots were fired. The two prepubescent boys, wearing camouflage shirts, pants, and hats, were caught near the school after the incident with handguns and rifles. In another fatal school shooting that year, three students were killed and five were injured in West Paducah, Kentucky, when a fellow student shot them as they left a prayer meeting. In Edinboro, Pennsylvania, a student gunned down a teacher and wounded two classmates, and in Springfield, Oregon, a disgruntled student brought a rifle into the cafeteria at Thurston High School and fired indiscriminately into a crowd, killing two students and wounding 22 others. These were not inner-city schools riddled with violence and crime; they were all schools in quiet towns where violence—at least publicly displayed violence—was uncommon.

Each of these cases caused a media frenzy. Headlines such as "The School Violence Crisis" and "School Crime Epidemic" were plastered across the pages of national newspapers and weekly news journals. The use of terms such as *crisis* and *epidemic* fostered the distinct impression that American schools were terribly dangerous and getting worse. From a statistical viewpoint, however, even with the rash of school shootings in 1997 and 1998, the probability of being killed at school was very low. More than 50 million students are attending more than 80,000 schools across the country; the vast majority of them never face the shock and horror experienced at places like Littleton and Jonesboro.[3] In fact, the most recent Bureau of Justice Statistics report on school violence has pointed out that more serious victimizations occur away from schools.[4] Without trying to minimize the pain and tragedy of these events, it is important to note that they are the exception rather than the rule. In fact, the headlines alleging a youth violence epidemic seemed a little late, particularly as the juvenile arrest rate for murder had already peaked a few years earlier and was on the decline.[5] Moreover, whereas there were 44 school murders in 1992–1993, there were only 20 in 1998–1999.[6]

What was the trend in juvenile murder leading up to the Jonesboro incident? Exhibit 1.1 displays the homicide victimization rate for children under

Exhibit 1.1 Homicide Victimization Rates per 100,000 for Children and Youth, 1976–1999

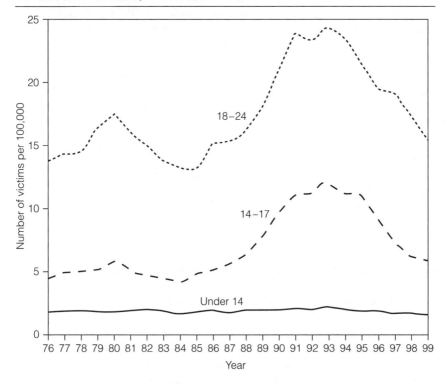

SOURCE: James A. Fox and Marianne W. Zawitz, *Homicide Trends in the United States* (Washington, D.C.: Bureau of Justice Statistics, U.S. Department of Justice, 2001).

the age of 14, juveniles between the ages of 14 and 17, and juveniles between the ages of 18 and 24 from 1978 through 1999. This exhibit shows that the rate at which juveniles were murdered peaked in 1993 at a level more than double that of the early 1980s. By 1996, the juvenile murder rate was the lowest it had been in the decade, even though it was still more than 50% higher than the rate in the early 1980s. During this time period, the murder rate for children under the age of 14 remained relatively constant. In short, although the horrific scenes played out in news reports of the school shootings understandably shocked the United States, our nation had been experiencing a shock wave of juvenile murder long before these events, but many of the victims' names had never made it into the national news. In fact, when these dramatic and horrific school shootings occurred, our schools were actually safer than they had been for almost 10 years.

The crime waves declared in the headlines are usually just waves of media attention. As Joel Best explains, "reporting that crime is stable—or even decreasing—makes a less compelling story." Through increased media attention in the form of feature stories on news shows and in newspapers and increased attention on talk shows, a few isolated incidents can come to be perceived by the public as full-blown epidemics and social problems. To be sustained as a social problem, of course, these crimes must be adopted by activists and by government officials. As Best describes, "the issue becomes the focus of legislative hearings and new laws; the criminal justice system changes to address the new crime by keeping track of reported incidents or devising programs to deal with the problem; researchers begin studying the new crime; and so on."[7]

Media attention to specific crime incidents can also be selective. For example, no national headlines called for action when an 11-year-old boy was shot and killed in Chicago in 1999 because he had allegedly shorted an 18-year-old on drug money. And in the same year, the media largely ignored the shooting of two teenagers outside a Baltimore nightclub when the easy availability of guns turned an argument lethal.

Several more recent media cases help to further illustrate our point. On December 26, 2000, 42-year-old Michael M. McDermott walked into his place of employment, an Internet consulting firm just outside of Boston, and shot and killed seven colleagues.[8] Apparently angry because his company had agreed to garnish his wages for taxes he owed to the IRS, he came into the lobby armed with an assault rifle, a 12-gauge shotgun, and a semiautomatic handgun and immediately opened fire. Most of his victims worked in the accounting department of the firm, which he apparently blamed for the decision to begin garnishing his wages. This story received a tremendous amount of national attention. Just two days later, on December 28, another mass murder occurred in Philadelphia, in which another seven people were shot and murdered. However, unless you live in the Philadelphia area, you probably didn't hear about it. In this case, four masked individuals broke into a reputed crack house, gathered everyone together, robbed them, made them lie face down, and then opened fire. Seven people, four of them teenagers, died, and three others were wounded.[9] According to the police, the murders may have been related to a gang dispute over territory.[10] Why didn't this case receive more media attention? Was one set of victims more innocent? Was the tragedy of the victims in Philadelphia any less because they were in a drug house or because they were people of color? Do certain types of victims receive more media attention than others?

Another example illustrating the selective nature of media representation is probably familiar to most of us. On the evening of June 12, 1994, Nicole Brown Simpson and Ronald Goldman were murdered in front of Nicole's condominium. Attacked first, Nicole Brown Simpson was evidently knocked unconscious and then stabbed several times with a knife. The assailant then turned to Ronald Goldman, a waiter in the restaurant where Nicole had eaten that night, who was returning sunglasses that she had forgotten. Trapped in the entrance area, unable to retreat, Ronald Goldman quickly succumbed to lethal knife thrusts. Returning to Nicole Brown Simpson, who was still alive but stunned or unconscious, the assailant pinned her to the ground and killed her with a knife slash across the neck, almost decapitating her. The ensuing publicity about the double murder shocked and mesmerized the nation, especially when it be-

Exhibit 1.2 Number of Intimate Partner Homicides by Sex of Victim, 1976–1998

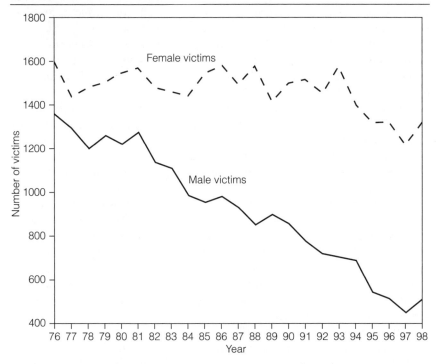

SOURCE: James A. Fox and Marianne W. Zawitz, *Homicide Trends in the United States* (Washington, D.C.: Bureau of Justice Statistics, U.S. Department of Justice, 2001).

came known that the prime suspect, who was eventually arrested and put on trial, was Nicole's estranged husband, football legend O. J. Simpson.[11] Following his arrest, the criminal and civil trials enthralled and titillated television viewers around the globe. Viewers tuned in daily to see the latest deliberations and courtroom procedures unfold live in front of their eyes. This case became one of the most celebrated trials of the twentieth century.

According to the media portrayals that followed the incident, intimate murder had become one of our nation's leading social problems. Whereas many social scientists and feminists lauded the long overdue attention given to the topic, all acknowledged that what many media pundits called an epidemic was nothing new. Every year, nearly 1,500 women are murdered by their intimate partners, yet rarely do these incidents make even local news broadcasts. Moreover, at the time Nicole Brown Simpson was murdered, intimate-perpetrated murder by men and women was actually on the decline. Exhibit 1.2 displays the number of intimate murder victims by the sex of the victim from 1976 through 1998. As can be seen, the total number of intimates killed dropped from nearly 3,000 per year in 1976 to fewer than 2,000 in 1998. But nowhere did this statistical trend appear in the news during the Simpson trial. The fact that more than 1,500 women are killed by their partners each year remains a tragedy, but why did the media not acknowledge the decrease? Obviously, such a headline would not be as attention grabbing as "Nicole's Death Evidence of Alarming Trend." Of course, most victims' rights advocates were understandably supportive of the increased attention because they had long known that women are significantly more likely to be killed by someone they know and perhaps love than by the stereotypical stranger lurking in the bushes.

In addition to the many other women who were killed by their partners in June of 1994, there were other victims who went largely unnoticed, even by local newspapers. For example, on June 11, 1994, the night before Nicole Brown Simpson was murdered, in the same city, a 22-year-old woman was killed. She was entering her car after making a stop at a convenience store and had just picked up her crying infant daughter to comfort her when a bullet slammed through the windshield, narrowly missing her child but striking her in the chest. Her sister-in-law, who was also in the car, rushed the young mother to a local hospital, but it was too late; she was pronounced dead shortly after arrival. Evidently, a member of one gang had spotted rival gang members and opened fire with a handgun, managing only to hit an innocent victim who just happened to be in the wrong place at the wrong time. The name of this woman was Rene Hurtado. Her murder received one column on one day in the Metro section of the *Los Angeles Times*.[12]

Other murders, involving multiple victims, also occurred in June 1994. For example, on June 5, in San Marino, a suburb of Los Angeles, a high school graduation party resulted in the deaths of two teenagers. After a confrontation with the disc jockey and other guests, several teens were ejected from the party. Later that evening, some of these unwanted guests returned for revenge. Two of the teens, a young man armed with a semiautomatic rifle and a young woman armed with a handgun, opened fire on the guests, leaving two dead and seven wounded.[13] Did you hear about this incident? Probably not. Yet it remains, with many others, a terrible and shocking indictment of a society in which petty conflicts all too often erupt into lethal violence. Unfortunately, most of these incidents pass with scarcely a ripple, except among the immediate families of those involved.

So why do certain murders attract so much more attention and condemnation than others? Are certain killings considered more newsworthy than others? Are some murders inherently more interesting, tragic, dramatic, or important? Indeed, we may ask why some murders never even appear in the news coverage of crime. In a study of Los Angeles murders, for example, one journalist found that the families of murder victims reported that the murders of their loved ones "had not merited a single line in the newspaper or even a brief mention on the local news."[14] Are they considered too ordinary or too mundane? As Richard Corliss suggests, "items on the news shows get more dramatic and sentimental. Everything is just a story, with a moral, a giggle, or a lingering sting."[15]

In the media today, crime and violence pervade the images we watch on local and national news broadcasts and prime-time entertainment shows. Unfor-

tunately, many of these programs only serve to reinforce stereotypical, erroneous notions about who is most likely to be killed in this country and by whom.
Because our understanding of murder is largely shaped by the media, it is necessary to briefly discuss the topic of crime reporting.

As the cases we have just examined reveal, the reporting of violent crime is
marked by extreme disparity in the amount and the content of coverage. These
cases illustrate that news coverage of murder is not as complete or as accurate
as one might expect. Media images of crime are often misleading and biased
because the reporting emphasizes sensational elements of crime and because the
reported frequencies for different types of crime rarely reflect the actual frequencies of occurrence. The least common forms of crime typically receive the
most news attention.

Various studies have found that murder, the least common form of violent
crime, is reported more often and in greater depth than other, more prevalent
types of violent crime.[16] This overrepresentation in reporting may serve to mis-
lead the consumers of crime news, because it suggests a greater frequency of
occurrence of some offenses relative to others. This is true not only in terms of
the frequency of murder reporting but also in regard to the types of murder reported. For example, Stephen Cain found that the murders most often reported
by newspapers are atypical ones, such as mass murders, assassinations, gangland
killings, and particularly vicious, cruel, or dramatic murders.[17] Although admittedly dramatic and embodying the worst characteristics of homicides, these
types of murder are certainly not a representative cross-section of murder in
the United States. According to Cain, about 5% of all murders garner the vast
majority of newspaper reporting, whereas the remaining 95% are perceived as
"mundane, banal, and usually lowlife,"[18] and therefore not worthy of any
significant coverage. Indeed, the definition of newsworthiness is antithetical to
proportionality and representativeness in coverage, because the unusual event
stands apart and is therefore considered more noteworthy and of greater interest to the reader. As Ray Surrette points out, "Crime news thus takes the rare
crime event and turns it into the common crime image."[19]

These stereotypical portrayals of crime in the media are inextricably linked
to our perceptions, because media images are a primary source for the opinions
and beliefs of many people.[20] Surveys, for example, have shown that for most
people (95% in one study), the primary source of knowledge on crime was the
mass media.[21] People who watch television frequently tend to perceive the
world around them as dangerous and scary, and women who watch more news
shows perceive themselves as being more vulnerable to victimization than other
women.[22] Even criminal justice college students are not immune to this phenomenon.[23] In Surrette's words, it is evident that we live "in two worlds: a real
world and a media world,"[24] and this media world often helps shape our understanding of the real world.

In sum, the evidence indicates that the mass media constitute the principal
source of information on crime for many people. Unfortunately, this source
tends to be unrepresentative and incomplete in its crime-reporting patterns. It
is not surprising that many people develop false and fragmentary notions of violent crime in the United States, which often guide their beliefs about appro-

priate social policy choices. We should remember W. I. Thomas's famous dictum that what people believe to be real is real in its consequences.[25] In other words, although a person's beliefs may be incomplete or factually erroneous, they are acted upon as if true, and their impact is accordingly real. This results in well-meaning individuals voting, creating legislation, and lobbying for policy or social reform on the basis of faulty information. The resulting policies, of course, often produce unsatisfactory results. More generally, the backdrop of murder and mayhem presented by the media helps create and maintain our society's psychic landscape—a landscape that is often riddled with a sense of fearfulness and insecurity.

FEAR OF CRIME AND PUBLIC POLICY

At present in the United States, the *fear* of violent crime—of which murder is generally considered the worst—ranks as one of the most pervasive and malign realities of life. The National Research Council has reported that "in cities, suburban areas, and even small towns, Americans are fearful and concerned that violence has permeated the fabric and degraded the quality of their lives. . . . Violent deaths and incidents that result in lesser injuries are sources of chronic fear and a high level of concern."[26] In general, when people discuss the fear of crime, they are largely talking about the fear of violence. Zimring and Hawkins point out that people do not express the same levels of fear about property loss as they do for personal injury: "Lethal violence is the most frightening threat in every modern industrial nation. The obvious reason why lethal violence is a priority concern is the importance people attach to personal survival. Physical survival, security from assault, freedom from the pain inflicted by serious intentional injuries are among the most basic interests citizens have. . . . The effectiveness of insurance and compensation schemes to ease the pain of property crime when compared with the impossibility of restoring life and health is an additional reason why serious violence is the central reason citizens fear predation."[27]

Today, the fear of violent crime is a top concern for many people. For example, in 1998, 41% of all Americans surveyed reported feeling afraid to walk alone at night in their neighborhood and were fearful of being victimized by various types of crimes.[28] They also defined crime as one of the top issues facing the country.[29] This heightened perception of fear continues to be a reality for many Americans in spite of consistent decreases in violent crime during the 1990s.

Exhibit 1.3 illustrates that during the 1990s, Americans continued to experience consistently high levels of fear even though the actual rates of violent offending decreased dramatically during this time. From 1988 to 1998, national rates of crime decreased by 13.1%, and the murder rate declined by 19%.[30] In short, Americans continue to be fearful of violent crime and have enacted laws and policies accordingly, even though the actual risk of victimization has eased dramatically. In fact, national opinion polls showed that for many voters, crime was the number one concern during the 2000 presidential election.[31]

Exhibit 1.3 Percentage of Population Reporting Fear of Walking Alone and Feeling Unsafe at Home at Night

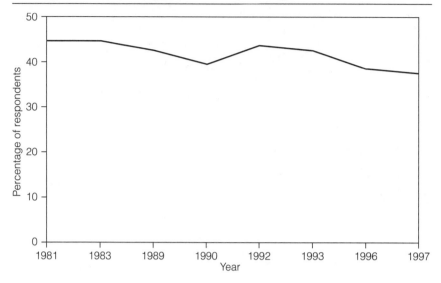

SOURCE: George Gallup Jr., *The Gallup Poll Monthly,* 318 (Princeton, N.J.: Gallup Poll), pp. 51–52.

Fear surrounding more specific types of murder has also increased. For example, the school shootings in the last few years have significantly threatened parents' perceptions of their children's safety at school. In fact, the Gallup Organization has reported that the percentage of parents who fear for their children's safety at school rises and drops dramatically after a school shooting. Exhibit 1.4 illustrates the dramatic increase in parents' fear after the Columbine shooting in Colorado on April 21, 1999.[32] To combat this fear, literally thousands of school boards across the country have spent millions of dollars on metal detectors, armed guards, and violence prevention training for their students. Do these programs actually work? Well, the rigorous empirical studies that have evaluated these programs are not so promising.[33] Nevertheless, politicians continue to spend millions of dollars on such programs, lest they appear soft on crime.

The point is that how we *feel* about crime—that is, the extent to which we as individuals and as a nation are threatened by it—is directly related to how crime is represented in the media. Moreover, our nation's fearfulness of violent crime is in turn inextricably related to public policies aimed at reducing and mitigating the consequences of such crime. Legislators at the federal and state levels are eager to appear tough on crime, and they enact legislation accordingly. In fact, many politicians rely on violence and crime as powerful issues about which they can mobilize support to get elected or reelected.

Since the late 1960s, six significant crime bills have been signed into law at the federal level, the latest of which was passed in 1994.[34] This most recent anticrime effort—the most expensive in history—added the death penalty to

Exhibit 1.4 Percentage of Parents Who Fear for Their Children's Safety at School

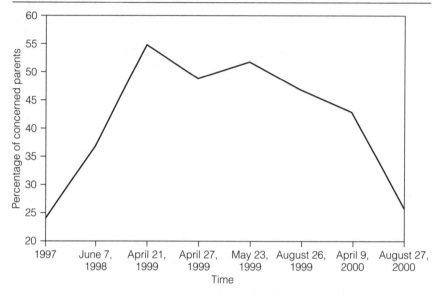

SOURCE: Darren K. Carlson, *Majority of Parents Think a School Shooting Could Occur in Their Community.* http://www.gallup.com/poll (retrieved February 2001).

dozens of federal offenses, allocated $23 billion for law enforcement (this includes the $9.7 billion for prisons), and directed another $6.1 billion for crime prevention programs."[35] One cannot help but wonder about the ultimate effectiveness of these and other get-tough policies, given that they are so often based on flawed information. Wendy Kaminer echoes this position when she writes, "Criminal justice debates are strikingly irrational, as are many criminal justice policies."[36] The failure of most crime control strategies to appreciably or even perceptibly affect crime rates certainly suggests that many of these efforts have been misguided at best. This has not gone unnoticed. A report of the National Criminal Justice Commission asserts that "the Commission's fundamental conclusion is that the criminal justice system is in crisis. Citizens in record numbers report that they feel unsafe on their streets and in their homes. As Americans have become more concerned about crime, the criminal justice system has become less effective at reducing it."[37]

This suggests that our society must address the problem of crime and violence in an informed and rational manner, making decisions based on documented empirical evidence rather than on distorted media images. Strategies and policies that are clearly ineffective and self-defeating must be discarded. Obviously, the first step in such a process is to educate ourselves about the *reality*, not the rhetoric, of the problems of crime and violence. Herein lies one of the primary goals of this book.

The intent of this book is to provide a comprehensive and factual overview of the trends, patterns, and characteristics of murder in American society. Moreover, we will provide an empirical assessment of the factors that are related to its occurrence. We choose to focus on murder because it is generally conceded to be the most serious and the most final of violent crimes. The irreversibility of murder sets it apart from assault, rape, and robbery, which, although serious and traumatic, do not cost the victims their lives. Furthermore, murder is worthy of attention for other reasons as well. Writing on the advantages of studying murder, Monkonnen asserts that "first, of all criminal offenses, homicide is the least definitionally ambiguous. Second, it is the most likely to be reported and 'cleared' by arrest; today the arrest of the accused killer follows about three fourths of all homicides. And, third, in some sense it constitutes an offense which indexes other forms of personal violence."[38]

Although Monkonnen is referring to historical analysis, his assertion also holds true for contemporary investigations; a discussion of murder reveals much about patterns of violence in general. The ways in which Americans kill each other tell us much about the processes and interactions that can lead to violence.

A project such as this benefits from the existence of two separate nationwide reporting systems. The data on criminal homicide, therefore, tend to be fairly extensive. The focus of this book is to guide the reader through a discussion concerning the nature and patterns of murder in the contemporary United States. The data we use come primarily from the Federal Bureau of Investigation's *Uniform Crime Reports,* from the National Center for Health Statistics' vital statistics, and from the large body of homicide research generated by social scientists. Our goal is to provide an up-to-date and informed overview of the magnitude and context of murder in America, paying particular attention to current trends and patterns. But first we must spend a bit of time defining what is sometimes called "murder most foul."

DEFINING MURDER

Although many people use the terms murder and homicide interchangeably, the two words are quite distinct. *Homicide* is a general term for the killing of a human being, whereas *murder* refers to the specific legal category of criminal homicide. Having said that, this book does use the terms *murder, homicide,* and *criminal homicide* interchangeably for narrative purposes and for ease of discussion.

The legal definitions of murder vary from state to state (depending on individual state legal codes), but we can briefly review some of the main characteristics and categories of criminal homicide that are commonly employed in individual state statutes. Generally, three types of homicide are recognized: excusable, justifiable, and murder. The 18th-century English lawyer Sir William Blackstone once wrote that the first had no guilt, the second had a little, and the third was the worst crime humans could perpetrate.[39] These words still capture the essence of the distinction between different types of killing. Exhibit 1.5 outlines the different types of homicide and their interrelationships.

Exhibit 1.5 Legally Defined Types of Homicide

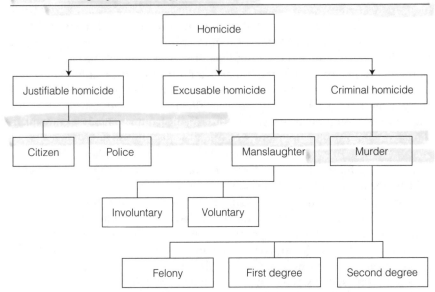

Excusable homicides are accidental or unintentional killings. For a killing to be ruled excusable, it must be shown that the killers did not act with negligence. If they were negligent, typically the killing will be considered a type of manslaughter. Although a degree of fault or blame may be assigned to the killer, it is not enough to constitute a criminal homicide. An example of an excusable homicide might involve a driver who runs over a pedestrian because of some unavoidable situation. The driver may bear some responsibility because of her or his actions, but those actions are not regarded as criminal.

Justifiable homicides are killings judged to be acceptable because they occurred in defense of life or property. This kind of homicide is considered to have been perpetrated out of necessity and, as such, no legal fault or blame attaches to the killer. There are two types of justifiable homicide: those committed by law enforcement officers in the line of duty, and those committed by private citizens in defense of life or property. Individual statutes may vary, but generally speaking, individuals may kill to protect their own lives or the lives of others if an assailant is judged to be engaged in life-threatening behavior. In some states, the mere presence of an intruder in a home is deemed a sufficient threat to the lives of the inhabitants to justify killing the intruder.

Murders are illegal killings and can be classified into different hierarchical categories depending on certain criteria. *First degree* murders are generally committed with both premeditation and deliberation. *Premeditation* refers to the knowledge and intention to kill, and *deliberation* implies that the killing was planned and thought about rather than committed on impulse. In other words, the killer must have considered the consequences of his or her actions and then consciously decided to kill. This contemplation does not need to take a long time but may occur quite quickly in the moments or even seconds before the murder. These types of murders are often characterized as being cold-blooded; according to the language of common law, the killing is committed with *malice aforethought.* The penalty for first degree murder is typically life imprisonment or death. *Second degree* murders are considered slightly less serious than first degree, because they do not involve premeditation or deliberation. In second degree murder, people kill because they exhibit extreme indifference for the life of another and intend to seriously injure them.

In addition to first and second degree murder, we also have the category of *felony murder,* which occurs during the commission of another felony. Felony murder involves the unintentional killing of a person in the course of a felony crime (such as robbery). There is tremendous variation in the specific legal definitions of felony murder, but generally speaking, the felony must be a violent one or must pose a great danger to someone's life. In some jurisdictions, it is possible for a felon to be found guilty of felony murder even if the person killed was a co-felon killed by the intended victim or by a law enforcement officer. Interesting enough, felony murder convictions are one of the most common pathways to death row, because felony murders, by definition, take place during the commission of a dangerous felony, so when a murder does occur, it is usually considered a type of first degree murder.[40]

Finally, there are criminal homicides in which the degree of responsibility is generally considered less than for murder because of an absence of malice. This type of killing, known as *manslaughter,* can be either voluntary or involuntary. An example of *voluntary* manslaughter might involve someone killing another person while overwhelmed by emotion or passion. An example of *involuntary* manslaughter might involve a person acting recklessly and killing someone unintentionally. For example, in 2001 in the state of Colorado, a reckless skier going exceptionally fast was convicted of involuntary manslaughter after he crashed into and killed another skier.

Although the legal criterion for defining homicide types based on intent or state of mind is the most widely used method for defining and classifying different kinds of killing, other typologies have also been developed. Richard and Carolyn Block, for example, rely on what they term "homicide syndromes."[41] Their system differentiates expressive from instrumental homicides. *Expressive* homicides are killings perpetrated as an expression of anger, rage, frustration, or some other emotional or psychological state, whereas *instrumental* homicides are killings performed for some ulterior motive, such as profit. This type of classification allows one to distinguish murders based on the underlying impulses of the offender. Some scholars, however, have argued that all violence is at some level instrumental, because even the most anger-driven killer is seeking to remove an obstacle, defend his or her status, or control someone's behavior.[42]

In contrast, Robert Silverman and Leslie Kennedy rely not on motivation but on relational distance to define homicides.[43] Their analysis concentrates on how well the offender and the victim knew each other. Best perceived as a continuum, relational distance can range from the most intimate, as in killings of spouses, to the most impersonal, as in murders of complete strangers. Depend-

Exhibit 1.6 Motivation-Based Homicide Types

Criminal enterprise homicide
  Contract (third party) killing
  Gang-motivated murder
  Criminal competition homicide
  Kidnap murder
  Product tampering murder
  Drug murder
  Insurance/inheritance-related death
    Individual profit murder
    Commercial profit murder
  Felony murder
    Indiscriminate felony murder
    Situational felony murder

Personal cause homicide
  Erotomania-motivated killing
  Domestic homicide
    Spontaneous domestic homicide
    Staged domestic homicide
  Argument/conflict murder
    Argument murder
    Conflict murder
  Authority killing
  Revenge killing
  Nonspecific-motive killing
  Extremist homicide
    Political extremist homicide
    Religious extremist homicide
    Socioeconomic extremist homicide
  Mercy/hero homicide
    Mercy homicide
    Hero homicide
  Hostage murder

Sexual homicide
  Organized sexual homicide
  Disorganized sexual homicide
  Mixed sexual homicide
  Sadistic murder

Group cause homicide
  Cult murder
  Extremist murder
    Paramilitary extremist murder
    Hostage extremist murder
  Group excitement homicide

SOURCE: John E. Douglas, Ann W. Burgess, Allen G. Burgess, and Robert K. Ressler, *Crime Classification Manual: A Standard System for Investigating and Classifying Violent Crimes.* Copyright © 1992 by Lexington Books. This material is used by permission of John Wiley & Sons, Inc.

ing on the relational distance, the trends, patterns, and nature of the individual homicides can vary dramatically.

Traditionally, the FBI has classified murder into the following circumstance-based categories: felony murder, suspected felony murder, argument-motivated murder, miscellaneous non-felony murder, and murder with unknown motives.[44] More recently, however, the FBI's National Center for the Analysis of Violent Crime has developed a classification system for homicide based solely on motivation.[45] Rather than identifying types of killing through a focus on intent, premeditation, and deliberation, this new method focuses on the victim, the crime scene, and the interaction between the victim and the offender.[46] In this approach, there are four primary categories of murder with numerous subcategories, as detailed in Exhibit 1.6.

A quick perusal of this exhibit indicates the wide range of motives in homicide events. The four primary types of homicide are (1) criminal enterprise, (2) personal cause, (3) sexual, and (4) group cause. The subcategories range from individual to collective acts of violence and from instrumental to expressive mo-

Exhibit 1.7 Comparison of Organized and Disorganized Offender Profiles

Organized Offender	Disorganized Offender
Average to above-average intelligence	Below average intelligence
Socially competent	Socially inadequate
Skilled work preferred	Unskilled work
Sexually competent	Sexually incompetent
High birth order status	Low birth order status
Father's work stable	Father's work unstable
Inconsistent childhood discipline	Harsh discipline as a child
Controlled mood during crime	Anxious mood during crime
Use of alcohol with crime	Minimal use of alcohol
Precipitating situational stress	Minimal situational stress
Living with partner	Living alone
Mobility with car in good condition	Lives/works near the crime scene
Follows crime in news media	Minimal interest in news media
May change jobs or leave town	Significant behavior change (e.g. drug or alcohol use)

SOURCE: Wayne Petherick, *Crime Profiling: How It Was Started and How It Is Used.* http://www.crimelibrary.com/criminology/criminalprofiling2/ (retrieved February 29, 2000). © 2002 Courtroom Television Network LLC. All rights reserved.

tivation. This categorization is a powerful and sophisticated tool that has many practical applications for the investigation of murder.

These categories are based on years of work investigating and profiling violent offenders. *Profiling* is grounded in the premise that offenders' personalities and motivations are revealed in the specific nature and characteristics of their criminal behavior. In other words, the *how* often reveals much about the *why* and the *who*.[47] Although profiling has only recently received widespread attention through the work of various FBI investigators and through several widely publicized scandals involving profiling based on racial characteristics, the techniques involved in profiling are actually much older and date back to the 1800s.[48] Based on sociological and psychological principles, investigators build a profile of an unknown individual that is determined by the type of crime committed and the distinguishing characteristics of the criminal act. To begin with, investigators gather as much evidence as possible from the crime scene and arrange it in order to reveal patterns. The investigators then try to reconstruct the series of events that led up to the crime and, based on this reconstruction, create a profile of the background, physical, and behavioral characteristics of the offender.[49] One distinguishing characteristic of the FBI's profiling strategies lies in their characterization of the offender as either *organized* or *disorganized*. Exhibit 1.7 illustrates the differences between these two types of offenders. Although these typologies have their critics, the practice of distinguishing between organized and disorganized offenders is one of the most widely taught and practiced investigative tools.

There are other murder classification schemes, but those reviewed here help illuminate the multifaceted nature of criminal homicide. Americans murder each other in a great many ways for a multitude of reasons. Our understanding of this, however, is largely dependent on the quality of the homicide data that are available.

MEASURING MURDER

On June 21, 1994, two young boys playing in a dry riverbed in Phoenix, Arizona, found the partial skeleton of a Hispanic woman in her 50s. An *Arizona Republic* article reported that the body had apparently been there for several months before being discovered, and the police were treating the case as a homicide.[50] Was this woman a murder victim, or did the police investigation subsequently reveal some other, less sinister reason for her death? Because the newspaper did not follow up this story, it remains unclear if the body was ever identified and whether there was enough evidence to determine the cause of death or to pursue an investigation. It is entirely possible that this particular case was never resolved. Perhaps this death, like so many others, remains a mystery. Did someone get away with murder, or did this unfortunate woman succumb to an accident? Regardless of the results of the investigation, this woman's death illustrates the problems inherent in enumerating murder statistics. If this woman truly was a murder victim, her killing never appeared in any data on homicide.

In our country, many murders go uncounted every year. For example, one group of murder victims at high risk of going unrecorded are infants and children. One of the most dramatic investigations of this problem was conducted by the *Washington Post*.[51] Reporters from the *Washington Post* created a database of causes of death for 2,379 Washington, D.C., area children younger than five who died from 1993 through 1995. Of the 790 children on average who died annually from all causes, only a few were officially recorded by the police as homicide victims: 14 in 1993, five in 1994, and 10 in 1995. When experts examined the details of each death, however, they estimated that four to five times as many intentional killings had actually occurred. In other words, many possible murders were recorded as something else. Not counted in the list of homicides, for example, was Ebony Brown. Ebony was born prematurely, weighing only three pounds and 13 ounces. She didn't leave the hospital until she was seven weeks old, and she was soon hospitalized again for severe diaper rash and a viral infection. But by September 15, 1994, when she was two months old and was sent home from the hospital again, she was up to six pounds and nine ounces. Eight weeks later, Ebony was dead. Her mother told the police that she found Ebony unconscious at about 8:45 in the morning, and a hospital pronounced her dead 45 minutes later. An autopsy found numerous healed and healing fractures, including four fractured ribs and a broken bone in her arm. She also had multiple scrapes on her tiny body and severe diaper rash. She weighed just seven pounds; in two months, she had gained less than half a pound. The D.C. medical examiner's office ruled at the time that the cause of

Ebony's death was undetermined. Thus, no criminal investigation was undertaken, even though the evidence clearly suggested that she was a victim of abuse.

Infants are just one subgroup of murder victims at risk of going unrecorded. Other vulnerable groups include elderly, mentally challenged, and homeless people. The case of Ebony Brown, however, vividly illustrates that the sources of data on crime and murder are flawed and incomplete. Because of the multitude of ways in which murders are committed and the ways in which they are reported and recorded, crime data are inherently imperfect reflections of the true magnitude of murder. Perhaps the best summation of the flawed nature of crime data was offered by Thorsten Sellin, who stated that "the value of a crime statistic for index purposes decreases as the distance from the crime itself, in terms of procedure, increases."[52] In other words, at each step of the data-gathering process, cases are lost because they are not discovered (as with the belated discovery of the body in Phoenix), because they are not defined as criminal (as with Ebony Brown), or because they are not reported because people are scared, do not want to get involved, or do not want to get friends or family in trouble. Of those murders that come to the attention of the police, only a proportion are ever investigated; of those investigated, only a fraction end up being cleared by an arrest; and so on down the line. The more information is filtered through the justice system, the less value it has. Because the validity of the data is inextricably linked to the validity of the generalizations made in this book, we present an overview of the two primary data sources used to measure murder in this country: the *Uniform Crime Reports* (UCR) and the National Center for Heath Statistics (NCHS) data.

The FBI's Uniform Crime Reports

Begun in the 1930s, the Federal Bureau of Investigation's Uniform Crime Reporting program is one of the best known and most widely used sources of national level crime statistics.[53] Based on the crimes that become known to the police, the UCR program provides information on a variety of crimes known as *index offenses* (such as murder and non-negligent manslaughter, forcible rape, robbery, aggravated assault, burglary, larceny theft, motor vehicle theft, and arson). They are referred to as index offenses because they are used to gauge the overall level of crime in the United States. Because individual states define individual crimes somewhat differently, the UCR defines murder and non-negligent manslaughter as the willful killing of one human being by another. Marc Riedel summarizes it this way: "As a general rule, any death due to injuries received in a fight, argument, quarrel, assault, or commission of a crime is counted as a murder or non-negligent manslaughter."[54] All participating agencies use this definition for reporting purposes, even though they may use somewhat different criteria for murder investigations in their own jurisdictions.

The UCR program collects detailed information on all murders known to the police, including the number of victims and offenders for each homicide event; the age, sex, race, and ethnicity of the victim and, if known, of the perpetrator; the weapons used; the relationship between the victim and the offender; and the circumstances of the murder. Therefore, the UCR program can present a fairly detailed description of the characteristics of murder in this country. This information is contained in the *Supplementary Homicide Report* (SHR) section of the UCR.

One important shortcoming of the UCR, however, concerns the issue of missing data. For various reasons, participating agencies sometimes fail to submit their reports. For example, in its preliminary report for 1996, the FBI noted that the states of Alabama, Delaware, Florida, Illinois, Kansas, Kentucky, and Montana did not submit any data for 1996 or submitted data only for cities over 100,000 in population.[55] This lack of reporting can occur for a variety of reasons, including personnel or time constraints, political issues, and the quality of record keeping. Regardless of the reason, the lack of reporting obviously affects the completeness and quality of the data produced.

Problems also exist with the ways in which the classification of murder occurs. Gary Kleck points out that some killings ultimately ruled noncriminal by prosecutors or judges (such as justifiable and excusable homicides) have been reported to the FBI as criminal homicides, because that is how the police originally defined them.[56] Conversely, in all likelihood the reverse sometimes occurs, with the police recording certain killings as noncriminal homicides that later turn out to be criminal. Although the FBI requests that agencies update their reports when further information is uncovered, this often does not happen, which results in miscoded cases being used to compute national and local homicide rates.[57]

Classification problems also exist in terms of categorization. Some researchers have found, for example, that the coding of the circumstances of homicides was sometimes unreliable, especially in situations with unclear or ambiguous motivations.[58] In sum, much depends on how individual police officers interpret the context of a death based on their individual biases, training, and the complexity of the situation. Though not insurmountable, these problems do limit the quality of the UCR data and the findings generated with them.

National Center for Health Statistics

In contrast to the UCR data, the Vital Statistics section of the National Center for Health Statistics does not rely on police data and, as such, does not suffer as much as the UCR from the problem of underreporting. Tapping into the vast system for registering all deaths in the United States, the NCHS information is based on mortality data collected from death certificates that are filled out by officials such as medical examiners.[59] This source provides an unsurpassed wealth of information on the victim (such as age, sex, and race) and on other relevant characteristics such as the type of weapon used in the killing. The major shortcoming of the NCHS data, however, is that they include no information on the offender. No analyses of the victim–offender relationship or of motivational factors are therefore possible. Another significant problem is that medical examiners may sometimes misclassify the cause of death, listing a killing as accidental or natural when, in fact, it may have been murder.[60]

Despite the problems associated with them, these two major data sets provide the primary sources on the characteristics of criminal homicide in the

United States. Several studies have found a high rate of agreement between the UCR homicide data and the NCHS homicide data.[61] Although research has indicated that differences sometimes exist between these two data sets at the county level, these discrepancies should not affect any analysis or discussion that broadly examines major patterns and trends at the state, regional, or national level.[62] In short, the majority of the evidence encourages the acceptance of these data sources as having some reliability and validity for measuring murder in America.

ORGANIZATION OF THE BOOK

This book is structured into chapters focusing on the major issues surrounding murder. Although the discussion of murder in terms of discrete qualities and characteristics is somewhat undesirable, it is partly unavoidable. Murder is a complex phenomenon, composed of sometimes distinct and sometimes interconnected attributes. To meaningfully describe murder, however, these components must be disentangled in order to identify common contextual characteristics. We have therefore divided these qualities into separate chapters.

Chapter 2 begins with a brief historic overview of homicide in the United States that illustrates the historic pervasiveness of lethal violence. A discussion follows of the variability of homicide rates across nations, over time, and by region. Various explanations are presented that attempt to explain these disparate patterns and trends in criminal homicide. Finally, this chapter presents a brief overview of the epidemiological patterns of murder victimization and perpetration in America.

Chapter 3 explores the various theories and models that attempt to explain murder. Generally speaking, most theories that attempt to explain lethal violence focus either on the individual or on the structural level. In this chapter, we provide a brief overview of some of the most popular theoretical explanations at each level and discuss their ability to explain criminal homicide in the United States.

In chapter 4, we focus on the contextual characteristics of murder. Here we highlight the notion that murder is not just an event but a process. That is, many criminal homicides are preceded by a series of escalating interactions between the victim and the perpetrator that are influenced by a variety of contextual and situational factors. Research has indicated that many murders occur at the end of an interpersonal conflict that evolves through distinct and identifiable stages. Chapter 4 reviews these interactive processes and presents a discussion of the ways in which these conflicts intensify into violence, sometimes with lethal consequences.

Chapter 5 offers a discussion of the nature of murders that occur between family members, including parents who kill their children and children who kill their parents. One major focus of this chapter concerns intimate partner homicide, which has emerged as a significant issue within the broader context of familial violence.

In chapter 6, we turn our attention to multiple-victim murders, or multicides as they are sometimes known. The vast majority of criminal homicides involve a lone offender and one victim, but multicides garner the lion's share of media attention. This chapter compares and contrasts three primary types of multicide. After a discussion of the characteristics of mass murder and spree murder, a detailed review of the patterns and types of serial murder is presented.

Chapter 7 discusses the role of alcohol, narcotics, and firearms in the perpetration of murder. In the United States, most murders are committed with firearms—more specifically with handguns. This chapter explores the dynamics of the relationship between firearms and lethal interactions. Similarly, the literature indicates that drugs and alcohol are a common ingredient of many homicides. We therefore discuss the business of illegal drugs, crimes committed to support habits, and drug and alcohol use prior to violent social interactions.

No book on murder would be complete without a discussion of capital punishment. Chapter 8 offers such a discussion. The death penalty is often justified in terms of its ability to deter potential criminal homicides. This chapter examines the accuracy of this argument and explores the recent history of capital punishment and the ways in which it is being applied in the United States.

Chapter 9 focuses on a discussion of the legal and social initiatives that may be useful in alleviating the perennially high rates of lethal violence in the United States. These suggestions and recommendations are compared and contrasted to existing policies and discussed in terms of their real and perceived effectiveness. This chapter also reminds us that criminal homicides have a terrible impact on families, communities, and society at large. Specifically, this chapter addresses the economic, social, and psychological costs that the families and friends of homicide victims must bear. We close the chapter with a discussion of the recent trend by states to enact victims' rights legislation.

NOTES

1. Stephen Cain, "Murder and the Media," in *The Human Side of Homicide,* ed. Bruce L. Danto, John Bruhns, and Austin H. Kutscher (New York: Columbia University Press, 1982), p. 73.

2. Joel Best, *Random Violence: How We Talk about New Crimes and New Victims* (Berkeley: University of California Press, 1999), pp.186–187.

3. Rene Sanchez, "Educators Pursue Solutions to Violence Crisis," *Washington Post,* May 23, 1998, p. A01.

4. Phillip Kaufman, Xianglei Chen, Susan P. Choy, Katharin Peter, Sally A. Ruddy, Amanda Miller, Jill K. Fleury, Kathryn A. Chandler, Michael G. Planty, and Michael R. Rand, *Indicators of School Crime and Safety: 2001.* NCES 2002-113/NCJ-190075 (Washington, D.C.:

U.S. Departments of Education and Justice, 2001).

5. Office of Juvenile Justice and Delinquency Prevention, *Juvenile Justice* (Washington, D.C.: U.S. Department of Justice, 2000).

6. Jack Levin and James Alan Fox, *Dead Lines: Essays in Murder and Mayhem* (Boston: Allyn & Bacon, 2001).

7. Best, *Random Violence,* p. 48.

8. Dan Eggen and Pamela Ferdinand, "7 Die in Massachusetts Office Shooting," *Washington Post,* December 27, 2000, p. A01.

9. Barbara Boyer, Monica Yant Kinney, and Clea Benson, "Police Search for Clues after Slaying of Seven. Four Gunmen Are Sought. A Rivalry between Drug Gangs

May Have Led to the Shootings, Police Say," *Philadelphia Inquirer,* December 30, 2000, p. A01.

10. Ibid.

11. Associated Press, "O. J. Simpson Civil Trial: Coroner Lays out Detailed Theories of Killings," *USA Today,* October 18, 1996.

12. Julio Moran, "Woman in Parked Car Slain as She Holds Baby," *Los Angeles Times,* June 12, 1994.

13. Vicki Torres and Kenneth Reich, "Killings at San Marino Party Blamed on Gangs," *Los Angeles Times,* June 7, 1994, pp. B7–B8.

14. Miles Corwin, *The Killing Season: A Summer inside an LAPD Homicide Division* (New York: Simon & Schuster, 1997), p. 7.

15. Richard Corliss, "A Star Trek into the X-Files," *Time,* April 7, 1997, p. 149.

16. J. Esterle, "Crime and the Media," *Jericho,* pp. 5–7 (1986); D. Graber, *Crime News and the Public* (New York: Praeger, 1980).

17. Cain, "Murder and the Media."

18. Ibid., p. 75.

19. Ray Surrette, *Media, Crime, and Criminal Justice: Images and Realities* (Pacific Grove, Calif.: Brooks/Cole, 1992), p. 14.

20. S. Barber, *News Cameras in the Courtroom* (Norwood, N.J.: Ablex, 1987); C. Stroman and R. Seltzer, "Media Use and Perceptions of Crime," *Journalism Quarterly,* 62, 340–345 (1985).

21. D. Graber, "Evaluating Crime-Fighting Policies," in *Evaluating Alternative Law Enforcement Policies,* ed. R. Baker and F. Meyer (Lexington, Ky.: Lexington Books, 1979).

22. Ted Chiricos, Sarah Eschholz, and Marc Gertz, "Crime, News, and Fear of Crime," *Social Problems,* 44, 342–357 (1997); George Gerbner and Larry Gross, "Living with Television: The Violence Profile," *Journal of Communication,* 26, 173–199 (1976).

23. A recent study found that most criminal justice majors frequently and significantly overestimated the extent of murder in the United States. See Margaret Vandiver and David Giacopassi, "One Million and Counting: Students' Estimates of the Annual Number of Homicides in the U.S." *Journal of Criminal Justice Education,* 8(2), 135–143.

24. Surrette, *Media, Crime, and Criminal Justice,* p. 81.

25. William I. Thomas, *The Unadjusted Girl* (Boston: Little, Brown, 1923).

26. Albert J. Reiss, Jeffrey A. Roth, and the National Research Council, *Understanding and Preventing Violence* (Washington D.C.: National Academy Press, 1993), p. 1.

27. Franklin E. Zimring and Gordon Hawkins, *Crime Is Not the Problem: Lethal Violence in America,* ed. Michael Tonry and Norval Morris, *Studies in Crime and Public Policy* (New York: Oxford University Press, 1997), p. 9.

28. George Gallup Jr., *The Gallup Poll Monthly* (Princeton, N.J.: The Gallup Poll, May, 1998).

29. Louis Harris, *The Harris Poll* (Los Angeles: Creators Syndicate, 1998).

30. Arizona Department of Public Safety Research and Planning, *Crime Trends in Arizona: 1988 through 1997 and Beyond* (Phoenix: Arizona Department of Public Safety, 1998).

31. George Gallup Jr., *The Gallup Poll Monthly* (Princeton, N.J.: The Gallup Poll, February, 2000).

32. Darren K. Carlson, *Majority of Parents Think a School Shooting Could Occur in Their Community.* http://www.gallup.com/poll/releases/pr010305c.asp

33. David C. Grossman, Jolly J. Neckerman, Thomas D. Koepsell, Ping-Yu Liu, Kenneth N. Asher, Kathy Beland, Darin Frey, and Frederick P. Rivara, "Effectiveness of a Violence Prevention Curriculum among Children in Elementary School: A Randomized Controlled Trial," *The Journal of the American Medical Association,* 277(20), 1605–1612 (1997).

34. Steven R. Donziger, ed., *The Real War on Crime: The Report of the National Criminal Justice Commission* (New York: Harper Perennial, 1996).

35. Ibid., p. 15.

36. W. Kaminer, *It's All the Rage: Crime and Culture.* (Reading, Mass.: Addison-Wesley, 1995).

37. Donziger, *The Real War on Crime,* p. xvii.

38. Eric H. Monkonnen, "Diverging Homicide Rates: England and the United States, 1850–1875," in *Violence in America: The History of Crime,* ed. Ted Robert Gurr (Newbury Park, Calif.: Sage, 1989), p. 82.

39. Thomas J. Gardner and Terry M. Anderson, *Criminal Law: Principles and Cases,* 7th edition (Belmont, Calif.: Wadsworth Thomson, 2000), p. 291.

40. Gardner and Anderson, *Criminal Law.*

41. Richard Block and Carolyn R. Block, "Homicide Syndromes and Vulnerability: Violence in the Chicago Community Area over 25 Years," in *Studies on Crime and Crime Prevention* (Stockholm: Scandinavian University Press, 1992).

42. J. Tedeschi and Richard B. Felson, *Violence, Aggression, and Coercive Action* (Washington, D.C.: American Psychological Association, 1994).

43. Robert A. Silverman and Leslie W. Kennedy, "Relational Distance and Homicide: The Role of the Stranger," *The Journal of Criminal Law and Criminology,* 78 (2), 272–308 (1987).

44. John E. Douglas, Ann W. Burgess, Allen G. Burgess, and Robert K. Ressler, *Crime Classification Manual* (New York: Lexington Books, 1992).

45. Ibid.

46. Ibid., p. 6.

47. Wayne Petherick, *Criminal Profiling: How It Was Started and How It Is Used.* http://www.crimelibrary.com/criminology/criminalprofiling2/ (retrieved February 29, 2000).

48. Ibid.

49. Ibid.

50. "Bones Believed to Be Those of Slaying Victim," *Arizona Republic,* June 24, 1994.

51. N. Lewis, "Across Area, Dozens of Suspicious Deaths," *Washington Post,* September 20, 1998, p. A01.

52. Thorsten Sellin, "The Bias of a Crime Index," *Journal of the American Institute of Criminal Law and Criminology,* 22, 335–356 (1931).

53. Victoria W. Schneider and Brian Wiersema, "Limits and Use of the Uniform Crime Reports," in *Measuring Crime: Large-Scale, Long-Range Efforts,* ed. Doris Layton-Mackenzie, Phyllis Jo Baunach, and Roy R. Roberg (Albany: State University of New York Press, 1990).

54. Marc Riedel, "Sources of Homicide Data," in *Homicide: A Sourcebook of Social Research,* ed. M. Dwayne Smith and Margaret A. Zahn (Thousand Oaks, Calif.: Sage, 1999).

55. Federal Bureau of Investigation, *Crime in the United States–1996, Uniform Crime Reports* (Washington, D.C.: U.S. Government Printing Office, 1997).

56. Gary Kleck, "Crime Control through the Private Use of Armed Force," *Social Problems,* 35, 1–22 (1988).

57. Joel Best, *Damned Lies and Statistics: Untangling Numbers from the Media, Politicians, and Activists* (Berkeley: University of California Press, 2001).

58. Colin Loftin, "The Validity of Robbery-Murder Classifications in Baltimore," *Violence and Victims,* 78, 259–271 (1986).

59. Marc Riedel, "Nationwide Homicide Data Sets: An Evaluation of the Uniform Crime Reports and the National Center for Health Statistics Data," in *Measuring Crime: Large-Scale, Long-Range Efforts,* ed. Doris Layton-Mackenzie, Phyllis Jo Baunach, and Roy R. Roberg (Albany: State University of New York Press, 1990).

60. Lawrence W. Sherman and R. H. Langworthy, "Measuring Homicide by Police Officers," *Journal of Criminal Law and Criminology,* 70, 546–560 (1979).

61. D. Cantor and L. E. Cohen, "Comparing Measures of Homicide Trends: Methodological and Substantive Differences in the Vital Statistics and Uniform Crime Report Time Series (1933–1975)," *Social Science Research,* 9, 121–145 (1980); Michael J. Hindelang, "The Uniform Crime Reports Revisited," *Journal of Criminal Justice,* 2, 1–17 (1974); Riedel, "Nationwide Homicide Data Sets."

62. Brian Wiersema, Colin Loftin, and David McDowall, "A Comparison of Supplementary Homicide Reports and National Vital Statistics System Homicide Estimates for U.S. Counties," *Homicide Studies,* 4 (4), 317–340 (2000).

2

★

A Murderous Society

Patterns of Murder
Past and Present

So America's history is contradictory. We are a free, democratic,
progressive, creative country of protected citizen rights, rule by law,
legal transfer of power, economic opportunity for at least most of our
citizens, and much more that is good. We are also a country in which
for more than two hundred years our people have insulted, injured,
assaulted, abused, raped, and murdered one another at levels that are
dismayingly high and seem to be growing.

ARNOLD P. GOLDSTEIN, 1996[1]

Our large towns swarm with idle, vicious lads and young men who have
no visible means of support. Our rural districts are infested with tramps. . . .
Violence is increasing and threatens our very existence.

RICHARD GRANT WHITE, 1880[2]

INTRODUCTION

As evidenced by the sentiments in these opening quotes expressed more than a
century apart, it is the fate of every society, including our own, to view its own
times as uniquely and increasingly stressful, disorganized, and violent. This belief probably stems from a combination of cultural ethnocentrism regarding time

and place, the immediacy of our own stressful experiences, and the persistence of a golden-age mythology that makes us view earlier times in a more idyllic light. It is common to hear people longing for the good ol' days when life was simpler and society was not falling apart. However, if history tells us anything, it is that this country has always had high rates of violent death and murder. From its very inception, violence and killing have been instrumental in the formation of American society and its value system.

As we observed in the last chapter, the media play a significant role in shaping and molding our perceptions. Such media attention in recent years has led Americans to become increasingly concerned with a society that has appeared ever more dangerous and lawless. Arnold Goldstein points out that "Much of the United States is scared out of its wits. Many of our citizens imagine a criminal lurking in each dark alley, a burglar casing each darkened home, a rapist eyeing a prospective victim from behind each rustling curtain."[3]

But how well founded are these fears? Do people accurately assess their chances of becoming a victim of crime, especially violent crime and murder? Perceptions of crime and violence are based largely on media sources that are usually neither accurate nor representative. Does this mean that people's fears are unjustified and groundless, or is there real cause for concern? In this chapter, we explore specific patterns and trends of modern murder in order to answer some of these questions.

It is also important to recognize the influence that historic forms of violence have had on the modern era. Today, compared to other industrialized nations, the United States has one of the highest rates of homicide. But we did not become a violent and dangerous society overnight; we have a long history of such violence. How we define ourselves, the ways in which we respond to conflict, and the values that we hold as truths are all guided and shaped by our cultural frames of reference. And because culture is shaped by time, events, and circumstances, our violent history is with us every day, guiding our decisions and helping to shape our actions. History, the Roman orator Cicero reminds us, illumines reality and provides guidance in daily life. In other words, our violent past affects the nature and distribution of modern American homicide. Not that because a country has had a violent past, a violent present is inevitable; on the contrary, there are plenty of examples of countries that have suffered a violent past and are now quite peaceful. Various European countries come to mind.

The impact of the past on the present is contingent on how that past is understood and interpreted. In the United States, our violent past has largely been mythologized and glorified. Historic figures are celebrated for their ability and willingness to engage in violence to protect American values and the American way of life. This type of imagery cannot help but affect the nature and patterns of modern American violence. As the historian Roger Lane explains, "habits, values, and attitudes are components of culture, and culture is the product of history. Americans are a diverse people, with a shared national history but a number of separate histories as well. These separate histories each have been very important in shaping homicide rates."[4] A brief review of American history quickly reveals numerous examples of widespread violence.

HISTORIC OVERVIEW OF VIOLENCE

Although the very first contacts between the European explorers and the native peoples of the Americas were usually quite friendly, relations often quickly degenerated into brutal and murderous conflict. Contemporary American society reveals that the native tribes were most commonly on the losing end. Throughout the westward expansion from the Eastern seaboard to the Pacific Ocean, disease, firearms, and greed combined with dehumanizing racist ideologies to kill millions of Native Americans.[5] As Ian Steele makes clear, "colonial North American history was not created in peace and interrupted by war; wars, rumors of war, and costs of war affected every generation of Amerindians and colonists. It is disturbing to recognize that modern North America was established amid such violence, but this sobering realization is better than accepting sanitized myths that make modern levels of violence seem like moral degeneration from some peaceful colonial or pre-colonial Arcadia."[6]

So, from the very beginning, violence was a central theme in the European colonization of the New World, not just a historic footnote. Some argue that this adversarial and destructive relationship still characterizes the association between the Native American and White cultures in the United States.[7]

Of equal historical importance is the War for American Independence. The founding of this country through revolutionary warfare, in the words of historian Richard Maxwell Brown, "served as a grand model for later violent actions by Americans on behalf of any cause . . . deemed good and proper."[8] Essentially, Brown argues that by choosing to gain independence through warfare rather than through diplomacy or some other nonviolent alternative, the founding fathers helped shape a reliance on violence as the preferred method of dispute and conflict resolution. Americans, according to Brown, have attitudes embedded within their value system that foster collective and interpersonal violence. In other words, the Revolution may have helped shape an American ethos or identity that relies on violence in a variety of settings and situations. More concretely, the Revolutionary War was accompanied by guerrilla combat, murder, and assassination, as rebels (who called themselves patriots) battled Tory loyalists on and off the battlefield. This brutal round of internecine conflict helped set the stage for further acts of American violence.[9]

Similarly, the years preceding the Civil War were marked by ever-increasing levels of violence, as pro-slavery forces fought abolitionists in contested states such as Kansas, known at the time as "bleeding Kansas."[10] In one infamous example from 1863, about 150 male residents of Lawrence, Kansas, an abolitionist stronghold, were murdered by pro-slavery raiders. The Civil War itself remains the bloodiest in American history, fought as it was between Americans and on American soil. The violence of this war left an indelible stamp on American culture in general and on the Southeast in particular. The Civil War also spawned decades of postwar feuding, as hatreds generated during the war spilled over into criminal violence and murder, families settled old scores and grudges and, in the process, often began new ones.[11] These feuds occurred "in a land so sensitive to insult, those indignities grew in the telling until no one could remember that they owed their origins to war. . . . Warfare almost became a way of life."[12]

In addition to feuding, lynching became common in the post–Civil War years, as southern Whites attempted to ensure that recently freed slaves did not challenge their authority and power or that those who did were made to pay for their temerity.[13] Robert Johnson contends that lynching arose because "southern Whites—beleaguered, afraid, and increasingly vengeful in the face of economic and social competition from free Blacks—sought alternatives to slavery that would allow them to control and ultimately exploit the Black population. . . . One strategy to preserve White supremacy featured sheer and often brutal violence. The aim: to reduce newly liberated African-Americans to slaves of fear, who would submit passively to the demands of the dominant White caste, quietly living out a segregated, inferior life."[14]

History tells us that lynching was used against any group that threatened the established and unequal social order—Mexicans, Cubans, Native Americans, and labor union organizers, for example—but we must recognize that the vast majority of lynchings occurred against African-Americans in the southeastern United States.[15] The alleged crimes for which individuals were lynched ranged from serious offenses such as murder and rape to very minor and trivial acts such as insolence or a misinterpreted stare.[16] In some ways, the alleged offense was merely the excuse to reinforce the normative codes that governed race in the South. In fact, the victim of a lynching did not have to be guilty of anything. Sometimes, a mob would simply victimize the first unlucky African-Americans they were able to acquire and punish them for the alleged crimes of another. This extralegal form of mob violence was often marked by beatings, castration, burning, and other tortures inflicted on the victims before they were murdered, often by hanging.[17] Afterward, the mob would sometimes pose for pictures with the victim's body.

Lynchings occurred well into the latter half of the twentieth century, as many Whites struggled against the social, political, and economic changes that slowly stripped them of traditional privileges and prerogatives. Lynching has largely died out, but the hatreds and fears that drove it have not. Hate groups are a malign reality of modern American life and contribute to a variety of violent acts involving race, ethnicity, sexual orientation, and religiosity. On June 7, 1998, in Jasper, Texas, for example, three young White men with links to White supremacist groups, kidnapped a 49-year-old African-American, beat him unconscious, and chained him by the ankles to the back of a pickup truck. Then they proceeded to drag him to his death on the country roads surrounding the small Texas town. Racially motivated violence such as this continues to be fostered by a variety of organizations dedicated to maintaining unequal arrangements in society.[18]

Violence was not confined to the southern regions of our country. The western frontier in the latter half of the nineteenth century was widely regarded as an extremely violent region. Although showdowns, gunfights, and ambushes were not as frequent as Hollywood movies would suggest, they were frequent enough to elevate the homicide rate to serious levels in many western communities. For example, Abilene, Kansas, in the early 1870s averaged a homicide rate of 76.6 per 100,000;[19] Ellsworth, Kansas, had a homicide rate of 421.9 per 100,000 in 1873; Dodge City, Kansas, weighed in with a rate of 160 per 100,000 in 1878; and Wichita, Kansas, had an average rate of 91.3 per 100,000 during the early 1870s.[20] On average, these rates were more than 10 times higher than our nation's overall homicide rate today. Whereas not all western communities were quite so dangerous, these rates do give a sense of the potential for extreme violence on the frontier and validate the reputation of this region as the Wild West. Interesting enough, Roger McGrath, in his study of several western mining towns, points out that these towns were otherwise relatively crime free. Robberies and thefts, for example, occurred rarely; yet these same communities suffered from extremely high homicide rates.[21] These high amounts of lethal violence typically involved young men spending time in saloons and getting into fights that ended with gunplay. According to McGrath's analysis, other citizens did not have much to fear from crime because it was largely confined to young men engaging in relatively consensual violence. This scenario of young men drinking and killing each other remains characteristic of a large proportion of lethal violence in this country today.

The western frontier also helped spawn a uniquely American response to lawlessness: vigilantism. Although some vigilante practices originated in the pre-revolutionary South—in many ways a frontier region at the time—it was in the western territories that these traditions truly flourished and evolved into a major phenomenon. In the absence of official law enforcement, many western communities formed vigilance committees composed of prominent members of the local community. These self-appointed guardians of the moral order enforced laws and apprehended and punished alleged criminals, guilty or not. Based on widely held sentiments of popular sovereignty, these vigilance committees often enjoyed widespread support from the communities they ostensibly served.

This tradition of private citizens taking the law into their own hands and meting out their conception of justice continues to haunt modern America. Contemporary examples include the case of Bernhard Goetz, the well-known "subway vigilante," who in 1984 shot four teens after they approached and allegedly threatened him in a New York City subway car.[22] Similarly, we can remember the case of the retired navy commander who shot and killed a neighborhood bully after warning public officials that he might "take matters into my own hands," or the case of Ellie Nessler who shot and killed the man accused of molesting her son during his first court appearance. Each of these examples illustrates that vigilante traditions are alive and well in contemporary American society.[23]

American cities have also been notoriously dangerous environments, prone to riots, murder, and mayhem.[24] As the population increased dramatically in the nineteenth century, largely through immigration, American cities were wracked with social upheavals as traditional institutions struggled to cope with the massive population influx. George Cole writes, "From 1830 to 1870 there was unprecedented civil disorder in the major cities. Ethnic conflict stemming from massive immigration, hostility toward nonslave Blacks and abolitionists, mob actions against banks and other institutions of property during economic declines, and violence in settling questions of morality created fears that democratic institutions would not survive."[25] As the riots during the 1960s and 1990s have indicated, America's cities continue this tradition of urban violence and remain hotbeds of violent crime. In July of 1964, long-simmering frustrations and resentment exploded in Harlem after two teenagers were shot and killed by New York City police officers in separate incidents.[26] This riot was soon followed by others in cities around the country. In the following summers, American cities repeatedly exploded in rioting. In the Watts district of Los Angeles, 34 people were killed in August of 1965. Newark, New Jersey, suffered 23 dead in July of 1967, followed by Detroit, where the body count reached 43.[27] More recently, the 1990s have seen a variety of urban protests and riots in many American cities, often following police shootings of minority citizens.

The history of labor relations is another arena in which Americans have played out violent actions against fellow citizens. During the first half of the twentieth century, violent conflict was often the norm, as union activists and striking workers fought it out with private detective agencies and police in their attempts to unionize. Of one such attempt in West Virginia, Phillip Foner writes, "The Cabin Creek–Paint Creek strike of 1912–1913 became one of the most violent labor battles in American history. The miners and their families were threatened, beaten, and murdered, and in self-defense, the miners armed themselves with guns, erected forts, and organized armed squads to protect their families and fight back."[28]

Another example of the violence endemic to the labor movement occurred in Colorado, when a tent city inhabited by striking miners and their families was attacked by the state militia in what became known as the Ludlow massacre.[29] Coal miners had been on strike against the Colorado Fuel and Iron Company, and after a month of sporadic violence in which 18 people were killed, the company decided to end the strike decisively. In the dark of night, the strikers' tents were doused with oil and set alight as the strikers and their families slept inside; as they awoke and tried to flee the flames, they were fired upon with machine guns. Many were wounded, and five men, two women and 13 children were killed.[30] This brutal attack sparked further violence, which did not end until federal troops were finally called in to resolve the conflict.[31]

These patterns of violence were not limited to mining but were prevalent in many industries in which the forces of unionization and workers' rights collided with those of unrestrained capitalism.[32] To read accounts of the histories of the logging, automobile, steel, and agricultural industries—to name just a few examples—is to recognize the pervasiveness of violence between labor and management. Roger Lane points out that "what was labeled 'labor violence' was often simply overlaid on traditional kinds of ethnic, political, and cultural differences that had long inspired murderous conflict."[33] As any study of recent strikes reveals, this heritage of violence in the labor movement is by no means a thing of the past.

Violence has also been an accompanying factor in many of the social reform movements that have changed our society. For example, prohibition created the necessary conditions for tremendous amounts of violence, as rival gangs sought to control the market and eliminate competition in what became a highly lucrative alcohol distribution business. During the 1960s and the 1970s, the anti–Vietnam war movement, the civil rights movement, and the women's liberation movement were all accompanied by enormous amounts of violence, both from those seeking change and social justice and from the established forces of law and order seeking to maintain the status quo. For example, at the 1968 Democratic National Convention in Chicago, police attacked and assaulted anti–Vietnam war activists and demonstrators in what has been widely documented as a police riot.[34] Throughout the South during the 1960s, civil rights demonstrators found themselves assaulted with clubs, dogs, cattle prods, and fire hoses as they struggled to achieve social, legal, educational, and economic equality.[35] Significant social change in this country has rarely been effected without a great deal of violence and bloodshed.

We should also remember that the United States has engaged in a great deal of warfare over the years. From the American Revolution to Desert Storm and Kosovo, American history reveals a country that has relied on its military in a variety of situations. Various scholars have suggested that such warfare contributes to higher rates of murder. These researchers assert that involvement in wars tends to legitimize the use of lethal force to resolve conflict and, thereby, increases the internal criminal homicide rate of a society. Because the state has chosen to kill when faced with difficult circumstances, the citizens of that state will also be more likely to choose force when confronted with conflict on an individual level.[36]

As this brief discussion shows, the golden age of America was not so golden as it is sometimes romanticized to have been. This past is still with us in many ways. The American frontier, for example, has been a powerful force in shaping popular mythologies about our heritage and who we are. In modern culture, cowboys and gunslingers have been re-created and transformed into heroic figures of epic proportions, renowned for their rugged individualism, self-sufficiency, and willingness to engage in violence. They have come to represent idealized metaphors for what it means to be an American, particularly a male American. This cultural symbolism identifies a specific vision of American masculinity that values self-sufficiency and self-protection—a man, in short, who doesn't back down and who handles his own problems, violently when necessary. Similarly, popular culture has glorified many violent criminals of the twentieth century, such as John Dillinger and Bonnie and Clyde, who are portrayed as oppressed underdogs fighting against a cruel system. Transformed in cinema and literature from brutal criminals into noble outlaws, their images are potent manifestations of the ways in which our past continues to influence our perception of who we are as a people and the violence that inevitably arises out of that portrayal.

In sum, our past illustrates that the lethal violence so disturbing to modern Americans is not unique to our own time period. Indeed, our modern patterns of criminal violence are but contemporary incarnations of a recurring historic theme. The past also continues to influence U.S. homicide rates in other ways. Much of the violence in the past, for example, was rooted in issues of race, ethnicity, and poverty. When we examine contemporary patterns of violent behavior, it is evident that these themes continue to play powerful roles in shaping the American experience with violence.

MURDER TRENDS IN
THE TWENTIETH CENTURY

In the twentieth century, the criminal homicide rate has fluctuated considerably, as illustrated by Exhibit 2.1. In broad terms, we find two major increases in the homicide rate during this century. An examination of Exhibit 2.1 shows that at the turn of the century, the homicide rate was relatively low (1.2 per 100,000 in 1900). However, for the next 30 years it rose quite dramatically, peaking in 1933 with a rate of 9.7 per 100,000. This rise was followed by a consistent decrease until the late 1950s, although the homicide rate never again reached the low levels found at the beginning of the century.

Beginning in the mid-1960s, we find the homicide rate beginning another upward cycle, culminating in a murder rate of 10.7 per 100,000 in 1980—the high point for the century. In the early 1980s, the murder rate declined slightly, until the mid-1980s, when the trend reversed itself again and increased for the next 10 years. Since the mid-1990s, the murder rate again has begun to diminish.

Exhibit 2.2 provides a more detailed examination of recent trends from 1960 to 1999. Although Exhibit 2.1 is derived from NCHS data and Exhibit 2.2 relies on UCR information, the trends during this time period appear to be virtually identical. Exhibit 2.2 reveals an increase during the 1960s that continued through the 1970s, followed by a slight decrease during the early 1980s, after which the murder rate again increased through the early 1990s. The latest trend since the 1980s seems to be a decrease in the amount of murders recorded.

How do social scientists explain these periodic swings in the murder rate? Several possible explanations have been suggested. To account for the first major increase in the murder rate (1900–1935), Roger Lane has suggested that some of the homicide boom can be attributed to the increased use of automobiles. Automobiles led to a large increase in pedestrian fatalities that often resulted in formal charges of murder.[37] This contention is supported by Eckberg, who similarly holds that the dramatic increase was due to many homicides being initially misclassified as accidental.[38] Because they made excellent getaway vehicles, automobiles also helped increase the rate of organized crime–related murders and armed robbery murders that relied on the speed and mobility of this new means of transportation.

After conducting race- and ethnicity-specific analyses for this 30-year increase, Lane found that several distinct waves of immigration also helped explain the upswing. During the first few decades of the new century, many northern cities experienced a population growth from two specific sources. First, many southern African-Americans migrated north looking for work and

Exhibit 2.1 Criminal Homicide in the United States, 1900–1999

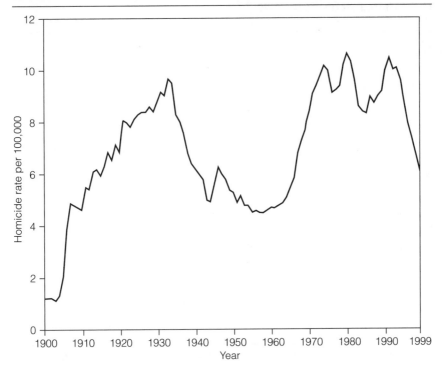

SOURCE: National Center for Health Statistics, *Vital Statistics in the United States, 1990–1999*.

opportunities and for an escape from the institutionalized racism so prevalent in the South. Many of these African-American immigrants became involved in violent crime when the hoped-for economic and social opportunities did not materialize, and they realized that they had exchanged southern rural poverty for poverty in northern urban slums. Second, during this time there was also an increase in immigration from Europe, especially from southern European countries such as Italy. Many of these immigrants likewise became involved in violent crime when the hoped-for land of opportunity did not live up to its promise. Supporting this argument, Ted Gurr's research illustrates that the upswing in murder rates was disproportionately high for African-Americans relative to Whites during the 1930s. Gurr attributes this to the fact that African-Americans were the hardest hit by the Great Depression.[39] Economic factors such as poverty and deprivation have long been identified as significant forces in promoting the perpetration of violence. As we will discuss in later chapters, race and ethnicity continue to be important correlates of modern American homicide for many of the same reasons.

Mark Haller, on the other hand, concentrates his explanation for the increased murder rates during the early twentieth century on the effects of prohibition, which went into effect in 1920. During this time, the sale and con-

Exhibit 2.2 Rates of Murder and Non-Negligent Manslaughter in the United States, 1960–1999

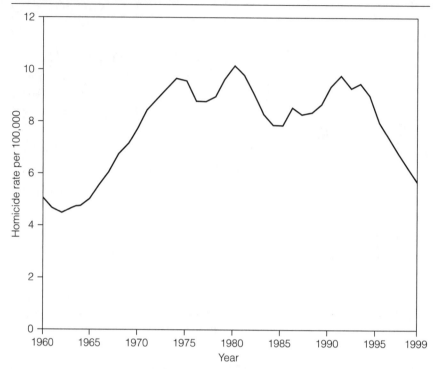

SOURCE: Federal Bureau of Investigation, *Uniform Crime Reports: Crime in the United States, 1960–1999.*

sumption of alcohol was illegal, but the demand remained high. Bootleggers engaged in a great deal of violence as they fought to control the market in illegal alcohol in ways that resemble the violent turf battles waged on our streets for the illegal drug trade today.[40] As gangs hijacked each other's alcohol shipments and fought to establish monopolies by eliminating competition, murder rates in many American communities skyrocketed. The most notorious case was the St. Valentine's Day massacre, in which members of Al Capone's gang disguised themselves as police officers and brutally gunned down members of a rival bootlegging gang.[41]

The last increase in murder rates of the twentieth century (1986–1991) has been largely explained through reference to the rise of crack cocaine. In the mid-1980s, a new form of cocaine known as *crack* became widely available. Created by cooking cocaine with sodium bicarbonate (baking soda) and water, crack cocaine is typically smoked. Crack cocaine produces a quick and very intense high that has been likened to the experience of an orgasm.[42] Unfortunately, the short duration of this high, combined with crack's ability to instantly and powerfully addict its users, quickly ensured a strong market demand. Moreover, the cheap price of crack cocaine, approximately $3 to $25 a vial, made this drug accessible to many more people.[43] Many scholars contend that the rise in homicide rates during the late 1980s came about because relatively well-armed young drug dealers competed viciously with each other to control this highly lucrative market. One study of crack-related homicides in New York City found that about 44% involved conflicts over territory, 18% involved dealers being ripped off, and another 11% concerned the collection of drug-related debts.[44] Needing to protect themselves and their business, young adults who "clocked" or worked in the drug trade increasingly turned to firearms to protect themselves and their product.[45]

The impressive decrease in the murder rate during most of the 1990s has been explained in a variety of ways. Garen Wintemute, for example, recently argued that the decline can be largely explained by the decreasing availability of handguns.[46] During the 1990s, various communities initiated aggressive legal and law enforcement tactics designed to get the guns off the streets by confiscating them, and other strategies focused on limiting dealers, sales, and buyers. Others have explained the decrease in homicide rates through reference to the increase in rates of incarceration or to the change in drug usage and distribution patterns.[47]

It is important to note that American homicide rates do not just vary over time but in space as well. Just as certain periods in U.S. history were more dangerous than others, certain regions of the country tend to be more unsafe than others.

REGIONAL DIFFERENCES

As Exhibit 2.3 illustrates, murder rates vary dramatically by region. During the 1980s and 1990s, approximately 42% of murders occurred in the southern states, more than twice the number that occurred in the western, midwestern, and northeastern regions. Why does the South have twice as many murders as other geographical areas? Attempts to explain this variance have generally focused on two competing arguments; the first argument stresses subcultural values, and the second argument emphasizes structural conditions such as poverty.

The South's historically higher rates of homicide have led various researchers to suggest a regional culture of violence native to the southeastern United States.[48] After the Jonesboro incident, various media pundits referred to this cultural explanation as the southern *gun culture*. But what is a so-called culture? Generally, *culture* is defined as "the beliefs, values, behavior, and material objects shared by a particular people."[49] Culture is a broad concept that refers to the intellectual and material tools that people use to make sense of the world around them. A *subculture,* on the other hand, is "a culture within a culture"[50]— that is, a group within a larger society that maintains a distinctive set of beliefs and customs, which may or may not be in opposition to those of the larger society. In a heterogeneous society such as the United States, with its wide range

**Exhibit 2.3 Murder by Region of the
United States, 1980–1989, 1990–1995**

Region	Average % of Murders, 1980–1989	Average % of Murders, 1990–1995
South	42.8	42.0
West	20.6	22.3
Midwest	19.2	19.3
Northeast	17.2	16.8

Percentages may not equal 100% due to rounding

SOURCE: Federal Bureau of Investigation, *Uniform Crime Reports: Crime in the United States, 1960–1999.*

of racial, ethnic, religious, and economic communities, many subcultures evolve as these groups struggle to define themselves and their place in the world.

Wolfgang and Ferracuti were among the first to suggest that some Americans hold subcultural value systems that condone, expect, and even encourage the use of violence to resolve interpersonal conflict.[51] Members of these groups more often perceive and define individual and group violence as legitimate. Wolfgang specifically asserted that "Quick resort to physical combat as a measure of daring, courage, or defense of status appears to be a cultural expectation. . . When such a culture norm response is elicited from an individual engaged in social interplay with others who harbor the same response mechanism, physical assaults, altercations, and violent domestic quarrels that result in homicide are likely to be relatively common."[52]

Extending this argument, some have suggested that because of the South's unique history, a regional culture has developed that is conducive to violent interactions. Several historical factors seem to be associated with the rise of a southern subculture of violence.

The first factor concerns the development of a southern tradition of masculine honor that is closely linked with reputation. This notion of *primal honor,* as it has been termed by Wyatt-Brown,[53] refers to a system in which men are expected to be violent in the defense of their good name and reputation. Nisbett and Cohen define this value system as a *culture of honor,* "based not on good character but on a man's strength and power to enforce his will on others. . . . The culture of honor differs from other cultures in that violence will be used to attain and protect this kind of honor."[54]

Southern men, the argument goes, are more likely to respond violently to insults or perceived attacks on their character. In addition to the regional disparities in homicide rates, research at the individual level has indicated that compared to men from other regions of the country, southern men are generally more supportive of defensive violence.[55]

A second element in the development of a culture of violence in the South concerns the legacy of slavery. Fox Butterfield suggests that "all this traffic in slaves, and the vast force needed to run a society based on bondage, was another major contributor to violence in the South. Slavery had a brutalizing effect that fell both on the bondsmen and their masters."[56] Although slavery was eventually abolished, the cultural values created under slavery persisted. Butterfield quotes a slave by the name of Charles Bell, who echoed this observation when he wrote, "It seems to be a law of nature that slavery is equally destructive to the master and the slave. For, whilst it stupefies the latter with fear, and reduces him below the condition of man, it brutalizes the former, by the practice of continual tyranny; and makes him the prey of all the vices which render human nature loathsome."[57]

Southern culture, then, placed a premium on values that legitimized the brutality of slavery, and these values have persisted into the modern era. Other scholars have referred to the historical imprint of the Civil War and the pursuant feuding and lynching as being instrumental in developing a more violent regional culture than in other areas of the country.[58]

The southern subculture of violence thesis, however, has not received much empirical support. One of the problems, of course, is how to statistically measure this thing called culture. Whereas some researchers have found evidence supporting subcultural explanations,[59] others have not. Robert Nash Parker, for example, found that structural indicators such as poverty were more powerful predictors of homicide rates than subcultural indicators such as region.[60] Others have similarly concluded that economic factors are more relevant than cultural factors to understanding why the South has such perennially high homicide rates.[61] *Poverty,* especially as it has affected certain minority communities, has been the focus of much of the research on murder. This line of investigation is supported by the finding that all across the country, regardless of region, most homicides are perpetrated by people living in poverty. Poor people, whether they are Black, White, Latino, Native American, or Asian-American, are more likely to kill than their racial or ethnic peers in the higher socioeconomic classes.[62] From this perspective, the levels of lethal violence in the South have more to do with poverty than with culture.

THE CHARACTERISTICS OF MURDER
IN THE UNITED STATES

So far, we have seen that murder in the United States has fluctuated across both time and space. We now turn to an analysis of murder that focuses on individual characteristics such as age, race, and sex. Although homicide rates have fluctuated tremendously over time, not everyone has been more vulnerable to murder simply because the overall rates were higher. As will become evident, the sharp increase in the murder rate during the late 1980s, for example, fell most heavily upon one specific group. In other words, a person's risk of becoming a murder victim has a lot to do with their age, sex, race, ethnicity, and class.

One of the questions posed at the beginning of this chapter asked whether people accurately assess their chances of becoming a victim of crime, especially violent crime and murder. One way of assessing the risk of dying as a result of a murder is to place this risk into the context of dying from other causes. For example, the Centers for Disease Control and Prevention tell us that in 1995, homicide was ranked as the fourteenth leading cause of death for the entire U.S. population. Clearly, being murdered does not rank among the most likely ways of dying when we consider the population as a whole. Accidents and various illnesses are more common causes of American deaths. However, if we examine the top five leading causes of death by age, sex, and racial group, we see a dramatically different reality. Exhibit 2.4 ranks causes of death for age groups between the ages of 5 and 44 years by sex and race for 1995.

As is evident from Exhibit 2.4, homicide was one of the top five killers of individuals in the youngest two age groups regardless of sex or race. Even more alarming is the finding that homicide is the leading cause of death for African-American men and women between the ages of 15 and 24. Moreover, whereas White men and women both appeared to decrease their risk of being murdered with increasing age relative to other causes of death, homicide remained a leading killer for African-Americans between the ages of 25 and 44. This demonstrates the fallacy of thinking of homicide as a homogeneous entity. Rather, homicide occurs differently depending on a variety of factors.

Exhibit 2.5 displays the average annual homicide victimization rates by age, sex, and race from 1995 through 1999. Young people between the ages of 18 and 24 show the highest rates of homicide victimization and offending. Men were six times more likely than women to have been the victims of homicide and nine times more likely to have been the offenders. African-Americans were six times more likely than Whites or members of other racial groups to have been the victims of homicide and eight times more likely to have been the offenders. Most of the murders were intraracial. For example, James Alan Fox and Marianne Zawitz estimate that during the past two decades, 86% of White victims have been killed by Whites, and 94% of African-American victims have been killed by African-Americans.[63]

How do these murder rate differentials across sex and race vary over the life span? In Exhibits 2.6 and 2.7 we see murder rates across the life span by age group, by sex, and by race, respectively, for 1994. From Exhibit 2.6, it is clear that men are more often the victims of murder than women throughout life. However, taking a closer look, it is clear that the differential between boys and girls skyrockets during late adolescence (ages 18–24). Although boys in the youngest age group (12–14) and men in the oldest group (65 and older) were still more likely to be killed than their female counterparts, this difference was not as great as that found in late adolescence.

An examination of the murder rates in Exhibit 2.7 reveals that compared to Whites, African-Americans have higher rates of murder victimization for all age groups. However, as with the pattern found across sexes, this disparity is particularly high among certain age groups, especially between the ages of 18 and 29. When examining the trends across both exhibits, we see that the youngest and the oldest in our society are less likely to be murdered compared to other individuals. After late adolescence, rates of murder drop precipitously

Exhibit 2.4 Top Five Leading Causes of Death in the United States in 1995 by Age Groups, Race, and Sex

	WHITE MEN		
Rank	Ages 5–14	Ages 15–24	Ages 25–44
1	Accidents and adverse effects	Accidents and adverse effects	Accidents and adverse effects
2	Malignant neoplasms	Suicide	Human immuno-deficiencyvirus (HIV)
3	Suicide	*Homicide*	Diseases of heart
4	*Homicide*	Malignant neoplasms	Suicide
5	Congenital anomalies	Diseases of heart	Malignant neoplasms

	BLACK MEN		
Rank	Ages 5–14	Ages 15–24	Ages 25–44
1	Accidents and adverse effects	*Homicide*	Human Immuno-deficiency virus (HIV)
2	*Homicide*	Accidents and adverse effects	*Homicide*
3	Malignant neoplasms	Suicide	Accidents and adverse effects
4	Human immuno-deficiency virus (HIV)	Diseases of heart	Diseases of heart
5	Chronic obstructive pulmonary diseases	Human immuno-deficiency virus (HIV)	Malignant neoplasms

	WHITE WOMEN		
Rank	Ages 5–14	Ages 15–24	Ages 25–44
1	Accidents and adverse effects	Accidents and adverse effects	Malignant neoplasms
2	Malignant neoplasms	*Homicide*	Accidents and adverse effects
3	Congenital anomalies	Suicide	Diseases of heart
4	*Homicide*	Malignant neoplasms	Suicide
5	Diseases of heart	Diseases of heart	Human immuno-deficiency virus (HIV)

	BLACK WOMEN		
Rank	Ages 5–14	Ages 15–24	Ages 25–44
1	Accidents and adverse effects	*Homicide*	Human immuno-deficiency virus (HIV)
2	Malignant neoplasms	Accidents and adverse effects	Malignant neoplasms
3	*Homicide*	Human immuno-deficiency virus (HIV)	Diseases of heart
4	Human immuno-deficiency virus (HIV)	Diseases of heart	Accidents and adverse effects
5	Diseases of heart	Malignant neoplasms	*Homicide*

SOURCE: R. N. Anders, K. D. Kochanek, and S. L. Murphy, "Report of Final Mortality Statistics," *Monthly Vital Statistics Report*, 45(11), Supp. 2. (Hyattsville, Md.: National Center for Health Statistics, 1995).

Exhibit 2.5 Average Annual Rates of Homicide Victimization and Offending per 100,000 Population by Age Group, Sex, and Race, 1995–1999.

Group	Victimization Rate per 100,000	Offending Rate per 100,000
Age		
Under 14	1.8	0.2
14–17	7.9	16.7
18–24	18.6	32.8
25–34	11.6	12.7
35–49	7.0	5.8
50 and over	3.1	1.7
Sex		
Male	12.1	14.3
Female	2.3	1.5
Race		
White	4.1	4.2
African-American	25.9	32.2
Other	3.8	4.3

SOURCE: Data obtained from James A. Fox and Marianne W. Zawitz, *Homicide Trends in the United States* (Washington, D.C.: Bureau of Justice Statistics, U.S. Department of Justice, 2001).

Exhibit 2.6 Rates of Murder Victimization per 100,000 by Age Group and Sex in 1994

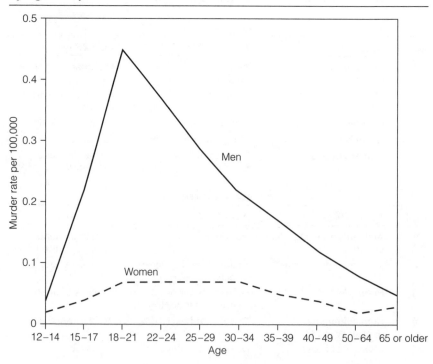

SOURCE: C. Perkins, *Age Patterns of Victims of Serious Violent Crime* (Washington, D.C.: Bureau of Justice Statistics, U.S. Department of Justice, 1997).

Exhibit 2.7 Rates of Murder Victimization per 100,000 by Age Group and Race in 1994

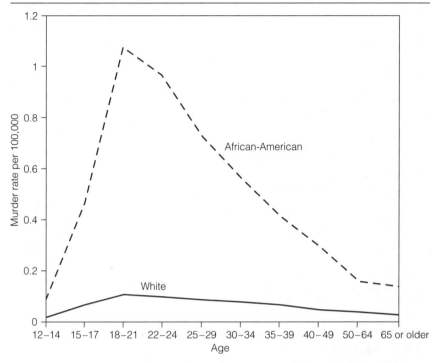

SOURCE: C. Perkins, *Age Patterns of Victims of Serious Violent Crime* (Washington, D.C.: Bureau of Justice Statistics, U.S. Department of Justice, 1997).

as we move through the life span. Thus, a central reality of homicide in the United States is that young African-American men are the most common murder victims.

RECENT TRENDS IN MURDER

Over the past two decades, certain groups in U.S. society have experienced tremendous volatility in their rates of homicide victimization and offending. Exhibit 2.8 displays homicide victimization rates by age group from 1980 through 1999. During the early 1990s, individuals between the ages of 14 and 24 experienced significant increases in their rates of homicide victimization. In fact, for juveniles, the homicide rate increased more than 150% from 1984 to 1993.[64] The rates of victimization for this age group have, however, declined in recent years.

Even steeper increases are observed in the rates of homicide offending for these age groups, as shown in Exhibit 2.9. In fact, homicide offending rates of

Exhibit 2.8 Homicide Victimization Rates per 100,000 Population by Age Group, 1980–1999

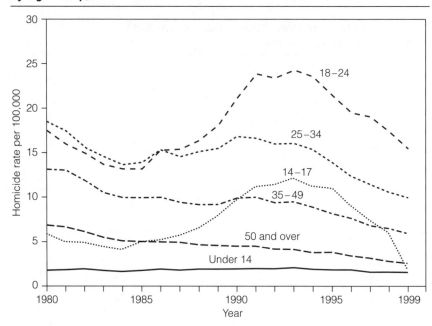

SOURCE: James A. Fox and Marianne W. Zawitz, *Homicide Trends in the United States* (Washington, D.C.: Bureau of Justice Statistics, U.S. Department of Justice, 2001).

Exhibit 2.9 Homicide Offending Rates per 100,000 Population by Age Group, 1980–1999

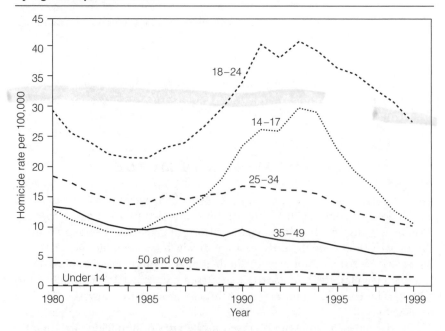

SOURCE: James A. Fox and Marianne W. Zawitz, *Homicide Trends in the United States* (Washington, D.C.: Bureau of Justice Statistics, U.S. Department of Justice, 2001).

Exhibit 2.10 Homicide Offending Rates per 100,000 by Age Group for White Men, 1980–1999

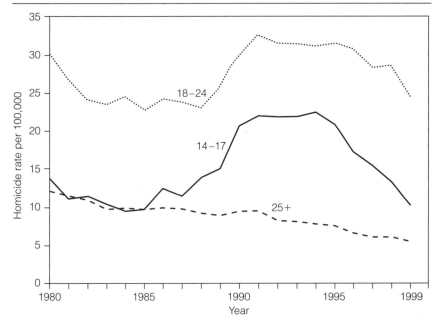

SOURCE: James A. Fox and Marianne W. Zawitz, *Homicide Trends in the United States* (Washington, D.C.: Bureau of Justice Statistics, U.S. Department of Justice, 2001).

14- to 17-year-olds exploded after 1985, surpassing those of 25- to 34-year-olds and 35- to 49-year-olds. Although offending rates for young adults have declined in recent years, they still remain higher than the rates observed in the early 1980s.

Examining the offending rates more closely, we see that this peak in the early 1990s was largely attributable to young African-American men. Exhibits 2.10 through 2.13 display the rates of offending by age, race, and sex from 1980 through 1999. The increase of the total homicide rate during the early 1990s was generally a young male phenomenon, and these exhibits illustrate that this increase largely involved the offending rates for African-American boys between the ages of 14 and 24. In fact, offending rates by race and sex over the age of 25 decreased during this time period. The only increase in rates of offending for women during this time was seen for girls between the ages of 14 and 17. Researchers examining city-level data have also found young men from other minority groups, such as Latinos, to be more vulnerable to homicide victimization than Whites during this time period.[65]

We have seen that young men, particularly African-American men, have been largely responsible for the explosion of murder in the early 1990s. Another factor contributing to this epidemic was the easy availability of handguns. Handguns are by far the most popular weapon for the commission of murder. More than 51% of the murder victims in 1999, for example, were killed with a handgun. An additional 14% were killed with other guns, and 13% were

Exhibit 2.11 Homicide Offending Rates per 100,000 by Age Group for African-American Men, 1980–1999

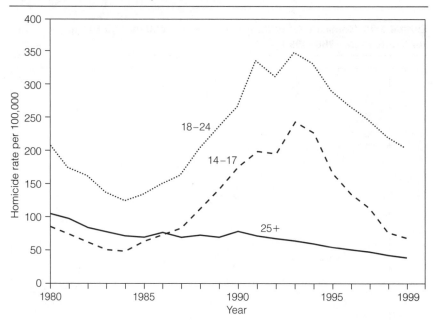

SOURCE: James A. Fox and Marianne W. Zawitz, *Homicide Trends in the United States* (Washington, D.C.: Bureau of Justice Statistics, U.S. Department of Justice, 2001).

Exhibit 2.12 Homicide Offending Rates per 100,000 by Age Group for White Women, 1980–1999

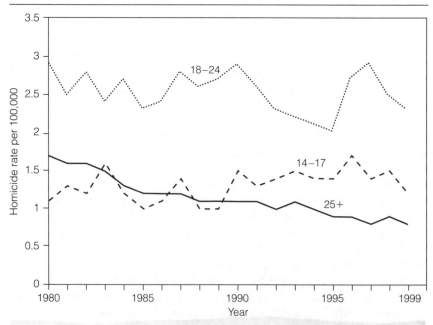

SOURCE: James A. Fox and Marianne W. Zawitz, *Homicide Trends in the United States* (Washington, D.C.: Bureau of Justice Statistics, U.S. Department of Justice, 2001).

Exhibit 2.13 Homicide Offending Rates per 100,000 by Age Group for African-American Women, 1980–1999

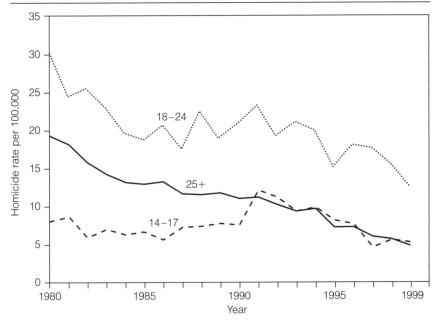

SOURCE: James A. Fox and Marianne W. Zawitz, *Homicide Trends in the United States* (Washington, D.C.: Bureau of Justice Statistics, U.S. Department of Justice, 2001).

killed with knives or other sharp instruments. Exhibit 2.14 displays the number of murder victims killed by various weapons during the 1980–1999 time period. Whereas the use of other weapons, including knives and other guns, has remained relatively constant over time, the use of handguns in the commission of murder skyrocketed during the early 1990s.

As we alluded to earlier, the spike in murder rates for young men in the late 1980s and early 1990s may be largely explained by the increase in firearm usage by young drug dealers. Supporting evidence for this explanation is most often found at the city level of analysis. For example, after examining homicide events categorized by weapon, age, and location (for instance, small versus large cities), Alfred Blumstein concluded that the increase in murder rates was primarily driven by young men wielding handguns in large central cities. The factors responsible for this pattern are largely speculative, but most researchers, including Blumstein, agree that the illicit crack cocaine market played a large role. The introduction of crack in the mid-1980s created a huge, potentially lucrative market. Because young urban African-American men often see no other route to economic success, they are particularly vulnerable to the lure of the drug market. As Elijah Anderson writes, "For many impoverished young black men of the inner city, the opportunity for dealing drugs is literally just outside the door. By selling drugs, they have a chance to put more money into their

Exhibit 2.14 Number of Homicides by Type of Weapon Used, 1980–1999

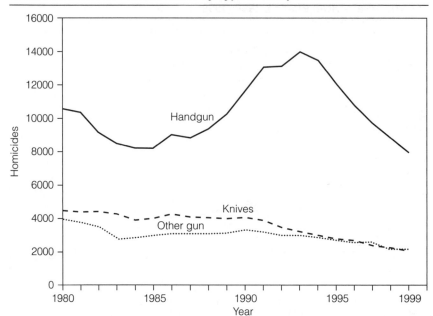

SOURCE: James A. Fox and Marianne W. Zawitz, *Homicide Trends in the United States* (Washington, D.C.: Bureau of Justice Statistics, U.S. Department of Justice, 2001).

pockets than they could get by legal means, and they can present themselves to peers as hip, in sharp contrast to the square image of those who work in places like McDonald's and wear silly uniforms."[66]

When drug markets became pervasive in inner-city neighborhoods, more and more young people chose to sell drugs and simultaneously to carry guns to protect themselves and their product. The mixture of young male machismo and bravado and territorial drug market disputes undoubtedly has the potential to result in lethal violence. The increased availability of firearms is a lethal ingredient to such a mix. As Blumstein states, "many of the fights that would otherwise have taken place and resulted in nothing more serious than a bloody nose can now turn into shootings as a result of the presence of guns."[67]

VICTIM–OFFENDER
RELATIONSHIPS IN MURDER

There are other informative ways in which we can disaggregate total rates of homicide, such as examining the relationship between the victim and the offender. Exhibit 2.15 displays the percentage of all male and female homicides in 1992 by victim–offender relationship. For cases in which the relationship between the victim and the offender was determined, large differences are ev-

Exhibit 2.15 Percentage of Male and Female Homicides in 1992 by Victim–Offender Relationship

	Female Victims	Male Victims
Victim–Offender Relationship		
Spouse/ex-spouse	18.0	2.2
Boy/girlfriend	10.3	1.4
Other relative	10.2	5.5
Friend/acquaintance	22.0	34.6
Stranger	8.6	15.0
Relationship not identified	30.9	41.3
Number of Incidents		
Relationship identified	3,454	10,351
Relationship not identified	1,547	7,824
Total number of incidents	5,001	17,635

In 41% of male homicides and 31% of female homicides, the victim–offender relationship could not be established. Therefore, readers are urged to use caution in interpreting these estimates.

SOURCE: Ronet Bachman and Linda Saltzman, *Violence against Women: Estimates from the Redesigned Survey* (Washington, D.C.: Bureau of Justice Statistics, U.S. Department of Justice, 1995).

ident across sexes in who is most likely to do the killing. Female victims of homicide are significantly more likely to be killed by an intimate, such as a husband, ex-husband, or boyfriend, than male victims are to be killed by intimates. In 1992, approximately 28% of female murder victims were known to have been killed by their intimate partners. In contrast, just over 3% of male homicide victims were known to have been killed by their intimate partners. Men, it appears, are more likely to be killed by acquaintances and friends than by intimates or strangers. What stands out most from this exhibit is that less than one in ten female homicide victims and less than two in ten male homicide victims were known to have been killed by strangers.

It is important to note that the relationship between the victim and the offender in a large percentage of these killings (39%) is never known, which may be explained in part by the decrease in arrest clearance rates for murder. According to the FBI, clearance rates decreased from 79% in 1976 to 66% in 1993 and increased slightly to 69% in 1999.[68] Evidence suggests that a significant portion of the unknown relationships may in fact be strangers. Marc Riedel, for example, points out that stranger murders often take longer for the police to solve because the obvious starting point for homicide investigations is the victim's family and friends.[69] Strangers are harder to identify as offenders, and these cases may initially be recorded on the monthly supplementary homicide reports as having an unknown relationship. As these forms are completed and submitted monthly, a case that takes more than a month to solve remains coded as having an unknown relationship.

Exhibit 2.16 Percentage of Murders by Relationship between Victims and Perpetrators

Relationship	1980–1989 (%)	1990–1995 (%)	Total Average (%)
Stranger	14.45	14.17	14.31
Known (includes family and non-family)	55.58	47.37	51.48
Unknown relationship	29.97	38.47	34.22
Family	16.54	12.21	14.38
Husband	3.1	1.62	2.36
Wife	4.96	3.93	4.45
Mother	0.68	0.58	.63
Father	0.92	0.78	.85
Daughter	1.18	1.08	1.13
Son	1.64	1.47	1.56
Brother	1.14	0.8	.97
Sister	0.22	0.17	.2
Other family	2.7	1.78	2.24
Non-Family (Known)	39	35.16	37.08
Acquaintance	29.74	27.12	28.43
Friend	4.22	3.57	3.9
Boyfriend	1.42	1.15	1.29
Girlfriend	2.26	2.35	2.31
Neighbor	1.36	0.97	1.17

SOURCE: Federal Bureau of Investigation, *Uniform Crime Reports: Crime in the United States, 1980–1995.*

The proportion of homicides in which the offender is classified as unknown is also increasing. Exhibit 2.16 details the relationship between victims and offenders for 1980–1989 and for 1990–1995. Clearly, the percentage of killings in which the victim–offender relationship is unknown has increased from approximately 30% in the 1980s to an average of almost 40% during the first half of the 1990s. It is improbable that *all* of these unknown relationship cases involve strangers, but a significant proportion of them may indeed involve stranger-perpetrated homicides. City-level analyses also provide evidence for this supposition. For example, in one study of murders in Dade County, Florida—which includes the city of Miami—William Wilbanks found that although official statistics recorded 11% of homicides as stranger perpetrated, when he added the killing of felons and instances of felons killing citizens—both categories involving strangers—the percentage of stranger homicides increased to 24.9%.[70] Similarly, Robert Silverman and Leslie Kennedy's review of homicide research studies revealed that stranger-perpetrated murders represented a range of 12% to 22% of all homicides depending on the location and the time under study.[71] In another study of homicide in eight cities, Marc Riedel and Margaret Zahn found that stranger murders ranged from 14.3% to 29% of all homicides, with an average of 23.5%.[72] Stranger homicides, then, may actually constitute a more significant proportion of homicides than official statistics initially seem to indicate. This is important because the fear of crime is more accurately described as the fear of being victimized by a stranger.[73] As Robert Sampson points out, "it is the possibility of attack by strangers that seems to engender the most intense feelings of vulnerability and fear."[74] Similarly, Joel Best asserts that "we do not fear 'crime'; we fear the carjackers, the sexual predators, the drive-by shooters—the strangers who attack without warning or provocation."[75] Because of this perceived vulnerability, stranger homicides assume a significance in our minds that is out of proportion to their actual occurrence. As the literature suggests, stranger-perpetrated homicides may account for at most one in four homicides.

So far, we have seen that homicide victimization rates vary dramatically across time, space, and demographic characteristics such as sex, age, and race. Although the primary focus of this book is on murder in America, it is important to frame the American experience with homicide within the broader international context. How do patterns of homicide in the United States compare to other countries? Where do we rank internationally?

INTERNATIONAL COMPARISONS

Is a criminal homicide rate of 10 per 100,000 relatively high or comparatively low? When we compare the incidence of murder to that of other crimes, we find that it actually occurs relatively infrequently. The FBI reports that in 1992, a motor vehicle theft occurred every 20 seconds, larceny theft every 20 seconds, rape every 5 minutes, and murder once every 22 minutes.[76] In other words, compared to other crimes—especially property offenses—homicide is a relatively infrequent event. As the FBI points out, this *crime clock* method of comparison should not suggest a periodicity of perpetration; rather, it represents a ratio of crime incidence to fixed time intervals. Although the crime clock is not a good tool for analysis, it does present a way to compare the relative frequency of perpetration. The less serious an offense, the more frequently it typically occurs.

However, when we contrast the murder rate in the United States to that in other societies, a very different picture emerges. Before making such comparisons, a word of caution is in order. Cross-national crime comparisons must be done carefully because of several methodological limitations. There is a fair amount of variability in how individual countries define crime, how they gather their data, and the ways in which they report them. This makes it somewhat difficult to compare crime rates between countries.[77] However, even with the problems of cross-national crime statistics, it is still possible to make rough comparisons in order to highlight international differences in crime.

Exhibit 2.17 compares murder rates in 20 selected countries including the United States. Although a variety of nations are included, the most important comparisons concern the United States in relation to the industrialized nations included in the exhibit. Evidently, the murder rate in the United States far exceeds that of other countries with similar economic, political, and social characteristics. Comparable countries in Europe, for example, have murder rates far below that endured by Americans. Messner and Rosenfeld report that in 1992,

Exhibit 2.17 Cross-National Comparison of Murder Rates for Selected Countries that are Socioeconomically Comparable to the United States

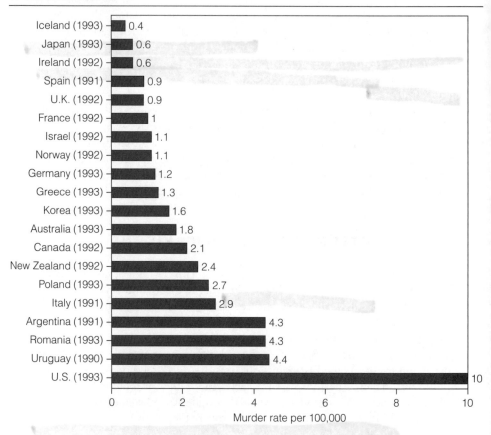

Country	Murder rate per 100,000
Iceland (1993)	0.4
Japan (1993)	0.6
Ireland (1992)	0.6
Spain (1991)	0.9
U.K. (1992)	0.9
France (1992)	1
Israel (1992)	1.1
Norway (1992)	1.1
Germany (1993)	1.2
Greece (1993)	1.3
Korea (1993)	1.6
Australia (1993)	1.8
Canada (1992)	2.1
New Zealand (1992)	2.4
Poland (1993)	2.7
Italy (1991)	2.9
Argentina (1991)	4.3
Romania (1993)	4.3
Uruguay (1990)	4.4
U.S. (1993)	10

SOURCE: United Nations, *Demographic Yearbook, 1994* (New York: United Nations, 1996).

the city of St. Louis, with a population of about 390,000, had more murders than the entire region of Scotland, with a population of 5,100,000.[78]

Of course, there are countries in the world with rates of murder that are as high or higher than those experienced in the United States. Exhibit 2.18 displays the U.S. murder rate in comparison to countries that have murder rates in excess of those experienced in this country. According to U.N. data, Colombia, with a murder rate of 89.6 per 100,000, suffers from the highest murder rate in the world. Colombia also happens to be a country that for years has been waging an internal conflict against drug cartels and against revolutionary movements intent on overthrowing the government. It is safe to assume that many killings in Colombia are related to these two sources of violence. Many of the other countries with high murder rates are former members of the Soviet Union. During the 1990s, these countries experienced tremendous civil

Exhibit 2.18 Cross-National Comparison of Murder Rates for Selected Countries that Are Socially and Politically Less Stable than the United States

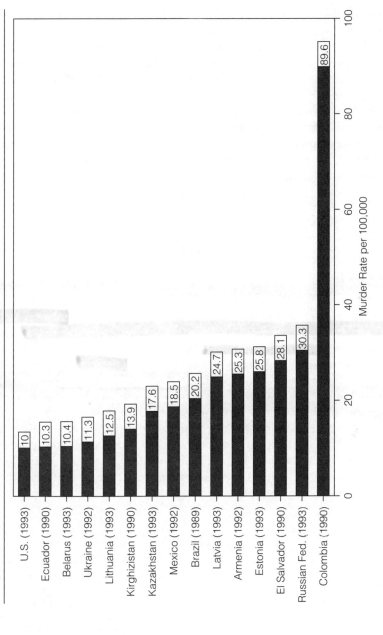

SOURCE: United Nations, *Demographic Yearbook, 1994* (New York: United Nations, 1996).

and political unrest as the Soviet bloc disintegrated and these countries transitioned from communism to democracy and from centralized forms of market relations to free-market capitalism. These social, political, and economic changes have often been accompanied by revolution, social unrest and disorganization, and increases in organized crime, which go a long way in explaining the high rates of murder in these countries. Noticeably absent from Exhibit 2.18 are the European and other industrialized nations of the world, which, as Exhibit 2.17 illustrates, experience much lower murder rates. Thus, in contrast to other stable industrialized nations, the average rate of murder we experience in the United States places us in the company of countries undergoing internal conflict and catastrophic change. In short, our nation experiences far higher murder rates than similar countries around the world.

SUMMARY

Why is the United States so much more dangerous than other, comparable societies? Similar to the subculture of violence thesis, some have argued that American culture in general—not just specific subcultures—tolerates and encourages the use of violence in many social interactions and settings.[79] Others contend that economic deprivation best explains the variation in homicide rates across nations.[80] Still others point to the role of firearms in helping to produce such high rates of violence. Regardless of the explanation, the fact remains that the United States has an unusually high rate of murder and, as such, is one of the more dangerous of modern industrialized nations.

This chapter has illustrated that criminal homicide is not a uniform phenomenon but rather has varying patterns based, for example, on region, sex, age, and race. The burden of murder falls unequally on the shoulders of different populations, and it is to the particular dynamics of these issues that we turn our attention in the next chapter.

NOTES

1. Arnold P. Goldstein, *Violence in America: Lessons on Understanding the Aggression in Our Lives* (Palo Alto, Calif.: Davies-Black, 1996), p. 7.

2. Richard Grant White, *The North American Review* (1880).

3. Goldstein, *Violence in America,* p. 13.

4. Roger Lane, *Murder in America: A History,* ed. David R. Johnson and Jeffrey S. Adler, *The History of Crime and Criminal Justice Series* (Columbus: Ohio State University Press, 1997).

5. Bartolomé de Las Casas, *The Devastation of the Indies* (Baltimore: The Johns Hopkins University Press, 1974); Francis Jennings, *The Founders of America: From the Earliest Migrations to the Present* (New York: W. W. Norton, 1993); David E. Stannard, *American Holocaust: The Conquest of the New World* (New York: Oxford University Press, 1992); Ian K. Steele, *Warpaths: Invasions of North America* (New York: Oxford University Press, 1994); Russell Thornton, *American Indian Holocaust and Survival: A Population History since 1492*

(Norman: Oklahoma University Press, 1987); Tzvetan Todorov, *Facing the Extreme: Moral Life in the Concentration Camps,* trans. Abigail Pollak and Arthur Denner (New York: Henry Holt, 1996).

6. Steele, *Warpaths.*

7. Ward Churchill, *A Little Matter of Genocide: Holocaust and Denial in the Americas: 1492 to the Present* (San Francisco: City Lights, 1997).

8. Richard Maxwell Brown, "Historical Patterns of Violence," in *Violence in America: Protest, Rebellion, Reform,* ed. Ted Robert Gurr (Newbury Park, Calif.: Sage, 1989), p. 23.

9. Richard Maxwell Brown, *Strain of Violence* (New York: Oxford University Press, 1975); Brown, "Historical Patterns of Violence."

10. Brown, "Historical Patterns of Violence"; Brown, *Strain of Violence.*

11. Kai T. Erickson, *Everything in Its Path: Destruction of Community in the Buffalo Creek Flood* (New York: Simon & Schuster, 1976); V. C. Jones, *The Hatfields and the McCoys* (Atlanta: Mockingbird Books, 1948); William Lynwood Montell, *Killings: Folk Justice in the Upper South* (Lexington: University Press of Kentucky, 1986); A. L. Waller, *Feud: Hatfields, McCoys, and Social Change in Appalachia, 1860–1900* (Chapel Hill: University of North Carolina Press, 1988).

12. Erickson, *Everything in Its Path,* p. 56.

13. W. Fitzhugh Brundage, *Lynching in the New South: Georgia and Virginia, 1880–1930* (Urbana: University of Illinois Press, 1993); J. M. Inverarity, "Populism and Lynching in Louisiana, 1889–1896: A Test of Erickson's Theory of the Relationship between Boundary Crisis and Repressive Justice," *American Sociological Review,* 41, 262–280 (1976); C. D. Phillips, "Exploring Relations among Forms of Social Control: The Lynching and Execution of Blacks in North Carolina, 1889–1918," *Law and Society Review,* 21(3), 361–374 (1987); Stewart E. Tolnay and E. M. Beck, *A Festival of Violence: An Analysis of Southern Lynchings, 1882–1930* (Urbana: University of Illinois Press, 1995); Stewart E. Tolnay, E. M. Beck, and J. L. Massey, "Black Lynchings: The Power Threat Hypothesis Revisited," *Social Forces,* 67(3), 605–623 (1989).

14. Robert Johnson, *Death Work: A Study of the Modern Execution Process* (Belmont, Calif.: West/Wadsworth, 1997), pp. 32–33.

15. Brundage, *Lynching in the New South;* Robert P. Ingalls, *Urban Vigilantes in the New South: Tampa, 1882–1936* (Gainesville: University Press of Florida, 1988); Tolnay and Beck, *A Festival of Violence.*

16. Tolnay and Beck, *A Festival of Violence.*

17. Brundage, *Lynching in the New South;* Tolnay and Beck, *A Festival of Violence.*

18. Vincent Coppola, *Dragons of God: A Journey through Far-Right America* (Atlanta: Longstreet Press, 1996); Raphael S. Ezekiel, *The Racist Mind: Portraits of American Neo-Nazis and Klansmen* (New York: Viking, 1995); John George and Laird Wilcox, *American Extremists: Militias, Supremacists, Klansmen, Communists, and Others* (Amherst, N.Y.: Prometheus, 1996); Barbara Perry, *In the Name of Hate: Understanding Hate Crime* (New York: Routledge, 2001).

19. A rate per 100,000 is a statistical construct that allows us to compare communities with different populations. In this example, the rate tells us the number of victims there would be out of every 100,000 individuals in the population.

20. Clare V. McKanna Jr., *Homicide, Race, and Justice in the American West, 1880–1920* (Tucson: The University of Arizona Press, 1997).

21. Roger D. McGrath, "Violence and Lawlessness on the Western Frontier: The History of Crime," in *Violence in America,* ed. Ted Robert Gurr (Newbury Park, Calif.: Sage, 1989).

22. George P. Fletcher, *A Crime of Self-Defense: Bernhard Goetz and the Law on Trial* (New York: Free Press, 1988).

23. Matthew Fordahl, "Former Navy Commander Convicted of Killing Bully." *San Diego Source,* June 6, 1996. http://sddt.com/files/librarywire/96wireheadlines/06_96/DN96_06_06_cg.html; "Chronology of Events in Case of Woman Who Killed Son's Alleged Molester." *San Diego Source,* June 13, 1996. http://sddt.com/

files/librarywire/96wireheadlines/06_96/
DN96_06_13_cae.html

24. Brown, "Historical Patterns of Violence"; Brown, *Strain of Violence.*

25. George F. Cole, *The American System of Criminal Justice,* 7th edition (Belmont, Calif.: Wadsworth, 1995), p. 137.

26. Lane, *Murder in America.*

27. Ibid.

28. Philip S. Foner, *The History of the Labor Movement in the United States: The AFL in the Progressive Era, 1910–1915,* vol. 5 (New York: International Publishers, 1980), p. 186.

29. Foner, *The History of the Labor Movement in the United States,* pp. 196–213.

30. Richard O. Boyer and Herbert M. Morais, *Labor's Untold Story* (New York: United Electrical, Radio, and Machine Workers of America, 1971).

31. Brown, "Historical Patterns of Violence."

32. See, for example, Jeff Ferrell and Kevin Ryan, "The Brotherhood of Timber Workers and the Southern Trust: Legal Repression and Worker Response," *Radical America,* 19, 54–74 (1985).

33. Lane, *Murder in America,* p. 157.

34. Frank Donner, *Protectors of Privilege: Red Squads and Police Repression in Urban America* (Berkeley: University of California Press, 1990).

35. S. Dale McLemore and Harriett D. Romo, *Racial and Ethnic Relations in America,* 5th edition (Boston: Allyn & Bacon, 1998).

36. Dane Archer and Rosemary Gartner, *Violence and Crime in Cross-National Perspective* (New Haven, Conn.: Yale University Press, 1984); Dane Archer and Rosemary Gartner, "Violent Acts and Violent Times: A Comparative Approach to Postwar Homicide Rates," *American Sociological Review,* 41, 937–963 (1976); Rosemary Gartner, "The Victims of Homicide: A Temporal and Cross-National Comparison," *American Sociological Review,* 55, 92–106 (1990); S. Landau and D. Pfefferman, "A Time Series Analysis of Violent Crime and Its Relation to Prolonged States of Warfare," *Criminology,* 26, 489–504

(1988); V. W. Sidel and R. C. Wesley, "Violence as a Public Health Problem: Lessons for Action against Violence by Health Care Professionals from the Work of the International Physicians Movement for the Prevention of Nuclear War," *Social Justice,* 22(4), 154–170 (1996).

37. Roger Lane, "On the Social Meaning of Homicide Trends in America," in *Violence in America: The History of Crime,* ed. Ted Robert Gurr (Newbury Park, Calif.: Sage, 1989).

38. D. Eckberg, "Estimates of Early Twentieth-Century U.S. Homicide Rates: An Econometric Forecasting Approach," *Demography,* 32, 1–16 (1995).

39. Ted Robert Gurr, "Historical Trends in Violent Crime: Europe and the United States," in *Violence in America: The History of Crime,* ed. Ted Robert Gurr (Newbury Park, Calif.: Sage, 1989).

40. William B. Sanders, *Gangbangs and Drive-Bys: Grounded Culture and Juvenile Gang Violence* (New York: Aldine De Gruyter, 1994).

41. Mark H. Haller, "Bootlegging: The Business and Politics of Violence," in *Violence in America: The History of Crime,* ed. Ted Robert Gurr (Newbury Park, Calif.: Sage, 1989).

42. Howard Abadinsky, *Drugs: An Introduction,* 4th edition (Belmont, Calif.: Wadsworth Thomson, 2001).

43. Daniel Cork, "Examining Space–Time Interaction in City-Level Homicide Data: Crack Markets and the Diffusion of Guns among Youth," *Journal of Quantitative Criminology,* 15(4), 5–24 (1999).

44. Paul J. Goldstein, Henry H. Brownstein, and Patrick J. Ryan, "Crack and Homicide in New York City, 1988: A Conceptually Based Event Analysis," *Contemporary Drug Problems,* 16, 651–687 (1989).

45. Cork, "Examining Space-Time Interaction"; David T. Courtwright, *Violent Land: Single Men and Social Disorder from the Frontier to the Inner City* (Cambridge, Mass.: Harvard University Press, 1996); James Alan Fox and Marianne W. Zawitz, *Homicide Trends in the United States* (Washington, D.C.: Bureau of Justice Statistics,

Department of Justice, 2001); Robert Nash Parker and Kathleen Auerhahn, "Drugs, Alcohol, and Homicide: Issues in Theory and Research," in *Homicide: A Sourcebook of Social Research,* ed. M. Dwayne Smith and Margaret A. Zahn (Thousand Oaks, Calif.: Sage, 1999).

46. Garen Wintemute, "Guns and Gun Violence," in *The Crime Drop in America,* ed. Alfred Blumstein and Joel Wallman, *Cambridge Studies in Criminology* (Cambridge, U.K.: Cambridge University Press, 2000).

47. Bruce Johnson, Andrew Golub, and Eloise Dunlap, "The Rise and Decline of Hard Drugs, Drug Markets, and Violence in Inner-City New York," in *The Crime Drop in America,* ed. Alfred Blumstein and Joel Wallman, *Cambridge Studies in Criminology* (Cambridge, U.K.: Cambridge University Press, 2000); William Spelman, "The Limited Importance of Prison Expansion," in *The Crime Drop in America,* ed. Alfred Blumstein and Joel Wallman, *Cambridge Studies in Criminology* (Cambridge, U.K.: Cambridge University Press, 2000).

48. Raymond Gastil, "Homicide and a Regional Culture of Violence," *American Sociological Review,* 36, 412–427 (1971); Sheldon Hackney, "Southern Violence," *American Historical Review,* 74, 906–925 (1969).

49. John J. Macionis, *Society: The Basics,* 2nd edition (Englewood Cliffs, N.J.: Prentice Hall, 1994), p. 28.

50. Rodney Stark, *Sociology,* 6th edition (Belmont, Calif.: Wadsworth, 1996), p. 48.

51. Marvin Wolfgang and Franco Ferracuti, *The Subculture of Violence* (London: Tavistock, 1967).

52. Marvin Wolfgang, *Patterns of Criminal Homicide* (Philadelphia: University of Pennsylvania Press, 1958), pp. 188–189.

53. Bertram Wyatt-Brown, *Southern Honor: Ethics and Behavior in the Old South* (Oxford, U.K.: Oxford University Press, 1982).

54. Richard E. Nisbett and Dov Cohen, *Culture of Honor: The Psychology of Violence in the South* (Boulder, Colo.: Westview Press, 1996).

55. C. G. Ellison, "An Eye for an Eye? A Note on the Southern Subculture of Violence Thesis," *Social Forces,* 69, 1223–1239 (1991).

56. Fox Butterfield, *All God's Children: The Bosket Family and the American Tradition of Violence* (New York: Alfred A. Knopf, 1995), p. 21.

57. Charles Ball quoted in Ibid., pp. 21–22.

58. H. C. Brearley, "The Pattern of Violence," in *Culture of the South,* ed. W. T. Couch (Chapel Hill: University of North Carolina Press, 1934); Richard Maxwell Brown, "Southern Violence: Regional Problem or National Nemesis? Legal Attitudes toward Southern Homicide in Historical Perspective," *Vanderbilt Law Review,* 32, 225–250 (1979); Gastil, "Homicide and a Regional Culture of Violence"; Hackney, "Southern Violence"; John Shelton Reed, "To Live—and Die—in Dixie: A Contribution to the Study of Southern Violence," *Political Science Quarterly,* 3, 429–443 (1971).

59. Lin Huff-Corzine, Jay Corzine, and David C. Moore, "Southern Exposure: Deciphering the South's Influence on Homicide Rates," *Social Forces,* 42, 906–924 (1986); Steven F. Messner, "Regional Differences in the Economic Correlates of the Urban Homicide Rate: Some Evidence on the Importance of Cultural Context," *Criminology,* 21, 477–488 (1983); Steven F. Messner, "Regional Racial Effects on the Urban Homicide Rate: The Subculture of Violence Revisited," *American Journal of Sociology,* 88, 997–1007 (1983).

60. Robert Nash Parker, "Poverty, Subculture of Violence, and Type of Homicide," *Social Forces,* 67, 983–1007 (1989).

61. Jo Dixon and Alan J. Lizotte, "Gun Ownership and the 'Southern Subculture of Violence'," *American Journal of Sociology,* 93, 383–405 (1987); Douglas J. Guthrie, "From Cultures of Violence to Social Control: An Analysis of Violent Crime in U.S. Counties with Implications for Social Policy," *Berkeley Journal of Sociology,* 39, 67–99 (1994–1995); M. Dwayne Smith and Robert Nash Parker, "Type of Homicide and Variation in Regional Rates," *Social Forces,* 59, 136–147 (1980).

62. James F. Short, *Poverty, Ethnicity, and Violent Crime,* ed. John Hagan, *Crime and Society* (Boulder, Colo.: Westview Press, 1997).

63. Fox and Zawitz, *Homicide Trends in the United States.*

64. Cork, "Examining Space–Time Interaction."

65. Ramiro Martinez Jr., "Homicide among Miami's Ethnic Groups: Anglos, Blacks, and Latinos in the 1990s," *Homicide Studies,* 1(1), 17–34 (1997).

66. Elijah Anderson, *Code of the Street: Decency, Violence, and the Moral Life of the Inner City* (New York: W. W. Norton, 1999), p. 114.

67. Alfred Blumstein, "Youth Violence, Guns, and the Illicit-Drugs Industry," *The Journal of Criminal Law and Criminology,* 86(1), 30 (1995).

68. Federal Bureau of Investigation, *Crime in the United States—1976–1999, Uniform Crime Reports* (Washington, D.C.: U.S. Government Printing Office).

69. Marc Riedel and Margaret Zahn, "Stranger Violence: Perspectives, Issues, and Problems," *The Journal of Criminal Law and Criminology,* 78(2), 223–258 (1987).

70. William Wilbanks, *Murder in Miami: An Analysis of Homicide Patterns and Trends in Dade County (Miami, Florida, 1917–1983)* (Lanham, Md.: University Press of America, 1984), p. 35.

71. Robert A. Silverman and Leslie W. Kennedy, "Relational Distance and Homicide: The Role of the Stranger," *The Journal of Criminal Law and Criminology,* 78(2), 272–308 (1987).

72. Riedel and Zahn, "Stranger Violence."

73. Various scholars have suggested that the fear of crime is essentially the fear of strangers. See, for example, John Conklin, *The Impact of Crime* (New York: MacMillan, 1975).

74. Robert J. Sampson, "Personal Violence by Strangers: An Extension and Test of the Opportunity Model of Predatory Victimization," *The Journal of Criminal Law and Criminology,* 78(2), 328 (1987).

75. Joel Best, *Random Violence: How We Talk About New Crimes and New Victims*

(Berkeley: University of California Press, 1999), p. xi.

76. Federal Bureau of Investigation, *Crime in the United States—1991, Uniform Crime Reports* (Washington, D.C.: U.S. Government Printing Office, 1992).

77. For a detailed review of the problems in comparing cross-national crime statistics, see Archer and Gartner, *Violence and Crime in Cross-National Perspective.*

78. Steven F. Messner and Richard Rosenfeld, *Crime and the American Dream,* 2nd edition (Belmont, Calif.: Wadsworth, 2001), p. 4.

79. Richard Maxwell Brown, *No Duty to Retreat: Violence and Values in American History and Society* (New York: Oxford University Press, 1991); Brown, *Strain of Violence;* R. Elias, "A Culture of Violent Solutions," in *The Web of Violence: From Interpersonal to Global,* ed. J. Turpin and L. R. Kurtz (Urbana: University of Illinois Press, 1997); Richard Slotkin, *The Fatal Environment: The Myth of the Frontier in the Age of Industrialization, 1800–1890* (New York: Harper Perennial, 1985); Richard Slotkin, *Gunfighter Nation: The Myth of the Frontier in Twentieth Century America* (New York: Harper Perennial, 1992); Richard Slotkin, *Regeneration through Violence: The Mythology of the American Frontier, 1600–1860* (New York: Harper Perennial, 1973); R. B. Toplin, "Violence and Culture in the United States," in *The Culture of Violence,* ed. K. Rupesinghe and Rubio C. Marcial (Tokyo: United Nations University Press, 1994).

80. William R. Avison and Pamela L. Loring, "Population Diversity and Cross-National Homicide: The Effects of Inequality and Heterogeneity," *Criminology,* 24, 733–749 (1986); Henry B. Hansman and John M. Quigley, "Population Heterogeneity and the Sociogenesis of Homicide," *Social Forces,* 61, 206–224 (1982); Harvey Krahn, Timothy F. Hartnagel, and John W. Gartrell, "Income Inequality and Homicide Rates: Cross-National Data and Criminological Theories," *Criminology,* 24, 269–295 (1986); Steven F. Messner, "Societal Development, Social Inequality, and Homicide: A Cross-National Test of a Durkheimian Model," *Social Forces,* 64, 225–240 (1982).

3

Why We Kill

Explaining Murder
in America Today

This case fills me with exhaustion and hopelessness. Another young
man dies by violence in this city, for no good reason, and another
young man stands before me to be sentenced for the crime.

JUDGE WILLIAM QUARLES, 2001

CIRCUIT COURT JUDGE, BALTIMORE[1]

What we need to see—if we are to understand violence and to prevent
it—is that human agency or action is not only individual; it is also,
unavoidably, familial, societal, and institutional. Each of us is
inextricably bound to others—in relationship. All human
action (even the act of a single individual) is relational.

JAMES GILLIGAN[2]

INTRODUCTION

In 1996, homicide rates in many American cities decreased significantly from
the previous years. Even so, in many cities, the toll of lethal violence remained
significant and costly. Nashville, Tennessee, for example, experienced 97 fatalities from homicides and police shootings.[3] Here are just a few of the individuals
behind those impersonal statistics.[4] On January 5, 17-year-old Aaron Tackett

was shot to death in front of two witnesses after an argument during a game of cards. On January 13, 15-year-old Tijonne Jones was shot in the back after an argument with two other teens. Anthony Robinson died on January 24. He had been shot in a drive-by shooting on December 27 as he was standing on the sidewalk in front of his house. Nineteen-year-old D'Angelo Lee and his 18-year-old cousin Gregory Ewing were both murdered on February 28. They were killed execution style while trying to sell cheaply made firearms. On March 22, 21-year-old Michael Vaughn was shot and killed during a robbery, and on the 24th of the same month, 26-year-old Kenneth Frierson got into an argument with another man over a woman and was fatally shot. On April 16, Terry Torrod Carter was shot and killed in the parking lot of a restaurant after a drug deal miscarried.[5] And so on.

These examples are but a small sampling of the murders in Nashville during the first few months of 1996. Of the killings mentioned here, the majority involved young African-American men killing other young African-American men. These cases, along with the homicide statistics presented in the last chapter, reveal one of the central realities of murder in the United States; namely, that it typically involves young non-White men killing other young non-White men. All demographic groups suffer some risk of homicide victimization and perpetration, but young non-White men are disproportionately at risk.

Even with the steady decrease in homicide victimization during the latter half of the 1990s, far too many Americans still fall victim to lethal attacks. In 1999, for example, 15,530 people are known to have been murdered in the United States.[6] It is important to note that whereas some segments of our society have experienced extreme fluctuations in their vulnerability to murder, other group patterns of victimization have remained relatively unchanged. Despite these year-to-year fluctuations, the people most vulnerable to murder in this country, both as victims and as offenders, continue to be our nation's young men, particularly from minority groups.

In this chapter, we will introduce the leading contemporary theories used to explain patterns and trends in homicide offending. Our goal in this chapter is to provide an overview of the underlying individual- and social-level factors thought to be responsible for the extraordinarily high levels of murder in American society.

EXPLANATIONS OF
HOMICIDE OFFENDING

Researchers who study the causes of homicide can typically be categorized into two groups—those who study the causes of homicide offending at the individual level, and those who examine the factors related to variation in homicide rates across ecological units such as nations, states, and cities. Researchers who concentrate on individuals generally explore various biological, psychological, and experiential characteristics of offenders.

Individual-Level Explanations

The purpose of individual-level explanations of murder is to examine why particular people are more likely to commit murder than others—that is, to explain homicide with reference to things that happen to or within individuals. It should be noted that most of these explanations are not unique to the offense of murder. Murder is often characterized as an event that takes place at the extreme end of a continuum of assaultive behavior. Keith Harries, for example, contends that homicides and assaults represent essentially similar behaviors that differ only in their outcome; one results in death and the other in nonlethal injury. What separates an assault from a homicide may simply be the lethality of the weapon available during a conflict situation. For example, a quarrel that ends in a knife fight is less likely to result in murder than one in which a handgun is readily available. Furthermore, the victim of a gunshot wound is less likely to die if adequate medical resources are available, such as shock trauma emergency rooms, than a gunshot victim in a remote and isolated area. A long delay in emergency medical response, such as sometimes happens in certain inner-city neighborhoods, also affects the likelihood of death.

Support for this notion of an *assault continuum* comes from offending data. For example, data indicate that the majority of homicide offenders have been involved in other types of offending behavior prior to committing the homicide. That homicide offending is intertwined with other forms of criminal offending further supports the notion that the criminological theories used to explain violent forms of offending in general may also be helpful in explaining homicide offending in particular. In other words, most theories and explanations of crime and violence in general are also useful in explaining some of the characteristics of and motivations for murder.[8]

Control Theories The premise of control theories of homicide is that murder will occur in the absence of restraint or control against it. Unlike many other theories that seek to explain why homicide occurs, control theories assume that homicide is an offender's quick and easy solution to some vexing problem (a store clerk reluctant to hand over the goods, a sexual rival) and will occur without much in the way of motivation. Rather than asking the question, "What causes people to commit homicide?" the control theorist would ask, "What causes people to resist the inclination to commit homicide and to conform to the prohibitions against it?" The key to explaining homicide for control theorists, therefore, is to explain what prevents its perpetration.[9] The classic statement of the control theory explanation of rule breaking or criminal conduct comes from Travis Hirschi: "The question, 'Why do they do it?' is simply not the question the theory is designed to answer. The question is, 'Why don't *we* do it?' There is much evidence that we would if we dared." The answer is that most people are controlled or restrained from committing homicide by something or someone.

Different control theorists have somewhat different solutions to the problem of control. One of the most prominent control theories was developed by the sociologist Travis Hirschi. Hirschi originally developed control theory to explain delinquency, but it can also be applied to homicide. According to Hirschi, people restrain themselves from committing crimes like homicide, when they have successfully forged what he calls a *social bond* with conventional society.[10] Think of the social bond as the tie or cord of responsibility that connects an individual to the society of which he or she is a part. When this social bond is strong, people refrain from committing deviant acts like homicide. When the social bond is not formed or is weak, a person is at a greater risk of committing homicide or any other act of rule breaking.

Hirschi argues that there are four components to the social bond: (1) attachment, (2) commitment, (3) involvement, and (4) belief. *Attachment* is the emotional element of the social bond and represents one's personal relationships with other people (such as spouses, parents, neighbors, or employers) that could be placed in jeopardy when committing a criminal act like homicide. For example, if I refrain from killing another person because I believe that it will cost me valued social relationships, attachment is working to control me. *Commitment* refers to possessions, valued roles, or expected benefits that would be lost if one were to commit a crime. For example, if I refrain from killing a business rival because I fear that I would be discovered and would lose my own company, then I am controlled by my conventional commitments. Likewise, I may be restrained from killing because I aspire to go to college, to be a member of the bar, or to join the armed services—if so, conventional commitments are controlling me. *Involvement* is the time and energy dimension of the social bond. If one is busy at work or involved with family or church, one has much less time for partying or socializing, which is the setting in which most homicides occur. Finally, *beliefs* are the moral dimension of the social bond. Very frequently, people refrain from committing serious crimes such as homicide because they believe them to be wrong. Moral beliefs and values may act to limit violent and other criminal behavior.

Subsequent to his original development of social control theory, Hirschi collaborated with another criminologist, Michael Gottfredson, to produce a different kind of control theory. In their 1990 book, *A General Theory of Crime,* Gottfredson and Hirschi have outlined a very broad theory of illegal and inappropriate conduct that would include homicide.[11] Gottfredson and Hirschi argue that crime and what they call "analogous acts" (such as smoking, gambling, and excessive drinking and eating) are due to individuals lacking self-control. Self-control is the ability to resist behaviors that involve immediate and easy gratification. Killing an acutely annoying family member or shooting a store clerk during an armed robbery would involve such immediate and easy gratification. People with low self-control find themselves unable to resist the temptation of homicide and, according to the theory, such people would find it difficult to resist other acts that also provide quick satisfaction. According to Gottfredson and Hirschi, individuals without self-control are usually impulsive, nonverbal, and inclined toward physical risk taking, all of which are elements that in certain conflict situations can lead to violence.[12]

Techniques of Neutralization In 1957, Gresham Sykes and David Matza developed neutralization theory to explain how delinquents neutralize their conformist beliefs to engage in criminal activity.[13] Essentially, Sykes and Matza argue that young offenders develop a series of justifications before the offending in order to allow them to engage in the criminal behavior. These justifications or *techniques of neutralization* serve to nullify the conventional values that might prevent them from perpetrating the crime. Specifically, Sykes and Matza identified the following five neutralization techniques: *denial of responsibility*, in which acts are perceived as being caused by forces beyond one's control; *denial of injury*, in which the harm or damage is dismissed or minimized; *denial of the victim*, which asserts that the victim somehow caused their own victimization; *condemnation of the condemners*, which argues that everybody is corrupt, so one's own deviancy is not problematic; and *appeal to higher loyalties*, which justifies the action because it is not taken for selfish, individualistic reasons. Over the years, this theory has been used to explain a variety of crimes, including embezzlement, pilfering, and genocide.[14] In particular, Robert Agnew found that neutralization techniques were used to assist in justifying violent behavior.[15] For example, many individuals who kill justify their violence before the act by convincing themselves that their victims "have it coming" because of their actions or words; this is an example of denying the victim. Similarly, gang members who kill rival gang members because in their own eyes they are protecting their territory are relying on appeal to higher loyalties to excuse their behavior.

Social Learning Theory The premise of social learning theory is that criminal behavior such as homicide occurs because it has been learned and reinforced.[16] Essentially, this perspective suggests that people's experiences combine with their perceptions and beliefs to shape their behavior. In many ways, social learning theorists have suggested that this type of learning occurs through a process of behavioral modeling that involves *imitation*.[17] Such modeling can be derived from family and friends, from environmental experiences such as witnessing violence in the community, and from media sources. Part of this process involves learning to be violent, which can be done simply by watching someone else engage in violence and seeing that person get rewarded for it either financially or in terms of status and prestige. For example, people who commit acts of serial killing frequently have a history of being sexually or physically abused. A consistent relationship is also found in the empirical literature between exposure to violence as a child and one's own use of violence, including homicide, as an adult.[18] Conceivably, being victimized or witnessing the victimization of others early in life may teach individuals that violence, even lethal violence, is an effective and acceptable way to solve one's problems. As a result, when confronted by difficulties in their own lives, such individuals may well resort to the problem-solving strategies they have experienced and learned. In addition to personal experiences with violence, Hollywood's glamorization of violence and the violence found in many video games may serve to teach those who witness it that violence is acceptable. The fear is that those who watch violence in the movies, on television, or in video games will become brutalized and more tolerant of violence in their own lives. Certainly, a great deal of research indicates that viewing violent images in the media affects our attitudes about violence and our willingness to engage in aggressive behavior.[19]

Another way of learning violent or homicidal behavior is through social *reinforcement,* in which the behavior is both learned from and reinforced by the social actions of others. In this type of learning, we repeat the behaviors that others who are important to us say are good, while not repeating the behaviors that these others do not reward. Gang members, for instance, frequently tell new members that standing up for the honor of the gang is both good and necessary and that real men are tough and can fight. In fact, many gangs "jump in" or beat up new members to determine if they are hardy enough and have enough heart to join.[20] Behaviors that are reinforced and rewarded in gang life include verbal threats and intimidation, physical assault, and, if necessary, killing others who disrespect the gang's turf or fellow gang members. Behaviors that are *not* reinforced include verbal reconciliation or other forms of nonviolent conflict resolution. In the course of belonging to a gang, therefore, gang members learn that violence is not only permissible but required. In fact, in some situations they learn precise forms of violence such as how to use knives or how to fire assault rifles. They are also taught that in situations requiring violence, the use of nonviolent action is forbidden. In short, the gang teaches violent behavior, rewards violence, and punishes nonviolence. As a result of the social reinforcement of physical aggression, including homicide, by other gang members, homicide is more common in gang conduct than in other social groups. We must remember that the members of these gangs find acceptance and belonging within these groups; consequently, there is a powerful compulsion to conform to the norms of the gang. As one gang member explains, "A gang gave me a sense of love. They would do anything to help me, and I would do anything to help them."[21] Too often, that *anything* includes homicide.

The criminologist Larry Siegel summarizes the main elements of social learning theory that contribute to aggressive behavior as follows:

1. An event that heightens arousal—such as a person's frustrating or provoking another through physical assault or verbal abuse.

2. Aggressive skills—learned aggressiveness responses picked up from observing others, either personally or through the media.

3. Expected outcomes—the belief that aggression will somehow be rewarded. Rewards can come in the form of reducing tension or anger, gaining some financial reward, building self-esteem, or gaining the praise of others.

4. Consistency of behavior with values—the belief, gained from observing others, that aggression is justified and appropriate, given the circumstances of the current situation.[22]

Rational Choice Theories In spite of the colloquialism that crime doesn't pay, sometimes crime does pay, and sometimes it pays better than noncriminal behavior. The argument of rational choice theories of crime is that a crime such as homicide is more likely to occur whenever an individual is rewarded in such a way that the benefits received from committing the crime are greater than the costs.[23] In other words, crimes like homicide are more likely to be committed when they are profitable—either financially or emotionally—for someone to commit. The key notion of rational choice theory, therefore, is that people who commit homicide are frequently rational beings—at least rational enough to consider the benefits and costs of their conduct—and choose the behavior that maximizes the rewards and minimizes the costs.

How can homicide be considered rational conduct? People who engage in violence to protect their self-image make a conscious choice about the value of their reputation or status. A lethal outcome may be seen as regrettable but unavoidable. For example, a man unhappily married to a wealthy woman can either attempt to outlive her—which is very unlikely unless he is much younger than she is, because women have a longer life expectancy than men—or he can "do her in." In killing his rich wife, the man stands to receive a vast sum (his reward or the benefits of the crime), and he will attempt to minimize the cost by making it look like an accident. The historical record suggests that this is not as far-fetched a scenario as it might initially appear. In similar fashion, rivals in a drug market can either attempt to negotiate over the disputed territory, or they can attempt to have the other one killed. A person robbing a convenience store will often feel that the only way to escape detection is to kill the clerk as well as any witnesses to the crime. As the offender may see it, no witnesses equals no conviction.

Even homicides that seem to be driven by some deep-seated psychological problem can be analyzed and understood as rational behaviors. As James Gilligan asserts, "even the most apparently 'insane' violence has a rational meaning to the person who commits it."[24] The serial killer Jeffrey Dahmer, for example, took a great deal of care in selecting his victims and disposing (by freezing or eating) of their body parts to minimize the chance that he would be noticed by the police. His apparent goal was to find or create (through lobotomizing) a person who could love and accept him for what he was. Even bizarre conduct, therefore, can have an element of perverted rationality to it.

Biological and Psychological Theories Over the centuries, there have been numerous attempts to explain violence and homicide with reference to biological or psychological causes. These explanations of homicide often make intuitive sense to us. When we read about a brutal murder, frequently our first question is, "What's wrong with the person who did that?" We may conclude that the murderer must be very different from the rest of us. But is this accurate, or is it merely a convenient way for us to distance ourselves from the perpetrator? Despite the fact that diagnosed psychopaths make up only about 10% of the criminal population, such perspectives remain very popular with the public, primarily because the belief that the people who commit such heinous acts are different from ourselves makes us feel more secure about our environment and ourselves.

Recently, scholars interested in crime have put forth the argument that violence and homicide are linked to genetic, neurological, and biochemical factors.[25] This is especially relevant when we consider that most violence is perpetrated by men. Are men genetically predisposed to violence, or are they simply socialized into more aggression? David Courtwright observes that "young men, in short, are biologically primed for deeds that may have been reproductively advantageous in the distant past but are problematic in societies that have come to value disciplined competence over raw aggression."[26]

One popular theory about male violence has held that the most brutal acts of aggression are often committed by men who have an extra Y chromosome. Normally, men get the genetic mix of one X and one Y chromosome. Sometimes, however, a male child receives an extra Y chromosome at conception. These XYY men have been thought to possess "super-male" traits, including a proclivity to commit violent acts such as murder.[27] More recent research, however, has tended to discount a link between this extra Y chromosome and violent behavior.[28]

Violence among men has also been linked to some of the neurotransmitters that are secreted by the brain. The male hormone testosterone has been linked to violent crime, as has the neurotransmitter serotonin.[29] Low levels of serotonin have been linked with increased impulsiveness and aggression; high levels of testosterone are associated with belligerent behavior.[30] The psychologist Adrian Raine has argued that antisocial behavior is linked to a person's resting heart rate, noting that people who are antisocial frequently have a lower resting heart rate than social conformists. Raine suggests that a low resting heart rate may be associated with other characteristics that put one at risk for aggression and violent acts, such as a lack of anxiety, fearlessness, and a need for strong stimulation.[31] Fearlessness and lack of anxiety are important because these traits prevent one from being inhibited or deterred from committing violence by the possibility of its negative consequences or costs. A person without fear, in other words, cannot learn that the killing of another may come at high cost, such as loss of freedom or some other form of punishment. If a low resting heart rate indicates a state of underarousal, it may drive a person to seek heightened forms of excitement and sensation, including murder.

One of the more extreme biologically based theories of aggression and homicide has recently been developed by Martin Daly and Margo Wilson.[32] Essentially, Daly and Wilson argue that a theory of homicide must square with the most important known facts about homicide, such as that homicides are most likely to be committed by men against other men and between individuals not linked by biology (strangers and acquaintances) rather than between family members. They suggest that these patterns can be explained by the influence of certain evolutionary pressures. The key element is that members of a species have a self-interest in furthering their genetic kin. In other words, there is an instinctive drive to pass on one's genes to the next generation.

Several implications follow from this evolutionary drive. First, men need to make sure that they mate with the fittest women to better ensure that they pass on their genes. However, all men have this same drive, leading to competition among men for the fittest women. In evolutionary terms, it is in the self-interest of men to weed out the competition by killing other men. Hence, male homicide is most likely to be committed against other men. Second, in addition to ensuring that one's own personal genes are passed on, there is a self-interest in increasing the odds that one's biological family survives to pass on one's genes. As a consequence of this second imperative, homicidal aggression is more likely to be directed against individuals not in one's immediate biological family (strangers and acquaintances) rather than against family members. Of course, as we have seen, certain subgroups in our society *are* more likely to be killed by family members than by strangers. Another problem with this evolutionary theory of homicide is that it is unable to address the murder of one's own children.

In general, psychological and biological theories do not go very far in explaining the significant variation in homicide rates across geographic units such as cities and states. Even if we assume that "murder is an ever-present possibility in all cultures because its roots are biological. Murder is coded in our DNA,"[33] individual theories such as these cannot explain why some locations (cities, neighborhoods, and so on) have greater amounts of violence than others. They simply cannot explain why homicide offending differs so significantly from place to place or from time to time. As Jay Livingston asks, "If crime is the result of certain personality traits, why should those traits be more common to urban people than to those in the suburbs? Or to 15- to 20-year-olds rather than to 30-year-olds? Why should those traits be so much more prevalent in the United States than in Canada? And even in the United States, did the large increase in crime in the decade 1963–1973 mean that a greater proportion of psychopaths had been born into the population?"[34]

Implicit in these criticisms is the fact that all individual-based theories divert attention from the social sources of crime, such as poverty and inequality. For this reason, many researchers have turned to theoretical explanations at the societal level, often termed macro-level theories. Robert Sampson, one of the most prolific researchers into the relationship between community-level factors and rates of crime and violence, has repeatedly demonstrated that community-level factors such as social disorganization explain a significant amount of the variation in criminal victimization patterns across neighborhoods.[35] We examine the most prominent of these societal-level explanations next.

Macro-Level Explanations

Over the last 20 years, a great deal of research has attempted to explain the variations in homicide rates at particular aggregate levels, especially at the state and city levels. This research has variously explored the role of poverty, racial inequality, social disorganization, and cultural values in affecting murder rates. This research has come to be known as the *comparative homicide literature* because it compares homicide rates across geographic entities or across time with factors thought to be related to homicide offending.

The comparative homicide literature has examined many factors thought to predict homicide rates at the aggregate level, but the majority of this research has usually examined either social structural forces or cultural factors. Social structural explanations focus on the roles or statuses that people occupy and the behavioral expectations attached to those positions. Because most structural positions in society are hierarchically stratified, some positions are advantaged relative to others with respect to wealth, prestige, and power. Researchers examining the social structural factors related to homicide have focused on various elements of this social stratification, including social class, race, ethnicity, sex, and age.[36]

In contrast, cultural or subcultural explanations of homicide posit that the variations in homicide rates across geographic units are related to differences in the values, norms, and beliefs held by members of these units. Seminal work in this area has been conducted by Wolfgang and Ferracuti, who have argued that a subculture of violence exists among some groups in our society (such as men, African-Americans, or southerners). These subcultures, they believe, exhibit greater normative support for the use of violence in upholding such values as honor, courage, and manliness.[37]

Although most scholars who engage in this type of research acknowledge that both structural and cultural contexts play a role in explaining homicide rates, an empirical debate of sorts has emerged between advocates of structural versus cultural explanations. For example, opponents of cultural explanations of homicide typically argue that studies documenting an empirical relationship or correlation between culture and homicide have not adequately controlled for all relevant structural conditions.[38] Proponents of cultural explanations argue that it is equally plausible that some of the significant relationships found between structural conditions such as poverty and homicide levels may be attributed to unmeasured cultural differences linked to the units under study.

Social Structural Explanations Social structural explanations of homicide offending and victimization focus on the social circumstances in which people live. The comparative homicide literature has generally focused on two material or objective social conditions: economic deprivation and social disorganization.

Economic Deprivation The premise underlying the relationship between economic deprivation and homicide rates is that when individuals live in environments that are characterized by extreme poverty, the struggle for basic resources is intensified. This, in turn, can lead to an atmosphere of extreme powerlessness, anger, and anxiety.[39] It is not hard to imagine how such environments can provoke conflict situations that may lead to violence.

Researchers studying crime and violence in the United States recognized early the important role that socioeconomic conditions played in affecting rates of violence. For example, in the early part of the twentieth century, sociologists at the University of Chicago found strong associations between rates of delinquency and rates of poverty within corresponding areas of Chicago. A classic study by Clifford Shaw and Henry McKay in 1942 found that areas characterized by high rates of poverty consistently had high rates of crime over several decades, despite the fact that these areas were inhabited by different ethnic groups over the years. This was one of the first empirical attempts to demonstrate that the causes of crime and violence were rooted in the social structure of areas, independent of the individuals living in those areas.

But what is this concept of economic deprivation or poverty? In the comparative homicide literature, the measurement of poverty has not always been consistent, because different notions of what poverty is shape estimates of how prevalent it is and, thus, of its relationship to homicide rates.

Most of the poverty statistics seen in newspapers reflect a conception of poverty that was formalized by Mollie Orshansky of the Social Security Administration (SSA) in 1965 and subsequently adopted by the federal government and by many researchers.[40] She defined poverty in terms of an *absolute* standard, based on the amount of money required to purchase an emergency diet estimated to be nutritionally adequate for about two months. The idea is that people are truly poor if they can barely purchase the food they need and other essential goods. This poverty standard is adjusted for household size and composition (number of children and adults), and the minimal amount needed for food is multiplied by three, because a 1955 survey indicated that poor families spend about one third of their income on food. Thus, researchers interested in examining the relationship between poverty and homicide have analyzed rates of absolute poverty in comparison with homicide rates in a given location.

Some social scientists, however, contend that absolute measures of poverty do not capture the true essence of the environmental deprivation experienced by residents. Instead, they believe that a measure of *relative* poverty, sometimes referred to as *income inequality,* is a better indicator of economic deprivation. Poverty, from this perspective, should be defined in terms of what is typical in a given location at a particular time, not in terms of an absolute standard.[41] These theorists believe that it is poverty relative to observed wealth, not poverty in and of itself, that fosters violence. As Judith and Peter Blau explain, "socioeconomic inequalities undermine the social integration of a community by creating multiple parallel social differences which widen the separations between ethnic groups and between social classes, and it creates a situation characterized by much social disorganization and prevalent latent animosities. Pronounced ethnic inequality in resources implies that there are great riches within view but not within reach of many destined to live in poverty. There is much resentment, frustration, hopelessness, and alienation."[42]

Inequalities that are rooted in ascribed characteristics such as race are thought to be a particularly potent source of frustration. Researchers hypothesize that this is one reason why disadvantaged minority groups such as African-Americans are overrepresented as offenders and victims of homicide. In a society such as ours that fosters the notion that success is within the reach of everyone, people who cannot achieve their goals simply because of their race or ethnicity are likely to develop feelings of resentment and hostility that may be expressed through violence. Ironically, this generalized anger is typically expressed against other minority group members within reach, rather than against those who are the source of the resentment.

Researchers have also contended that racial segregation, which is the "cornerstone of urban inequality," has produced extreme conditions of disadvantage for minorities, particularly African-Americans left in central cities. Ruth Peterson and Lauren Krivo call these extreme conditions *concentrated disadvantage*.[43] Concentrated disadvantage is the extent to which disadvantaged group members disproportionately reside within a limited number of neighborhoods rather than being spread throughout an urban area. Several scholars have contended that it is this concentration of disadvantage, not simply absolute levels of poverty or inequality, that directly increases violence.[44] Courtwright explains it this way: "Ghetto violence is clearly a product of racial discrimination, as is the ghetto itself. Throughout American history racism has exacerbated violence and disorder in three distinct ways: by inspiring and rationalizing interracial attacks; by blocking intermarriage and family formation; and by impoverishing, isolating, and socially marginalizing minority groups."[45]

In support of this type of explanation, Darnell Hawkins has demonstrated that homicide rates vary tremendously within the larger African-American community.[46] African-Americans who are middle or upper class typically have lower homicide rates than poor African-Americans. Similarly, African-American youths living in nonmetropolitan communities have lower firearm homicide rates than African-American and White youths living in the inner cities;[47] this has led one scholar to conclude that "at low socioeconomic levels, Blacks have much higher risks of becoming homicide victims than do Whites. At higher socioeconomic levels, the difference between Blacks and Whites disappears and even reverses in one of the studies."[48]

Inequality has also been used to explain the relatively low rates of homicide offending by women. In this case, however, the focus is on the victimization of women and not on offending by women. The murder of women (perceived as the subordinate group) is interpreted as an expression of control by the dominant (male) group. In the same way that spousal abuse is explained as an expression of patriarchal power, the murder of women is seen as merely a more lethal expression of the same structural inequalities.

Strain/Anomie Some researchers have elaborated on the mechanisms of inequality even further, bringing together several related concepts under a larger conceptual umbrella. One such concept is *strain*, which assumes that under normal circumstances, people will restrain themselves and abide by societal rules, such as those that prohibit killing another. From this point of view, social conformity is given and rule breaking must be explained. According to strain theorists, violent crimes such as homicide are understood through reference to the extraordinary pressures that people may face.

In its simplest form, strain theory contends that deviance and criminality are the result of frustrated needs or wants. This frustration is generally believed to result from a breakdown in the balance between socially induced aspirations or goals and socially approved ways of achieving these goals. For example, one study of murderers found that they had indeed experienced tremendous amounts of frustration in their own lives that may have contributed to their homicidal actions.[49] For some theorists, this strain or pressure is mainly financial. According to strain theory, criminality (such as interpersonal violence) is a response to the actual or anticipated failure to achieve socially induced needs or goals (such as status, wealth, power, social acceptance, and so on). The sociologist Robert K. Merton was one of the first to articulate this kind of strain theory. He argued that American society places families with low incomes under tremendous strain, because it limits their access to conventional means of achieving financial success while at the same time holding out financial success as a goal that is realistically available to all. In the United States, monetary success is often viewed as a goal, but the means to achieve this goal legally, such as going to college and getting a high-paying job, are not within the reach of all Americans. Denied conventional opportunities for success, like a quality education and a good job, and yet wanting to achieve success, some people in this position may resort to illegal means to achieve their goals. From this perspective, drug dealing, with its attendant risks of violence, may be perceived as a means to acquire widespread goals of wealth through innovative (illegal) means.[50] Unfortunately, this form of innovation also increases the likelihood of an individual killing or being killed.

A more general version of strain theory was developed by Robert Agnew. Agnew argued in his *general strain theory* (GST) that strain can be produced by things other than blocked financial goals or a discrepancy between one's aspirations and expectations. He asserted that three types of experiences that individuals have may generate strain: (1) someone prevents them from achieving a goal that they value; (2) someone removes or threatens to remove something they possess and value; and (3) someone imposes or threatens to impose something they would find unfavorable or awful.[51]

According to Agnew, however, the experience of strain by itself is not sufficient for a crime such as homicide to occur. Strain must be accompanied by the emotion of anger and by the inability to cope with or adapt to that anger in order to generate sufficient motivation for committing a crime. Finally, the criminal or deviant act must be seen as a solution to the experience of strain. If, for example, people lose a lover to a sexual rival, they may feel strain because a valuable thing has been taken from them and their self-esteem has been threatened. Such people may be tempted to explain the loss as not due to any fault of their own but due perhaps to the selfishness of the lost lover and the meanness of the rival. Angry and upset, that person may be tempted to "do something about this" and get a gun and kill both the former lover and the rival, thus alleviating the source of strain. Similarly, drug dealers who kill rival dealers for infringing on their turf would likewise be removing a source of frustration.

Relying on Merton's earlier conceptualization, Steven Messner and Richard Rosenfeld have used the macro-level analogue of strain, called *anomie*, to explain the rates of serious offending, including homicide.[52] Anomie, in its most general formulation, is defined as a weakening in the normative regulation of behavior. Anomie theory asserts that diminished normative regulation results from an overemphasis on cultural goals, such as wealth and prestige, relative to the legitimate means of achieving them, like the availability of a college education or access to high-status jobs. This differential distribution of opportunities to achieve highly valued goals results in the American Dream not being equally attainable in America.

What exactly is the American Dream? Messner and Rosenfeld define it as "a commitment to the goal of material success, to be pursued by everyone in society, under conditions of open, individual competition."[53] According to Messner and Rosenfeld, four cultural values within American society contribute to anomie and, therefore, to crime in general and to violence in particular; these values are *achievement, individualism, universalism,* and *materialism.* Their description of materialism illustrates the connection of these values to the propensity for serious criminal offending:

> In American culture, success is signified in a profoundly significant way: by the accumulation of monetary rewards. Money is awarded special priority in American culture. . . . The point to emphasize here is not that Americans are uniquely materialistic, for a strong interest in material well-being can be found in most societies. Rather, the distinctive feature of American culture is the preeminent role of money as the 'metric' of success. . . . Monetary success is inherently open-ended. It is always possible in principle to have more money. Hence, the American Dream offers 'no final stopping point.' It requires 'never-ending achievement.' The pressure to accumulate money is therefore relentless, which entices people to pursue their monetary goals by any means necessary.[54]

In addition to explaining the comparatively high rates of offending by African-Americans, Messner and Rosenfeld assert that their theory can also account for the comparatively low rates of offending by women. Because women are much more engaged than men in the social institution of the family, they will exhibit different cultural orientations than men. Based on this argument, women should be more likely to balance economic values of materialism and individualistic competition with other values that are more consistent with familial roles. Messner and Rosenfeld contend that as a result, the anomic pressures of the American Dream will be somewhat tempered for women, thus explaining their decreased involvement in serious offending. Given the increasing economic pressures that impinge on the family, however, this supposed insulation may not always serve to inhibit women from offending in the future, particularly if the deindustrialization of the American economy continues.

The theory delineated by Messner and Rosenfeld actually combines elements of both culture and structure. The dominant value patterns of American culture "crystallize into the distinctive cultural ethos of the American Dream," which, in turn, encourages members of society to pursue the American Dream.[55] Because not everyone can achieve the dream legitimately, some may use illegitimate means, such as robbery or drug dealing, with all the attendant risks. Or, as others contend, the frustration and resentment experienced by some people because of their lack of resources may lead them to act aggressively toward available targets such as family members and friends. As Williams and Flewelling explain, "it is reasonable to assume that when people live under conditions of extreme scarcity, the struggle for survival is intensified. Such conditions are often accompanied by a host of agitating psychological manifestations, ranging from a deep sense of powerlessness and brutalization to anger, anxiety, and alienation. Such manifestations can provoke physical aggression in conflict situations."[56]

Social Disorganization Economic deprivation and inequality can also serve to break down a community's mechanisms for informal social control by eroding families and schools. This breakdown is known as *social disorganization.* The foundation for social disorganization originates in the argument that rapid social change is associated with increases in crime due to the breakdown of social controls. The term is generally used to describe conditions that undermine the ability of traditional institutions, such as families and schools, to govern social behavior. For example, Robert Bursik has defined social disorganization as the inability of a community structure to realize the common values of its residents and to maintain effective social control.[57]

Although it is related to other structural factors such as economic deprivation, social disorganization operates independently. For example, after analyzing violent crime rates over time, Wesley Skogan noted that although America's past is riddled with illiteracy, cyclical unemployment, and low wages, crime rates have tended to remain low where traditional agents of social control like the family and schools remained strong. Skogan concluded that "crime problems became worse when those agents lost their hold on the young."[58]

Cultural Explanations In general, cultural theories explaining homicide rate differentials suggest that murder occurs more often among certain groups because these groups endorse or at least tolerate the use of physical violence in settling quarrels or in upholding certain values such as honor and manliness. Jay Corzine and his colleagues, however, correctly point out that these theories do not assume that some groups are violent because their subculture approves of violence *in general.* They state, "Although it is probably true that every society includes some unsocialized individuals who place a high positive value on violence across the board, violence, and especially violence against one's group, is seldom positively sanctioned in any and all situations. Persons who are indiscriminately violent are viewed as dangerous, and societies and members of subcultures find formal and informal ways of controlling them. If approved at all, violence is deemed acceptable only in some situations (e.g., violations of the code of honor in organized crime families)."[59]

Based on this subcultural framework, researchers have delineated several subgroups within our society who they believe have, for various reasons, developed such a subculture.[60] For example, based on historical evidence and contemporary homicide rates, some researchers contend that people residing in the South of the United States are more violent than people residing in the North. Nisbett and Cohen, for example, contend that the South has developed what has been termed a *culture of honor.* One of the properties of this culture, they believe, is the necessity for men to appear strong and unwilling to tolerate an insult. They state that an individual "must constantly be on guard against affronts that could be construed by others as disrespect. When someone allows himself to be insulted, he risks giving the impression that he lacks the strength to protect what is his."[61]

Other subgroups identified as having developed such a subculture are minority populations in central-city ghettos who lack any opportunity for economic advancement. Neighborhoods in many central cities of the United States have lost well-paying manufacturing jobs. This loss, exacerbated by the continuing effects of racism, has produced a high level of social disorganization in these neighborhoods, including a substantial decrease in two-parent families and high rates of out-of-wedlock births to teenage mothers. Rose and McClain point out that African-Americans were among the last to make the transition from a rural agricultural workforce to an urban industrial one, with the result that they not only arrived in the cities after manufacturing industries began leaving, but they were disadvantaged relative to other groups who had already established themselves politically, economically, and socially.[62]

Researchers such as Elijah Anderson believe that as a result of these conditions, an oppositional subculture may have developed in such neighborhoods, particularly among young African-American men.[63] This *code of the streets,* as Anderson terms it, or *cool pose* as Majors and Billson label it, includes a heightened sensitivity to personal affronts by others and a strong emphasis on maintaining honor—that is, *respect*—at all costs, including one's life.[64] According to Anderson, "at the heart of the code is the issue of respect—loosely defined as being treated 'right' or being granted one's 'props' (or proper due) or the deference one deserves. . . . In the street culture, especially among young people, respect is viewed as almost an external entity, one that is hard-won but easily lost—and so must constantly be guarded."[65]

Adherents of this oppositional subculture, of course, would be predisposed to violence. An example of this involves one young man who felt that he had been insulted several times by another young man. In his own words, "I just stood there thinking. This niggah is gonna make me do something I didn't come here to do. Not only had he disrespected me again, but he'd done it in front of my lady. I had to do something. That's when I decided to shoot him."[66] And he did, fatally wounding his antagonist with a .22 caliber bullet to the chest. Moreover, residents in such settings who do not maintain such an orientation are also at increased risk of violence, because they may interact with people who have a street orientation and can become involved in violent altercations simply because they cannot avoid it.[67]

Similarly, Harold Rose and Paula McClain note that the vulnerability to homicide in America's cities is related to urban growth and the inability of young adult men to find successful and satisfying employment. After analyzing patterns of homicide in six cities from 1960 to 1985, Rose and McClain believe that a subculture of materialist aggression has emerged that is most often manifested in robbery homicides. They explain, "In Detroit and in other northern urban centers, we are witnessing the coming of age of a cohort socialized in an environment where instrumental violence has become entrenched. As a result, gratuitous, violent confrontations have become more commonplace. The changed demands of the mainstream economy, the lure of the irregular economy (e.g., drug trafficking), the strengthening of secular values, and the growing attractiveness of the street hustler as a role model fuel this situation."[68]

After examining more recent homicide trends from eight cities from 1985 to 1993, Rose and McClain found that the age of homicide victimization and offending was moving downward, with young Black men between the ages of 15 and 19 experiencing the most rapid growth since the late 1980s.[69] As we saw earlier, this is consistent with trends at the national level. Furthermore, as indicators of oppositionality in homicide cases, they examined trends in young male victimizations, drug-related homicide victimizations, gang-related victimizations, and gun-related victimizations among the target population of young Black men. Based on their analysis, Rose and McClain concluded that for a growing segment of young Blacks residing in certain neighborhoods, "the indirect effect of a globalizing economy has been to produce growing alienation from mainstream values and subsequently to promote lifestyles and behaviors associated with an oppositional culture among certain urban Black youth."[70]

Empirical Support for Structural and Cultural Explanations It is well beyond the scope of this book to summarize the proliferation of comparative homicide research that has attempted to test these theories. Suffice it to say that research has found mixed support for these theories at the aggregate level. For example, researchers testing the relationship between homicide rates and cultural orientations have found that the theoretical indicators used to measure a violent subculture both increase and decrease rates of homicide across geographic units, depending on the units under study (for example, states, cities, or metropolitan areas). Similar inconsistencies emerge for studies testing indicators of absolute poverty. Indicators used to measure levels of inequality have been more consistently related to homicide rates across geographical units.

Most scholars agree that the inconsistent nature of this research is related to a myriad of methodological problems inherent in the literature. A few of the primary problems are the following:

- Some geographical units used in the analyses, such as states or metropolitan areas, do not really represent homogeneous units. As such, a total rate of homicide for each unit does not represent the actual diversity of homicide offending or victimization that exists within each unit. Smaller and more homogeneous locales should be used to represent urban and rural areas.

- Some studies analyze the total homicide rate as if it represented a homogeneous category of lethal violence. However, the total homicide rate is composed of very different events that may be related to very different causal mechanisms. As Williams and Flewelling explain, "a violent cultural orientation, for example, is more likely to produce deaths that spring from heated arguments among intimates than to produce serial killings."[71] As such, homicide rates that are disaggregated by such indicators as victim–offender relationship and specific circumstances should be used.

- Measurement error occurs in some of the indicators used to measure particular theoretical constructs. For example, it is difficult to measure a cultural orientation to violence, because these orientations are inherently subjective and not directly observable at the aggregate level. For example, most of the literature has substituted regional location as a proxy for culture. This is obviously problematic. More innovative approaches are needed to remedy this measurement problem, such as using indicators of other cultural artifacts that represent justifications of lethal violence, like the imposition of the death penalty, subscriptions to violent magazines, and the rate of justifiable homicides within locales.[72]

- Researchers have described other problems inherent in the statistical analyses conducted in several studies, including (1) using two highly correlated indicators, such as absolute and relative measures of poverty, to predict homicide rates; and (2) ignoring outliers and other extreme cases in the analyses.[73]

Most authors concede that many methodological advances have been made in the comparative homicide literature, yet most agree that much work is still needed to advance our understanding of the factors related to fluctuations in homicide rates at community levels (such as states and cities). More refined analyses that have been performed during the past 10 years hold promise. For example, studies that rely on more homogeneous subcategories of homicide (such as race and victim–offender relationship) are beginning to illuminate the mechanisms by which social and cultural conditions explain different types of homicide offending.[74]

In sum, although many researchers typically place more emphasis on either structural or cultural explanations of homicide offending patterns, most also acknowledge the contribution of both influences in producing homicide rate differentials across subgroups in the population. Jay Corzine and his colleagues candidly describe their view of the debate between cultural and structural explanations as follows: "Although promoting the position that cultural factors influence homicide rates, we do not view ourselves as opponents of other perspectives. It is apparent to us that economic disadvantage is related to violence, including killing. . . . Our position is that a consideration of social structural variables is necessary but not sufficient to provide an explanation of homicide, and theories that include cultural differences between groups offer a promising avenue for advancing our understanding of killing."[75]

Steve Messner and Richard Rosenfeld, typically proponents of structural explanations of homicide and violence, similarly contend that an important task for future theorizing and research is to integrate structural and cultural factors in explanations of homicide: "Indeed, many structural arguments presuppose cultural dynamics, but these dynamics simply are left implicit. For example, the strain tradition emphasizes the extent to which structural location is associated with relative deprivation, which can generate motivations for lethal violence. For people to experience relative deprivation, however, they must have some end state that they anticipate that they will be unable to attain because of structural impediments. These end states are, in the final analysis, determined by culture."[76]

It is important to keep in mind the policy implications inherent in cultural and structural explanations of homicide. Most cultural theorists agree that subcultures that tolerate the use of violence in certain situations (for instance, an oppositional culture) most often emerge from structural conditions such as blocked economic opportunities or economic deprivation. As such, it is in our power to change these conditions. As Messner and Rosenfeld eloquently state, "if a given level of homicide reflects to a significant extent features of the social structure, it need not be an inevitable (nor invariant) fact of life. Social structures are ultimately created, sustained, and altered by the members of a society. The social production of homicide *can* be tempered when people have the collective will to do so."[77]

SUMMARY

In this chapter, we have described the most popular theories for explaining homicide at the individual and societal levels. Because homicide is not a homogeneous category but is made up of very different events, we also need a multitude of explanations to explain homicide. No one explanation is credible for explaining *all* types of homicide. What may not be so evident to you right now, however, is the relationship that theory has to our world in general and to public policy in particular. You may be asking yourself, "Why are these theories so important, and how are they linked to the study of homicide?" Well, virtually all policies that our government has implemented to combat violence in general and homicide in particular have been influenced by theory. For example, many of our recent policies, including "three-strike" laws and the use of capital punishment, implicitly assume that offenders are rational beings and can therefore be deterred from committing criminal acts (reflecting rational choice theory) by making punishments severe. If you don't think that theory is relevant to public policy, perhaps you should ask the thousands of offenders currently incarcerated across the United States their opinion on the matter!

So far in this book, we have examined the contextual characteristics of homicide at the aggregate level, including rates of offending by sex, age, race, ethnicity, the victim–offender relationship, the precipitating circumstances, and the weapons used in the murder. We have also examined where the United States ranks relative to other countries in its overall murder rate. Whereas this chapter has focused on theories of homicide offending, in the next chapter we refocus on the personal act of killing itself by examining the homicide event as it plays out at the individual level.

NOTES

1. Lee Gardner, "A Baltimore Killing Behind the Numbers," *Baltimore City Paper Online.* http://www.citypaper.com/2000-12-27/feature.htm (retrieved January 2, 2001), p. 2.

2. James Gilligan, *Violence: Our Deadly Epidemic and Its Causes* (New York: Grosset/Putnam, 1996), p. 7.

3. Deborah Highland, "Murder in Black and White: Behind the Statistics, Many See Nashville's Homicide Rate as a Symptom of Lost Hope," *The Tennessean,* January 1, 1997, p. 1A.

4. All of the reviewed cases were taken from Ibid.

5. Ibid.

6. James Alan Fox and Marianne W. Zawitz, *Homicide Trends in the United States* (Washington, D.C.: Bureau of Justice Statistics, Department of Justice, 2001).

7. Keith D. Harries, *Serious Violence: Patterns of Homicide and Assault in America,* 2nd edition (Springfield, Ill.: Charles C. Thomas, 1997).

8. For a more detailed description of individual-level theories of crime in general, see Raymond Paternoster and Ronet Bachman, *Explaining Criminals and Crime* (Los Angeles: Roxbury, 2001).

9. Travis Hirschi, *Causes of Delinquency* (Berkeley: University of California Press, 1969).

10. Ibid.

11. Michael R. Gottfredson and Travis Hirschi, *A General Theory of Crime* (Stanford, Calif.: Stanford University Press, 1990).

12. Ibid., p. 90.

13. Gresham M. Sykes and David Matza, "Techniques of Neutralization: A Theory of Delinquency," *American Sociological Review,* 22, 664–670 (1957).

14. Alex Alvarez, "Adjusting to Genocide: The Techniques of Neutralization and the Holocaust," *Social Science History,* 21(2), 139–178 (1997); G. S. Green, *Occupational Crime* (Chicago: Nelson Hall, 1990); D. M. Horning, "Blue Collar Theft: Conceptions of Property Attitudes toward Pilfering and Workgroup Norms in a Modern Industrial Plant," in *Crime against Bureaucracy,* ed. E. Smigel and H. L. Ross (New York: Van Nostrand Reinhold, 1979).

15. Robert Agnew, "The Techniques of Neutralization and Violence," *Criminology,* 32, 555–580 (1994).

16. Ronald L. Akers, *Social Learning and Social Structure: A General Theory of Crime and Deviance* (Boston: Northeastern University Press, 1998).

17. Albert Bandura, *Aggression: A Social Learning Analysis* (Englewood Cliffs, N.J.: Prentice Hall, 1973); Albert Bandura, "The Social Learning Perspective: Mechanisms of Aggression," in *Psychology of Crime and Criminal Justice,* ed. Hans Toch (New York: Holt, Rinehart & Winston, 1979); Albert Bandura, *Social Learning Theory* (Englewood Cliffs, N.J.: Prentice Hall, 1977).

18. Kathleen M. Heide, "An Integration of Psychological, Sociological, and Biological Approaches," in *Homicide: A Sourcebook of Social Research,* ed. M. Dwayne Smith and Margaret A. Zahn (Thousand Oaks, Calif.: Sage, 1999).

19. See, for example, Dave Grossman and Gloria Degaetano, *Stop Teaching Our Kids to Kill: A Call to Action against TV, Movie, and Video Game Violence* (New York: Random House, 1999); Madeline Levine, *Viewing Violence: How Media Violence Affects Your Child's and Adolescent's Development* (New York: Doubleday, 1996).

20. See, for example, Sanyika Shakur, *Monster: The Autobiography of an L.A. Gang Member* (New York: Penguin Books, 1993).

21. David T. Courtwright, *Violent Land: Single Men and Social Disorder from the Frontier to the Inner City* (Cambridge, Mass.: Harvard University Press, 1996), p. 239.

22. Larry Siegel, *Criminology,* 7th edition (Belmont, Calif.: Wadsworth/Thomson, 2000), p. 166.

23. Derek B. Cornish and Ronald V. Clarke, *The Reasoning Criminal* (New York: Springer Verlag, 1987).

24. Gilligan, *Violence: Our Deadly Epidemic,* p. 9.

25. Diana H. Fishbein, "Biological Perspectives in Criminology," *Criminology,* 28, 27–72 (1990); Adrian Raine, *The Psychopathology of Crime: Criminal Behavior as a Clinical Disorder* (San Diego: Academic Press, 1993).

26. Courtwright, *Violent Land,* p. 20; Diana H. Fishbein, *Biobehavioral Perspectives in Criminology* (Belmont, Calif.: Wadsworth/Thomson, 2001).

27. P. A. Jacobs et al., "Aggressive Behavior, Mental Sub-Normality, and the XYY Male," *Nature,* 208, 1351–1352 (1965).

28. Gregory Carey, "Genetics and Violence," in *Understanding and Preventing Violence: Biobehavioral Influences,* ed. Albert J. Reiss, Klaus A. Miczek, and Jeffrey A. Roth (Washington D.C.: National Academy Press, 1994).

29. Alan Booth and D. Wayne Osgood, "The Influence of Testosterone on Deviance in Adulthood: Assessing and Explaining the Relationship," *Criminology,* 31, 93–117 (1993); Raine, *The Psychopathology of Crime.*

30. Fishbein, *Biobehavioral Perspectives in Criminology.*

31. Raine, *The Psychopathology of Crime;* Pauline S. Yaralian and Adrian Raine, "Biological Approaches to Crime," in *Explaining Criminals and Crime,* ed. Ray Paternoster and Ronet Bachman (Los Angeles: Roxbury, 2001).

32. Martin Daly and Margo Wilson, "An Evolutionary Psychological Perspective on Homicide," in *Homicide: A Sourcebook of Social Research,* eds. M. Dwayne Smith and Margaret A. Zahn (Thousand Oaks, Calif.: Sage, 1999).

33. Michael P. Ghiglieri, *The Dark Side of Man: Tracing the Origins of Male Violence* (Reading, Mass.: Perseus Books, 1999).

34. Jay Livingston, *Crime and Criminology,* 2nd edition (Upper Saddle River, N.J.: Simon & Schuster, 1996).

35. Robert J. Sampson, "Local Friendship Ties and Community Attachment in Mass Society: A Multilevel Systemic Model," *American Sociological Review,* 53(5), 766–799 (1988); Robert J. Sampson and By-ron Groves, "Community Structure and Crime: Testing Social-Disorganization Theory," *American Journal of Sociology,* 94(4), 774–802 (1989); Robert J. Sampson and Stephen W. Raudenbush, "Systematic Social Observation of Public Spaces: A New Look at Disorder in Urban Neighborhoods," *American Journal Of Sociology,* 105(3), 603–651 (1999).

36. Steven F. Messner and Richard Rosenfeld, "Social Structure and Homicide: Theory and Research," in *Homicide: A Sourcebook of Social Research,* ed. M. Dwayne Smith and Margaret A. Zahn (Thousand Oaks, Calif: Sage, 1999).

37. Jay Corzine, Lin Huff-Corzine, and H. P. Whitt, "Cultural and Subcultural Theories of Homicide," in *Homicide: A Sourcebook of Social Research,* ed. M. Dwayne Smith and Margaret A. Zahn (Thousand Oaks, Calif.: Sage, 1999).

38. See, for example, Judith R. Blau and Peter M. Blau, "The Cost of Inequality: Metropolitan Structure and Violent Crime," *American Sociological Review,* 47, 114–129 (1982); Colin Loftin and R. H. Hill, "Regional Culture and Homicide: An Examination of the Gastil-Hackney Thesis," *American Sociological Review,* 39, 714–724 (1974); Colin Loftin and Robert Nash Parker, "An Errors-in-Variable Model of the Effects of Poverty on Urban Homicide Rates," *Criminology,* 23(2), 269–285 (1985); Robert Nash Parker, "Poverty, Subculture of Violence, and Type of Homicide," *Social Forces,* 67, 983–1007 (1989). For example, after examining homicide rates in 125 metropolitan areas, Blau and Blau unequivocally interpreted their findings as support for the structural explanation of violent crime: "These results imply that if there is a culture of violence, its roots are pronounced economic inequalities, especially if associated with ascribed position." Blau and Blau, "The Cost of Inequality," p.114.

39. Kirk R. Williams and Robert L. Flewelling, "The Social Production of Criminal Homicide: A Comparative Study of Disaggregated Rates in American Cities," *American Sociological Review,* 53(3), 421–431 (1988).

40. Gordon M. Fisher, "The Development and History of the Poverty Thresh-

olds," *Social Security Bulletin,* 55(4), 3–14 (1992).

41. Blau and Blau, "The Cost of Inequality." This article also provides a detailed discussion of the difference between absolute and relative measures of poverty.

42. Ibid., 119.

43. Ruth D. Peterson and Lauren J. Krivo, "Racial Segregation, the Concentration of Disadvantage, and Black and White Homicide Victimization," *Sociological Forum,* 14(3), 465–493 (1999).

44. Ruth D. Peterson and Lauren J. Krivo, "Racial Segregation and Black Urban Homicide," *Social Forces,* 71(4), 1001–1026 (1993); E. S. Shihadeh and N. Flynn, "Segregation and Crime: The Effect of Black Social Isolation on the Rates of Black Urban Violence," *Social Forces,* 74, 1325–1352 (1996).

45. Courtwright, *Violent Land,* pp. 30–31.

46. Darnell F. Hawkins, "What Can We Learn from Data Disaggregation? The Case of Homicide and African Americans," in *Homicide: A Sourcebook of Social Research,* ed. M. Dwayne Smith and Margaret A. Zahn (Thousand Oaks, Calif.: Sage, 1999).

47. Ibid.

48. Albert J. Reiss and Jeffrey A. Roth, eds., *Understanding and Preventing Violence: Social Influences,* Vol. 3 (Washington, D.C.: National Academy Press, 1993).

49. Stuart Palmer, *The Psychology of Murder* (New York: Crowell, 1960).

50. Robert K. Merton, *Social Theory and Social Structure* (New York: Free Press, 1957).

51. Robert Agnew, "Foundation for a General Strain Theory of Crime and Delinquency," *Criminology,* 30, 47–87 (1992).

52. Steven F. Messner and Richard Rosenfeld, *Crime and the American Dream,* 2nd edition (Belmont, Calif.: Wadsworth, 2001).

53. Ibid., p. 62.

54. Messner and Rosenfeld, *Crime and the American Dream,* pp. 63–64.

55. Messner and Rosenfeld, *Crime and the American Dream,* p. 64.

56. Williams and Flewelling, "The Social Production of Criminal Homicide," p. 423.

57. R. J. Bursik Jr., "Social Disorganization and Theories of Crime and Delinquency: Problems and Prospects," *Criminology,* 26, 519–552 (1988).

58. Wesley G. Skogan, "Social Change and the Future of Violent Crime," in *Violence in America: The History of Crime,* ed. Ted Robert Gurr (Newbury Park, Calif.: Sage, 1989), p. 244.

59. Corzine, Huff-Corzine, and Whitt, "Cultural and Subcultural Theories of Homicide," p. 44.

60. Jo Dixon and Alan J. Lizotte, "Gun Ownership and the 'Southern Subculture of Violence'," *American Journal of Sociology,* 93, 383–405 (1987); Lin Huff-Corzine, Jay Corzine, and David C. Moore, "Deadly Connections: Culture, Poverty, and the Direction of Lethal Violence," *Social Forces,* 69, 715–732 (1991); Lin Huff-Corzine, Jay Corzine, and David C. Moore, "Southern Exposure: Deciphering the South's Influence on Homicide Rates," *Social Forces,* 42, 906–924 (1986); F. E. Markowitz and Richard B. Felson, "Social Demographic Attitudes and Violence," *Criminology,* 36, 117–138 (1998); Walter B. Miller, "Lower Class Culture as a Generating Milieu of Gang Delinquency," *Journal of Social Issues,* 14(3), 5–19 (1958); John Shelton Reed, *One South: An Ethnic Approach to Regional Culture* (Baton Rouge: Louisiana State University Press, 1982); Harold M. Rose and Paula D. McClain, "Race, Place, and Risk Revisited: A Perspective on the Emergence of a New Structural Paradigm," *Homicide Studies,* 2(2), 101–129 (1998); Harold M. Rose and Paula D. McClain, *Race, Place, and Risk: Black Homicide in Urban America,* ed. John Howard and Robert C. Smith, *SUNY Series in Afro-American Studies* (Albany: State University of New York Press, 1990); H. P. Whitt, Jay Corzine, and Lin Huff-Corzine, "Where Is the South? A Preliminary Analysis of the Southern Subculture of Violence," in *Trends, Risks, and Interventions in Lethal Violence,* ed. Carolyn R. Block and R. L. Block (Washington, D.C.: National Institute of Justice, 1995).

61. Richard E. Nisbett and Dov Cohen, *Culture of Honor: The Psychology of Violence*

in the South. Boulder, Colo.: Westview Press, 1996), p. xv.

62. Rose and McClain, *Race, Place, and Risk.*

63. Elijah Anderson, "Code of the Streets," *Atlantic Monthly,* 273, 81–94 (1994); Elijah Anderson, *Streetwise: Race, Class, and Change in an Urban Community* (Chicago: University of Chicago Press, 1990).

64. Elijah Anderson, *Code of the Street: Decency, Violence, and the Moral Life of the Inner City* (New York: W. W. Norton, 1999); Richard Majors and Janet Mancini Billson, *Cool Pose: The Dilemmas of Black Manhood in America* (New York: Touchstone Books, 1992).

65. Anderson, *Code of the Street,* p. 33.

66. Courtwright, *Violent Land,* p. 237.

67. It should be noted here that other scholars, including William Julius Wilson, interpret the same code of the streets as a situational adaptation, not a reflection of a distinct subculture. See William Julius Wilson, *The Truly Disadvantaged: The Inner City, the Underclass, and Public Policy* (Chicago: University of Chicago Press, 1987); William Julius Wilson, *When Work Disappears: The World of the New Urban Poor* (New York: Alfred A. Knopf, 1996).

68. Rose and McClain, "Race, Place, and Risk Revisited," p.104.

69. The eight cities selected for the study were Atlanta, Detroit, St. Louis, and Los Angeles (which had been included in the original six cities), and Washington, D.C., New Orleans, Milwaukee, and Charlotte, N.C.

70. Rose and McClain, "Race, Place, and Risk Revisited," p.127.

71. Williams and Flewelling, "The Social Production of Criminal Homicide," p. 422.

72. Many researchers have used creative measurement strategies to indicate a geographic unit's support of violence. Archer and Gartner (1984) have demonstrated how the involvement of countries in war can increase a country's level of homicide; Bowers (1984) has shown how a state's use of the death penalty can also increase rates of homicide; Williams and Flewelling (1988) used a city's rate of justifiable homicide as an indicator of a violent cultural orientation; and Baron and Straus (1989) developed a *legitimate violence index* that measures a state's socially acceptable preferences for noncriminal violence in three broad areas: mass media having high violence content, governmental use of violence, and participation in legal or socially approved violent activities. See Dane Archer and Rosemary Gartner, *Violence and Crime in Cross-National Perspective* (New Haven, Conn.: Yale University Press, 1984); Larry Baron and Murray A. Straus, *Four Theories of Rape in American Society: A State-Level Analysis* (New Haven, Conn.: Yale University Press, 1989); W. J. Bowers, *Legal Homicide* (Boston: Northeastern University Press, 1984); Williams and Flewelling, "The Social Production of Criminal Homicide."

73. For a detailed review of these issues, see Karen F. Parker and Patricia L. McCall, "Structural Conditions and Racial Homicide Patterns: A Look at the Multiple Disadvantages in Urban Areas," *Criminology,* 37(3), 447–478 (1999); Karen F. Parker and Matthew V. Pruitt, *Social Science Quarterly,* 81(2), 555–570 (2000).

74. Kenneth Land, P. McCall, and L. E. Cohen, "Structural Co-Variates of Homicide Rates: Are There Any Invariances across Time and Space?" *American Journal of Sociology,* 95, 922–963 (1990); Graham C. Ousey, "Homicide, Structural Factors, and the Racial Invariance Assumption," *Criminology,* 37(2), 405–426 (1999); Peterson and Krivo, "Racial Segregation, the Concentration of Disadvantage, and Black and White Homicide Victimization;" Robert J. Sampson and William Julius Wilson, "Toward a Theory of Race, Crime, and Urban Inequality," in *Crime and Inequality,* ed. John Hagan and Ruth D. Peterson (Stanford, Calif.: Stanford University Press, 1995); M. Dwayne Smith, "Variations in Correlates of Race-Specific Urban Homicide Rates," *Journal of Contemporary Criminal Justice,* 8(2), 137–149 (1992).

75. Corzine, Huff-Corzine, and Whitt, "Cultural and Subcultural Theories of Homicide," p. 43.

76. Messner and Rosenfeld, *Crime and the American Dream,* p. 38.

77. Ibid.

4

Deadly Interactions

Exploring the Dynamics
of the Murder Process

When individuals and groups feel their "honor" is at stake, and an intolerable
degree of humiliation or "loss of face" would result from a failure to fight for
that honor, they may act violently. The loss of self-esteem is experienced
subjectively as the death of the self. People will sacrifice anything to prevent
the death and disintegration of their individual or group identity.

JAMES GILLIGAN[1]

There is no need to develop a special theory for homicide. . . . It makes more
sense to see acts of violence on a continuum, where fatal actions represent an
extremely harmful escalation of more mundane disagreements or coercive
actions. The fact that one party ends up dead need not make us change our
view of why these conflicts occur, although they clearly make our search for
answers about how to curtail this escalation to violence much more urgent.

LESLIE KENNEDY AND DAVID FORDE[2]

INTRODUCTION

On April 22, 1974, two military airmen attempted to rob a stereo store in the
town of Ogden, Utah. Somewhere along the way, a simple robbery turned into
a horrible orgy of violence that victimized the two salespeople and three oth-

ers who had the misfortune to come by the store during the robbery. After tying up their prisoners in the basement, the two would-be robbers subjected their victims to horrific tortures before shooting them in the head, some several times. These torments included rape, throttling, forcing victims to drink a drain cleaner containing hydrochloric acid, and forcing a pen into the ear of one of the victims. Incredibly, two of the victims survived the brutality, although both sustained massive injuries.[3] This case was an exceptionally brutal one and resulted in both perpetrators ultimately being sentenced to death. One psychiatrist who was hired to test the mental state of the murderers stated that "it's probably the most gruesome crime that's ever occurred in this state . . . the sadistic quality here, the unmitigated and unnecessary cruelty, the ingenuity and variety of indignities to the people. . . . this is the worst."[4]

In another case in 1993, a woman was shot and killed in a group home where she worked in Minneapolis. Evidently, a drunk teenager had been wandering around the neighborhood with a handgun and, on seeing her through the window, decided to try what it would be like to kill someone. He later told the police that he didn't know her and just wanted to find out if he could actually kill somebody.[5] As with the victims in the Utah case, the woman was the innocent and unwitting victim of a violent and lethal assault.

These types of crimes often exacerbate public fears. Not only were the unfortunate victims subjected to various outrages but they were victimized solely because they were in the wrong place at the wrong time. In the Utah case, a couple of the victims had simply entered the store to make a purchase; they had done nothing wrong and certainly did not deserve their fate. The woman in Minneapolis was busy at work when her life was suddenly and violently taken from her. These kinds of events tell people that anyone, anywhere can be a victim of violent crime. But is this an accurate perception? Does the Ogden, Utah, case represent a typical pattern of violent victimization? It is certainly an image that Hollywood has helped disseminate. For example, in the film *Regarding Henry,* actor Harrison Ford portrays Henry Turner, a successful and high-powered New York lawyer and family man. One fateful night, Henry walks into a convenience store around the corner from where he lives and interrupts a robbery in progress. Before he has a chance to react, he is shot and almost killed by the surprised and panicky robber. The film is largely about how Harrison Ford's character Henry survives the shooting and about the ways in which he and his family cope with the aftermath of the tragedy. This scenario typifies a common perception about murder victims; namely, that they are unfortunate people who happen to be in the wrong place at the wrong time. In the film, Henry is guilty of nothing except having the bad luck to accidentally surprise a desperate criminal. In short, Henry is the archetypal innocent victim of crime.

The reality of murder in the United States, however, is that not all victims are simply unlucky, and criminal homicides are not simply episodic events that just happen to people. Instead, we find that murders often evolve out of a complex series of interactions between the offender, the victim, and in many cases, an audience. The murder itself is only one possible outcome of many possible results and is contingent on a variety of factors. In these situations, all the actors are fully involved participants in the social drama leading up to someone's death. To begin to understand murder, therefore, it is important to recognize the dynamic nature of the typical homicide situation.

HOMICIDE EVENTS

Contrary to the aforementioned cases, the typical murder is not a by-product of another criminal act, such as a bank robbery that doesn't go according to plan, a rapist who kills his victim, or some other felony crime situation. Homicide does occur in these situations, but they are not the most common contexts for murder. Instead, we find that murders often result from fights or arguments with others. In other words, criminal homicide tends to result from conflictual social exchanges. The FBI classifies murder into different categories by situation, and Exhibit 4.1 details the frequency with which these different circumstances occur.

The five major categories of circumstance used by the FBI are felony, suspected felony, argument, miscellaneous non-felony, and unknown. As is quickly evident from an examination of Exhibit 4.1, murders committed during the perpetration of another felony do not constitute the largest category. During the 1980s and 1990s, this category constituted on average less than 20% of all murders. When suspected felony situations are added, they still only account for approximately 20 to 21% of all murders. It is possible that some of the murders in which the circumstances were unknown might have been felony related, but it is not likely that all of them were. So, in all probability, the category of unknown circumstances would not change the distribution dramatically.

Miscellaneous non-felony homicides constituted 17.4% and 21.2% of the total murders during the 1980s and 1990s, respectively. This category is made up of gangland or juvenile gang killings, sniper attacks, and various other situations. Interesting enough, this category also contains murders committed during an alcohol- or narcotic-induced brawl. Our perception of these murders is that they would be more appropriately categorized under the *argument* classification. A brawl essentially describes a conflict situation most typically arising from an argument, and it is therefore closely related to other argument circumstances.

During the last 20 years, the largest single category of criminal homicide was argument related (39.4% during the 1980s; 31.1% during the 1990s). Kenneth Polk labels these events *confrontational homicides* and they are characterized by altercations that evolve from verbal exchanges of insults into physical contests.[6] Adding to the lethality of this type of encounter, alcohol and drugs are frequently cited as contributory factors to the dispute and subsequent murder.[7] The typical scenario involves people who have been drinking or using other drugs getting into an argument that escalates and results in one of the participants killing the other. These characteristics dovetail with several other situational characteristics of murder. For example, Exhibit 4.2 summarizes the results of two studies examining criminal homicide by day of the week.

Exhibit 4.1 Circumstances of Murder, 1980–1989 and 1990–1995

	MEAN % OF MURDERS	
Circumstance	1980–1989	1990–1995
Felony Total	18.6	19.8
Robbery	9.7	9.7
Narcotics	3.5	5.8
Sex Offenses	1.4	0.8
Arson	1.0	0.7
Other Felony	3.0	2.9
Suspected Felony	3.1	0.8
Argument Total	39.4	31.1
Romantic Triangle	2.2	1.7
Property or Money	2.8	2.1
Other Arguments	32.7	27.3
Miscellaneous Non-Felony[a]	17.4	21.2
Unknown	21.6	27.1

Note: Percentages may not sum to 100% due to rounding.

[a]This category includes brawls due to alcohol or narcotics, gangland killings, juvenile gang killings, institutional killings, sniper attacks, and children killed by babysitters.

SOURCE: Federal Bureau of Investigations, *Uniform Crime Reports: Crime in the United States, 1980–1995.*

Exhibit 4.2 Homicides by Day of the Week

	% OF HOMICIDES	
Day of the Week	Lester's Analysis	Falk's Analysis
Monday	13.0	12.4
Tuesday	11.9	11.7
Wednesday	10.9	11.1
Thursday	11.9	12.6
Friday	13.7	15.1
Saturday	20.9	21.8
Sunday	17.9	15.3

SOURCES: Gerhard Falk, *Murder: An Analysis of its Forms, Conditions, and Causes* (Jefferson, N.C.: McFarland, 1990); and David Lester, "Temporal Variation in Suicide and Homicide," *American Journal of Epidemiology,* 109: 517–520 (1979).

David Lester's analysis of national homicide patterns in the early 1970s and Gerhard Falk's analysis of murders in Erie County, New York, for a 40-year period reveal strikingly similar patterns.[8] In each of these studies, the results clearly indicate that the great majority of murders take place during the weekend, and these findings would be even more pronounced if homicides that occur on Friday evenings, the prelude to the weekends, were included.

Why are weekends the deadliest times, and how does this relate to conflict-related murders? David Lester provides one possible answer that may well resonate with many college students: "The excess of homicides over the weekend has been attributed to increased alcohol consumption on weekends, together with the increased contacts between friends, family members, and acquaintances."[9]

In other words, weekends are times when people are more likely to drink and socialize, and during these times, arguments develop, some of which lead to physical violence and even death. This reality also corresponds with research indicating that most of these killings take place at night, which is why homicide detectives often assert that "our day begins when your day ends."[10]

Referring back to Exhibit 4.1, under the argument category, we find three subclassifications; romantic triangle; property or money; and other. Examining them, we find that overwhelmingly, most arguments are under the *other argument* subcategory. Just what are these other types of arguments? It is impossible to say with certainty, but we can speculate. In his analysis of murder, Gerhard Falk found that many argument murders were precipitated by seemingly trivial events such as a spilled drink or some other apparently minor disagreement. As Falk suggests, "these killings are indeed senseless, not only because the precipitating motives are so negligible, but also because there appears to be no gain for the killer in committing these murders except self-assertion and a desire to dominate the opponent."[11]

A review of the *Supplementary Homicide Report* forms completed by the Phoenix police department reveals very similar patterns. The forms are filled with brief summations of the circumstances such as "Disagreement over loudness of suspect's car stereo," "Shot while arguing with prostitutes," "Shot on freeway because suspect didn't like his driving," "Argument at pool hall, followed out to street and shot over racial argument," "Argument over business relationship," "Victim shot in a dispute over a dice game," and "Victim was stabbed due to disruptive behavior/drinking."[12] One murderer recalls just such a situation:

> I was over at my friend's place, just sitting around drinking whiskey with him and another guy. This other dude then came over, and we began shooting dice for half-dollars. After about an hour or so of shooting dice, I started feeling the whiskey and decided that I better be leaving. I told them that I had to go, and I picked up my dice and put them in my pocket. Then X jumped up and said, "What did you pick up those dice for?" I said, "Because I'm finished shooting, and I'm going to split." He said, "You can't quit now. You have to give me a chance to win back some of my money." I couldn't understand him coming down on me with that because I hadn't won that much money. I said, "Hey, man, I'm tired of shooting, and I've got to be somewhere now."
>
> Then he got right up in my face and said, "You're not quitting yet, motherfucker." I thought to myself, "There's no use trying to talk to him; reasoning with him is out of the question," so I said, "The hell if I'm not. I told you that I'm tired of playing." He stared at me with his eyes popping out of his head like he was crazy and said, "You dirty, no-good fucking ass punk." I figured then that I was in a hell of a situation.

I knew that the drunken fool wasn't in his right state of mind, and I got scared because I knew he carried a gun and didn't care what he did. I heard that he had killed a dude some time back.

I said, "Man, will you get the fuck out of my face?" But that sent him into a rage. He started swinging his arms side to side and calling me a motherfucking punk, and he spit in my face. I called him a dirty motherfucker, and he shoved me. I figured then that he wasn't going to be wasting much more time on me, and when he went into his coat, I thought that he was reaching for his piece. I knew then that I had to act quick, so I pulled out my pistol and shot the crazy damn fool before he could shoot me. I knew that he'd shoot me without any hesitation. I was just damn lucky that I had bought a gun after being mugged about a week before.[13]

Kenneth Polk's study of patterns of homicide in Australia has revealed similarly mundane precipitants such as challenging eye contact or real and imagined insults.[14] These are not what most people would consider to be legitimate provocations to kill. So why do these rather minor events trigger homicidal interactions?

What seems likely is that although the triggering event appears trivial to the outsider, it serves to elicit responses that elevate the conflict. In one sense, the homicidal interaction transforms into a reciprocal conflictual relationship centering around other issues such as honor, prestige, and self-respect. As James Gilligan asserts, "when individuals and groups feel their 'honor' is at stake, and an intolerable degree of humiliation or 'loss of face' would result from a failure to fight for that honor, they may act violently."[15] Gerhard Falk echoes this statement when he writes that "The causes of murder are not the trivial arguments or incidents that appear on police blotters or in newspapers. Instead, the causes of murder are the beliefs that Americans have about the maintenance of self-respect in a competitive culture."[16]

This suggests that argument-related murders are not caused by the initial precipitant, such as a loud stereo or bad driving, but by a culture that constrains how an individual can respond to that triggering insult or affront. The confrontation becomes one about saving face and maintaining a certain type of self-image. The homicide event is therefore a transformative, interactive process that is concerned less with the initial offense but more with culturally patterned responses to perceived threats and challenges. This metamorphosis becomes evident when we examine the different phases of murder scenarios.

MURDEROUS INTERACTIONS

Historically, a great deal of research and theorizing has been devoted to attempting to explain why certain people become homicide offenders. Recent efforts, however, have tried to frame violent behavior in a contextual analysis by simultaneously taking into account offenders, victims, and circumstances.[17] Conceptualizing a criminal or violent event in this way encourages us to view it as a social event. Thus, we can see that like other social events, violent events are evolutionary and sequential in nature, with a beginning and an end and, as such, can be systematically studied.

For example, Felson and Steadman have suggested the following tripartite model of murder: "The first stage involves verbal conflict, in which identities are attacked and attempts to influence an antagonist fail. The second stage involves threats and evasive action. Mediation, when it occurs, tends to occur at this point. Instigation of the conflict tends to occur during either the first or second stage. The third and final stage involves physical attack." [18]

David Luckenbill offers a more detailed model of the murderous scenario. After an in-depth analysis of 71 murders in one California county, Luckenbill concluded that murder is "a collective transaction. An offender, a victim, and possibly an audience engage in an interchange which leaves the victim dead." [19] Distinct phases are identifiable in the pattern of interaction that leads to murder. Luckenbill has categorized these phases into six stages that make up the typical criminal homicide transaction:

1. In stage 1, the eventual victim says or does something that is offensive to the eventual murderer. This may involve verbal insults, unwillingness to cooperate or acquiesce, or a physical, nonverbal gesture or communication. This phase marks the opening round of a series of interactions that become what Luckenbill terms a *character contest*. [20] As Luckenbill explains, a character contest is "a confrontation in which at least one, but usually both, attempt to establish or save face at the other's expense by standing steady in the face of adversity." [21]

2. Stage 2 involves the murderer interpreting the previous interaction as being personally offensive. Whereas the eventual victim may not have intended any offense, the offender perceives it as insulting or derogatory. In more than half of all cases, the offender's interpretation is mediated by bystanders and witnesses who help interpret what happened.

3. The third stage is a critical step, in that the offender has a variety of response options, including excusing or explaining away the offense, leaving the situation, or retaliation. Only the last response may result in a murder. Because this interactional scenario involves a character contest and because most of the possible responses involve losing face or prestige, the option of retaliation is the most commonly chosen response. In a small number of cases, Luckenbill found that the offender killed the victim at this point, but more typically, a verbal or physical retaliatory response was initiated.

4. Stage 4 in this escalating series of interactions again involves a choice, this time on the part of the victim, who can choose either to defuse the situation or to retaliate in turn. However, because a conciliatory response involves a display of what might be interpreted as cowardice or weakness on the part of the victim, it is not always the preferred choice. Luckenbill describes this phase as one in which the two participants reach an agree-

ment on the violent nature of their interaction. In other words, both parties perceive the situation in the same terms, as a confrontation to which the only appropriate response involves aggression and violence.

5. Stage 5 is the phase in which violence is typically used to resolve the character contest. In many cases, the offender procures a weapon that is at hand, briefly leaves the scene to get one, or converts into a weapon some object at hand, such as a lamp or a baseball bat. In approximately half the cases, the violence is over quickly, with the offender killing the victim after one shot, stab, or flurry of strikes.

6. The final stage marks the last phase of the scenario, with the offender either fleeing, remaining, or being held by bystanders and witnesses. The choice seems to be determined by the relationship between the victim and the offender and by the attitude the audience assumes toward the killer, whether supportive, hostile, or neutral.

The strength of David Luckenbill's analysis is his demonstration that murder involves an evolutionary transaction between the victim and the offender—a transaction that is often mediated by an audience. What is clear from this investigation is that homicides don't just happen, they develop out of a series of interactions. As Luckenbill writes, "the offender and victim develop lines of action shaped in part by the actions of the other and focused toward saving or maintaining face and reputation and demonstrating character. Participants develop a working agreement, sometimes implicit, often explicit, that violence is a useful tool for resolving questions of face and character."[22]

Others have found support for Luckenbill's conceptualization of the homicide event using other data. For example, Savitz and his colleagues reported that more than half the killings in their detailed review of homicide cases contained an informal contest of character or moral strength. These authors also noted that one or both of the people involved could have resolved the conflict before it resulted in death, but they failed to do so. In fact, about half the cases examined involved the victim initiating the personal confrontation. This scenario was originally coined *victim precipitation* by Marvin Wolfgang in 1958. Wolfgang defined the term as follows: "Victim precipitation is applied to those criminal homicides in which the victim is a direct, positive precipitator in the crime. The role of the victim is characterized by his having been the first in the homicide drama to use physical force against his subsequent slayer. The victim-precipitated cases are those in which the victim was the first to show and use a deadly weapon, to strike a blow in an altercation—in short, the first to commence the interplay or resort to physical violence."[23]

Wolfgang found that more than one fourth (26% of the 588 murders studied) of the criminal homicides in his sample were victim precipitated.[24] This illustrates that far from being passive unfortunates caught up in circumstances beyond their control, murder victims are sometimes active participants in the events leading up to their death. This is certainly not to argue that murder victims deserve to be killed. Victim precipitation theory is not intended to blame victims for their own murder. Rather, it illustrates that murder often involves a series of interactions between the victim and the offender. Thus, murder is often the outcome of a process in which the eventual victim was actively engaged. Again, to borrow David Luckenbill's words, "criminal homicide does not appear as a one-sided event with an unwitting victim assuming a passive, noncontributory role. Rather, murder is the outcome of a dynamic interchange between an offender, a victim, and, in many cases, bystanders."[25]

Although they do not dispute the concept of victim precipitation, Felson and Steadman conclude that murders are more complex than originally suggested by Wolfgang. They contend that it is sometimes difficult to classify murders as victim precipitated because the victims are typically not as aggressive as the offender.[26] Even with this critique, however, it is generally recognized that the victims sometimes play a crucial role in situations leading up to their murder. To ignore this element would produce a lopsided and incomplete understanding of how homicides occur. One murderer describes just such a situation in which the eventual victim played an active role in bringing about his own demise:

> I was sitting at a bar drinking a beer when this guy sitting next to me went to play the pinball machine. When he came back to the bar, he said, "You've been drinking my beer. I had a full can of beer when I went over to play that pinball machine." I said, "I ain't drink none of your beer." He said, "You better buy me another can of beer." I said, "Shit no, I ain't." At first I didn't know whether he really thought I had drank some of his beer or was just trying to bluff me into buying him a can, but when he later said, "You're gonna buy me another fucking can of beer," I knew then that he was handing me that to start some crap, so I knew for sure that I wasn't gonna buy him any beer. He told me again to buy him a beer. I said, "Hell no." I figured if I showed him that I wasn't gonna buy him a beer, he wouldn't push it, but he said, "You better go on and buy me another fucking beer." All I said then was, "I don't want any trouble; I'm just out of the pen, so go on and leave me alone, 'cause I ain't about to buy you any beer." He just kept looking. Then I started thinking he was out to do something to me. He pulled out a knife and made for me, and I shot him once in the arm. He kept on coming, so I had to finish him off. He was out to kill me.[27]

Clearly, in this example, the murder victim was not just an innocent bystander who was unaware of the potential for violence. Instead, he was actively engaged in the sequence of events that led to his own death.

In sum, all the aforementioned research has illustrated the interactive pattern of escalating tension that culminates in homicide. This is why Harries calls murder a process crime.[28] It should be clear that homicide is not always inevitable. Rather, it is contingent on the individual responses to the situation. At any point in the process, choices could be made that would de-escalate the conflict and end the interaction. Many confrontations do not result in murder because of the specific choices made. Maxfield asserts that murder should not be regarded as a crime but rather as an outcome.[29] Homicide is merely one out of many possible outcomes. Another way to look at it is to recognize that in many ways, murder is simply an assault that goes bad, and not all assaults end up being lethal. Blumstein points out that for every murder, there are 50 non-fatal assaults.[30] When arguments end lethally, it is often because the victim and the perpetrator both defined the situation as one in which violence was not only appropriate but preferred to a verbal or other nonviolent response.

A COMMENT ON HOMICIDE OFFENDERS

As we have discussed, a murderer usually kills only after a series of escalating interactions with the ultimate victim over ostensibly petty or mundane issues. The question is often asked, "How can someone kill for such superficial reasons?" This question is often asked rhetorically, but it also speaks to our apparent bewilderment in the face of seemingly bizarre behavior. One common response involves the portrayal of the offender as a monster. Popular novels and films portray murderers as psychotic, remorseless fiends, sometimes possessed of inhuman powers and abilities. Harry Marsh's research on the newspaper coverage of a murder case illustrates how reporting styles tend to stigmatize and denigrate offenders through sensational reporting that highlights the evil qualities of the perpetrator.[31] In the words of David Lester, "the general public often assumes that murderers are inevitably vicious criminals, potential assassins waiting for another chance to kill."[32] This demonization serves to distance us from the murderers and to explain their behavior in easily understood, if simplistic, terms. It also allows for feelings of moral superiority and for harsher punishment. We tend to be much more lenient toward those we can identify with or empathize with.

Implicit in this type of characterization is the assumption that murderers are motivated by primitive and evil impulses. Although this portrayal has a tremendous amount of appeal, our discussion of murder so far should illustrate that in reality, it is far from the truth. Instead, we usually find that murderers are typical people responding appropriately—as they see it—to specific situations and circumstances. Far from seeing themselves as wrong, perpetrators of murder perceive their violent behavior, at least at the time, as appropriate and necessary. Research evidence indicates that perpetrators of crime and violence feel justified in their actions; that is, they define the criminal act as a legitimate response to some behavioral or ethical breach on the part of their victim. As Donald Black states, "There is a sense in which conduct regarded as criminal is often quite the opposite. Far from being an intentional violation of a prohibition, much crime is moralistic and involves the pursuit of justice. . . .[33] Most intentional homicide in modern society may be classified as social control, specifically as self-help, even if it is handled by legal officials as crime."[34]

In other words, murderers often feel justified in their actions. As one violent offender expressed it, "If somebody fucked with me, I would righteously blow them away."[35] This perception of aggressive behavior as a form of self-help serves to legitimize the crime to the offender and perhaps even to others.[36] The concept of self-help refers to the tradition of private citizens dispensing justice themselves when official and legal mechanisms (such as the police) are seen as being unavailable or ineffective. Many killers see themselves as acting in the same tradition. Similarly, Jack Katz argues that killers often see themselves as acting for moralistic reasons.[37] As Katz writes, "violence erupts in situations that put at stake what the people involved momentarily regard as dimensions of the eternal good."[38] For example, one young man who assaulted someone who accosted his girlfriend described the event this way:

> I got mad as fucking hell then. First he won't stop checking out her body in front of me, next he makes the remark about her ass, then he squeezes her ass, and now he calls her a rag. After he called her a rag, that was it for me. He had now finally gone too far, so I grabbed a pool stick, tightened my grip around the thick part as hard as I could and swung it with all my might at his head. I broke the thin part of it across the side of his head, which knocked him off his feet. Then I quickly turned the stick around, jumped on top of him and started smashing him in the head with the thick end of the stick. I was fucking up the guy bad, blood was pouring out all over his head, neck and shoulders. Everybody in the pizza parlor then started screaming. "He's gone crazy, he's gone completely crazy. Call the police." My girlfriend started yelling at me, "Stop, stop, stop. You're going to kill him." I threw the bloody pool stick down on the floor, grabbed her by the hand and we ran out the door.[39]

Clearly, this individual felt that he was defending not only his honor but also that of his girlfriend. He felt justified in using violence because of the behavior of the other man, who had the temerity not only to hit on his girlfriend but to insult her as well. In his eyes, the victim had brought the violence upon himself. Of this perception, James Gilligan writes, "The first lesson that tragedy teaches is that *all violence is an attempt to achieve justice,* or what the violent person perceives as justice, for himself or for whomever it is on whose behalf he is being violent, so as to receive whatever retribution or compensation the violent person feels is 'due' him or 'owed' to him, or to those on whose behalf he is acting, whatever he or they are 'entitled' to or have a 'right' to; or so as to prevent those whom one loves or identifies with from being subjected to injustice. Thus, *the attempt to achieve and maintain justice, or to undo or prevent injustice, is the one and only universal cause of violence.*"[40]

In short, individuals who engage in violence, including lethal violence, typically define their actions as a necessary and positive step that they feel justified in taking.

Of course, in other cases, the situational dynamics just described are not present. Confrontational homicides follow a different pathway than intimate homicides or robbery homicides. It is to this latter type of homicide that we now turn our attention.

ROBBERY HOMICIDES

When we examine the dynamics of stranger homicides, we find that they tend to be quite distinct from homicides in which the victim is acquainted with or related to the perpetrator. This makes intuitive sense because people interact differently with their family and friends than with strangers. Although some stranger homicides follow the interaction patterns described by Luckenbill, most do not arise from those kinds of conflictual situations. Stranger homicides more typically arise from other felony situations. In other words, most stranger homicides occur either during or immediately after the perpetration of another crime. These kinds of killings may involve planned executions, contract killings, or kidnap murders.[41] However, the most common type of felony leading to homicide is robbery, followed in decreasing order of frequency by drug-related crimes, burglary, arson, rape, and motor vehicle theft.[42]

When one considers the characteristics of robberies, it is not surprising that they often end in murder. Robbery is defined as "the taking or attempting to take anything of value from the care, custody, or control of a person or persons by force or threat of force or violence and/or by putting the victim in fear."[43] As such, robbery is considered a violent crime as well as a property offense. Robbery is also a relatively common type of crime, with a rate of 220.9 per 100,000 population in 1995.[44] Typically, different forms of robberies are categorized based on location, including streets or highways, businesses, gas stations, convenience stores, homes, and banks.[45] In recent years, new forms of robbery have been developed as our society continues to change. For example, in response to better security on cars, which makes them harder to steal while parked and unattended, carjackings have increased in frequency. Similarly, ATM machines offer a new and potentially lucrative source of robbery locations.

Interesting enough, recent research has suggested that for some groups, robbery often occurs between acquaintances rather than between strangers.[46] Specifically, Felson, Baumer, and Messner assert that for poor young African-American men, more than a third of robberies involve perpetrators who target acquaintances. They argue that because many African-American men are less prone to report crime to the police and because information about valuables and other items is more easily obtained by acquaintances, young African-American men are particularly vulnerable to this type of victimization.

Commonly referred to as muggings, approximately 55% of robberies occur on streets and highways.[47] These tend to be fairly violent, with about one out of every three robberies resulting in injury to the victim. Most robbers recognize this potential, as evidenced by one offender who stated, "We try not to kill our victims. If we can avoid killing them, then we try not to. But if they force your hand, then you have to kill them. It's just that simple."[48] Another armed robber stated it this way:

> Robbing is an art, and the whole art of robbing is fear, and the main reason for robbing is to get what you came after—the money—and get away. You don't go there to hurt people. Sometimes you have to . . . but most good hustling dudes, especially with robbing experience, they never go out to hurt people. . . . Occasionally somebody says, "I ain't giving up nothing." But you can change his tune easy. You ain't got to kill him. Smack him with the gun or shoot him in the foot or kneecap, he give it right up. Knock his big toe off with one of them .45s, he give it up. . . . I know that I done a lot of cruel things, but it was something that I had to do at that particular moment for one reason or another. I have never did something unnecessary, especially when it comes to violence.[49]

As these accounts reveal, violence or the potential for violence is an important subtext that pervades all robbery interactions.

Robberies also often involve weapons. In 1997, 40% of robbers used a firearm, 38% relied on strong-arm tactics, 8% relied on some form of edged weapon, and 13% used some other form of weapon, such as a club or pipe. Robbery situations, therefore, present a high risk of serious injury or death because the prevalence of weapons serves to increase the likelihood of harm. If a gun is present, for example, and the victim resists the robbery, the fatality rate is much higher (9 per 100,000) than if no gun is present (1.4 per 100,000). According to Franklin Zimring and Gordon Hawkins, firearms are the primary reason why robberies are so dangerous.[50]

Regardless of the circumstances, robberies are remarkably similar in their perpetration. Typically, the robbers depend on sudden violence or the overt presence of a weapon to ensure the victim's compliance.[51] As Wright and Decker explain, they do this because "to be successful, armed robbers must take control of the offense from the start. They immediately have to impose on the interaction a definition favorable to their ends, allowing intended victims no room for negotiation."[52] This may involve surprising their victims, roughing them up, or brandishing a weapon. This kind of sudden, overwhelming attack serves to put the target victims in a helpless position and increase their fear, thus making them more vulnerable and less likely to mount an effective defense or even resist. A gun is particularly effective for this purpose because it is recognized to be a dangerous weapon. In one study of robbers, Wright and Decker found that overwhelmingly, the preferred weapons were guns because "a gun kind of speaks for itself."[53] For example, one robber's tactic was to come up behind his victims, push the gun to the back of their head so that they could feel it, and command, "Give it up, motherfucker, don't move or I'll blow your brains out."[54] Another tactic used by a robber was to "grab the victim by the neck and stick the gun to their head. Sometimes I don't even touch them, I just point the gun right in front of they face. That really scares people."[55] These tactics quickly establish a relationship in which the robber takes a position of dominance over the victim. Very often, this feeling of empowerment may be as important to the perpetrator as any actual money or valuables acquired. The payoff is sometimes the perception of power over someone rather than a financial reward. Here is how one robber expressed this feeling: "On one of my armed robberies me and a friend of mine . . . was standing up over the victims with these big old guns and these people were saying, 'Take the money! Take the money! Just don't shoot us!' I didn't have any intentions of shooting anybody anyway. But I'm just saying that when a person is telling me that, you are in control. You can either take their life like that or you can just let them live. That's what it is, a control thing. . . . You succeeded in having the authority to control people. You think about it and you say, 'I had this much control in my hands.' Really, it's an unexplainable thing."[56]

In these situations, what increases the probability that a threat will result in an actual act of violence? All the available evidence indicates that the most common reasons for the actual use of violence during a robbery are victims resisting, making sudden moves, or otherwise hindering the completion of the robbery.[57] One robber stated, "If they think I'm bullshitting, I'll smack them up they motherfucking head," and another noted that "you would be surprised how cooperative a person will be once he's been smashed across the face with a .357 magnum."[58] Others make more drastic use of violence by shooting the robbery victims, either to wound them or in many cases to kill them. In one offender's own words, "If I see he just trying to get tough, then sometimes I just straight out have to shoot somebody, just shoot 'em."[59] Given this propensity for intimidation and violence, it is easy to understand how robberies sometimes result in murder, especially when the target is a man. Although many robbery victims are women, they are not often killed because they tend to resist less and to cooperate more. Men, on the other hand, are more likely to fight back or otherwise practice noncompliance, thereby increasing the odds that the robber will end up killing them.[60] In some ways, therefore, robbery homicides exhibit the same characteristics as conflict-based ones. That is, both involve certain kinds of interactive patterns between the victim and the perpetrator, in which both are active participants.

Various scholars have pointed out that firearms in robberies are dangerous also because the victims may interpret the robbery as involving a more mortal threat and, consequently, will be more likely to resist.[61] For example, several years ago, two English tourists pulled over at a highway rest stop in Florida, and when two young men brandishing guns approached the car, the couple attempted to flee, and both were shot, one of them fatally.[62] In all likelihood, the guns tapping on the window provoked a panic reaction that led to the shooting. Aside from the actual or perceived resistance of the victim, other reasons for killing the target may be to remove an eyewitness or to help the robber escape the scene unhindered. Thus, for several reasons, the presence of firearms serves to increase the risk of killing during robberies.

The possibility of violence and murder is enhanced when we consider that most robberies are not planned or involve only minimal preparation.[63] The more spontaneous and haphazard the robbery, the more likely that something could go wrong and that the confrontation would end lethally. John Conklin, in his classic work on robbers, identified four primary types of robbers based on their motivations: professional, opportunist, addict, and alcoholic.[64] As three out of these four types are not individuals whom one would expect to engage in a lot of planning, this further illustrates the potentially explosive nature of many robberies. One would not expect addict robbers, for example, to handle frustration or unexpected situations calmly during high-stress and unplanned confrontations, particularly if they are in need of a fix. Even bank robberies, which Hollywood typically portrays as incredibly elaborate and well planned, are often spontaneous. For example, research indicates that most bank robbers had never even been in the banks they robbed and had no specific plan upon entry.[65]

SUMMARY

The goal of this chapter was to illustrate the fact that criminal homicides occur in a variety of different circumstances and that the perpetration of particular homicides often depends on the nature of the confrontation and on the nature of the relationship between the victim and the offender. Because the majority of murders are the result of a conflict situation between people who are least acquainted with one another, the analysis of murder as a social event offers important insights into the transformative and interactive nature of the homicide event. Moreover, when we examine murders that occur during the course of a robbery, we find a somewhat different dynamic at work, which relies on the sudden threat of violence to acquire valuables. In another sense, however, we find that robbery homicides, like confrontational ones, involve a distinctive process and sequence of events. Conflict and robbery homicides, however, encompass a process very different from the one typically found in killings between intimate partners. In the next chapter, we will explore murder between intimate partners and other family members.

NOTES

1. James Gilligan, *Violence: Our Deadly Epidemic and Its Causes* (New York: Grosset/Putnam, 1996), p. 97.

2. Leslie W. Kennedy and David R. Forde, *When Push Comes to Shove: A Routine Conflict Approach to Violence* (Albany: State University of New York Press, 1999), p. 7.

3. John E. Douglas, Ann W. Burgess, Allen G. Burgess, and Robert K. Ressler, *Crime Classification Manual* (New York: Lexington Books, 1992).

4. Quoted in Edward Green, *The Intent to Kill: Making Sense of Murder* (Baltimore: Clevedon Books, 1993), p. 110.

5. K. Diaz, "Slaying in Lino Lakes Apparently Capped a Night of Gunplay for Boy, Woman," *Star Tribune,* September 15, 1993.

6. Kenneth Polk, *When Men Kill: Scenarios of Masculine Violence* (Cambridge, U.K.: Cambridge University Press, 1994).

7. See, for example, Robert Nash Parker and Linda Anne Rebhun, *Alcohol and Ho-*

micide: A Deadly Combination of Two American Traditions (Albany: State University of New York Press, 1995).

8. Gerhard Falk, *Murder: An Analysis of Its Forms, Conditions, and Causes* (Jefferson, N.C.: McFarland, 1990); David Lester, "Temporal Variation in Suicide and Homicide," *American Journal of Epidemiology,* 109, 517–520 (1979).

9. Lester, "Temporal Variation in Suicide and Homicide," p. 519.

10. David T. Courtwright, *Violent Land: Single Men and Social Disorder from the Frontier to the Inner City* (Cambridge, Mass.: Harvard University Press, 1996); Falk, *Murder: An Analysis.*

11. Falk, *Murder: An Analysis,* pp. 21–22.

12. "Supplementary Homicide Reports," February, March, May, June, and November (Phoenix, Ariz.: Phoenix Police Department, 1991).

13. Quoted in Lonnie Athens, *Violent Criminal Acts and Actors Revisited* (Urbana: University of Illinois Press, 1997), pp. 44–45.

14. Polk, *When Men Kill.*

15. Gilligan, *Violence: Our Deadly Epidemic,* p. 97.

16. Falk, *Murder: An Analysis,* p. 21.

17. Christopher Birkbeck and Gary La Free, "The Situational Analysis of Crime and Deviance," *Annual Review of Sociology,* 19, 113–137 (1993); Kennedy and Forde, *When Push Comes to Shove.*

18. Richard B. Felson, and Henry J. Steadman, "Situational Factors in Disputes Leading to Criminal Violence," *Criminology,* 21 (1983), p. 70.

19. David F. Luckenbill, "Criminal Homicides as Situated Transaction," *Social Problems,* 25 (1977), p. 176.

20. Erving Goffman, *Interaction Ritual: Essays on Face-to-Face Behavior* (Garden City, N.Y.: Doubleday Books, 1967); Luckenbill, "Criminal Homicides as Situated Transaction."

21. Luckenbill, "Criminal Homicides as Situated Transaction," p. 177.

22. Ibid., pp. 185–186.

23. Marvin Wolfgang, *Patterns of Criminal Homicide* (Philadelphia: University of Pennsylvania Press, 1958); L. D. Savitz, "Official Statistics," in *Contemporary Criminology,* ed. L. D. Savitz and N. Johnson (New York: John Wiley, 1982), pp. 3–15.

24. Ibid., p. 252.

25. Luckenbill, "Criminal Homicides as Situated Transaction," p. 186.

26. Felson and Steadman, "Situational Factors in Disputes Leading to Criminal Violence."

27. Athens, *Violent Criminal Acts and Actors Revisited.*

28. K. D. Harries, *Serious Violence* (Springfield, Ill.: Charles C. Thomas, 1990).

29. Michael G. Maxfield, "Circumstances in Supplementary Homicide Reports: Variety and Validity," *Criminology,* 27, 671–695 (1989).

30. Alfred Blumstein, "Disaggregating the Violence Trends," in *The Crime Drop in America,* ed. Alfred Blumstein and Joel Wallman (Cambridge, U.K.: Cambridge University Press, 2000).

31. Harry L. Marsh, "University Professor or Sadistic Killer? A Content Analysis of the Newspaper Coverage of a Murder Case," in *Media, Process, and the Social Construction of Crime,* ed. Gregg Barak (New York: Garland, 1994).

32. David Lester, *Questions and Answers About Murder* (Philadelphia: Charles Press, 1991), p. 39.

33. Donald Black, "Crime as Social Control," *American Sociological Review,* 48 (1983), p. 34.

34. Ibid., p. 36.

35. Quoted in Athens, *Violent Criminal Acts and Actors Revisited,* p. 34.

36. Wesley G. Skogan, "Reporting Crimes to the Police: The Status of World Research," *Journal of Research in Crime and Delinquency,* 21, 113–137 (1984).

37. Jack Katz, *Seductions of Crime* (New York: Basic Books, 1988).

38. Ibid., p. 126.

39. Richard Rhodes, *Why They Kill: The Discoveries of a Maverick Criminologist* (New York: Alfred A. Knopf, 1999), p. 131.

40. Gilligan, *Violence: Our Deadly Epidemic,* pp. 11–12; emphasis in original.

41. See, for example, Douglas et al., *Crime Classification Manual;* Carl P. Malmquist, *Homicide: A Psychiatric Perspective* (Washington, D.C.: American Psychiatric Press, 1996).

42. Terance D. Miethe and Richard McCorkle, *Crime Profiles: The Anatomy of Dangerous Persons, Places, and Situations* (Los Angeles: Roxbury, 1998).

43. Federal Bureau of Investigation, *Crime in the United States–1995, Uniform Crime Reports* (Washington, D.C.: U.S. Government Printing Office, 1996), p. 26.

44. Ibid.

45. Miethe and McCorkle, *Crime Profiles.*

46. Richard B. Felson, Eric P. Baumer, and Steven F. Messner, "Acquaintance Robbery," *Journal of Research in Crime and Delinquency,* 37(3), 284–305 (2000).

47. Robert J. Meadows, *Understanding Violence and Victimization* (Upper Saddle River, N.J.: Prentice Hall, 1998).

48. Quoted in Richard T. Wright and Scott H. Decker, *Armed Robbers in Action: Stickups and Street Culture* (Boston: Northeastern University Press, 1997), p. 57.

49. Quoted in Katz, *Seductions of Crime,* p. 178.

50. Carolyn R. Block, "Patterns of Change in Chicago Homicides: The Twenties, the Sixties, and the Seventies," (Chicago: Statistical Analysis Center of the Illinois Law Enforcement Commission, 1980); Philip C. Cook, "Robbery Violence," *Journal of Criminal Law and Criminology,* 78, 357–376 (1987); Franklin E. Zimring and Gordon Hawkins, *Crime Is Not the Problem: Lethal Violence in America* (New York: Oxford University Press, 1997).

51. Jody Miller, "Up It Up: Gender and the Accomplishment of Street Robbery," *Criminology,* 36(1), 37–66 (1998).

52. Wright and Decker, *Armed Robbers in Action,* p. 96.

53. Ibid.

54. Quoted in Miller, "Up It Up," p. 48.

55. Quoted in Ibid.

56. Quoted in Wright and Decker, *Armed Robbers in Action,* p. 56.

57. Rosemary J. Erickson and Arnie Stenseth, "Crimes of Convenience," *Security Management.* http://www .securitymanagement.com/library/ 000236.html (retrieved October 1996).

58. Quoted in Miller, "Up It Up," p. 50.

59. Quoted in Ibid.

60. For a good discussion of this issue, see Michael P. Ghiglieri, *The Dark Side of Man: Tracing the Origins of Male Violence* (Reading, Mass.: Perseus Books, 1999), pp. 146–149.

61. See, for example, Katz, *Seductions of Crime;* Wright and Decker, *Armed Robbers in Action.*

62. Discussed in Kathleen M. Heide, *Young Killers: The Challenge of Juvenile Homicide* (Thousand Oaks, Calif.: Sage, 1999).

63. Floyd Feeney, "Robbers as Decision Makers," in *The Reasoning Criminal: Rational Choice Perspectives on Offending,* ed. Derek B. Cornish and Ronald V. Clarke (New York: Springer Verlag, 1986).

64. John Conklin, *Robbery and the Criminal Justice System* (Philadelphia: J. B. Lippincott, 1972).

65. Feeney, "Robbers as Decision Makers"; Marcus Felson, *Crime and Everyday Life,* ed. George S. Bridges, Robert D. Crutchfield, and Joseph G. Weis, *The Pine Forge Press Series in Crime and Society* (Thousand Oaks, Calif.: Pine Forge Press, 1998); S. Morrison and I. O'Donnell, "An Analysis of the Decision Making Processes of Armed Robbers," in *Crime Prevention Studies, Vol. 5, The Politics and Practice of Situational Crime Prevention,* ed. R. Homel (Mensey, N.Y.: Criminal Justice Press, 1996).

5

Dangerous Relations

Homicides in Families and Between Intimate Partners

For too long, the collective consciousness of contemporary Western society
has promoted an idyllic image of the family as a safe haven in an otherwise
turbulent, violent, and unsafe world. Closer examination of the nuclear
family, however, provides considerable evidence that this unit of social
organization is actually a fertile environment for deadly aggression.

JIM STRUVE[1]

INTRODUCTION

Darla Trice, a White 26-year-old woman, was killed on the night of April 24,
1994, after trying to murder her husband Charles Trice, a highway patrol officer for the state of Florida. Responding to a 911 call, police found Darla lying face up in a large pool of blood in the home office, and on the floor next
to her left hand was a small knife. Charles was slightly wounded in the chest
but, interesting enough, had no defensive wounds. According to Charles, the
couple had been in the process of divorcing, and he had gone to his office,
which was attached to the house, in order to retrieve some belongings. He
claimed that while he was in the office closet, he heard a noise, turned around,
and saw his wife approaching with a knife in her hand. According to his testi-

mony, he then heard his wife say, "I should have done this a long time ago," after which she stabbed him in the chest. He fell to his knees, grabbed a handgun, and shot his wife in the chest, killing her. At first blush, it seemed like a straightforward case of self-defense. However, on closer investigation, a different story began to emerge. Not only was the couple divorcing but Darla had taken out a restraining order on Charles because of his past abuse and his threats against her and their daughter Christina. Charles, it turned out, had been a very abusive husband, frequently beating Darla if meals were not prepared at a certain time or if the house was not as clean or orderly as he wanted it. Sometimes, he would put his gun to Darla's head and tell her he was going to kill her, and reportedly, he had often told her, "If you keep it up, I'll kill you. After I kill you, I'll kill Christina, and then I'll kill myself. And if I don't feel like killing myself and I want to keep Christina, believe me, I'll get off, and you know I will." Charles was also very possessive and jealous, and during the separation that preceded their divorce, Charles found out that Darla had begun seeing another man. In many ways, Charles Trice was a prototypical male abuser. Abusers are usually extremely jealous, controlling, and possessive, and they feel especially threatened during a separation or divorce. Most abusers who kill their intimate partners have a long history of violence against those partners.[2] Eventually, Charles Trice was arrested on first degree murder charges and, after a court trial, was convicted for the murder of his wife. Sadly, the social recognition and legal protection for battered women such as Darla Trice often comes much too late to help them.

The mythology surrounding the all-American family has typically envisioned it as a safe haven where members can find respite and safety from the outside world around them. Beginning in the 1940s, however, cracks in the foundation of this safe haven began to be publicly recognized, and the mythology surrounding the family began to unravel. Radiologists began noticing unexplained multiple fractures in the x-rays of infants and small children. In 1962, Dr. C. Henry Kempe and his colleagues published the now-famous article "The Battered-Child Syndrome" in the prestigious *Journal of the American Medical Association,* defining this syndrome as "a clinical condition in young children who have received severe physical abuse, generally from a parent or foster parent."[3]

Social consciousness concerning violence in the family expanded in the 1970s when women's rights groups brought the crimes of rape and intimate partner assault to the forefront of public awareness. In 1980, the results of the first national survey to estimate the amount of family violence was published. The numbers were shocking. The authors Murray Straus, Richard Gelles, and Suzanne Steinmetz concluded, "Drive down any street in America. More than one household in six has been the scene of a spouse striking his or her partner last year. Three American households in five (which have children living at home) have reverberated with the sounds of parents hitting their children. Where there is more than one child in the home, three in five are the scenes of violence between siblings. Overall, every other house in America is the scene of family violence at least once a year."[4]

In the 1980s, Americans learned about another form of family violence—elder abuse and neglect. Of course, all these types of violence are not new; what is new is the social, legal, and scholarly recognition of these phenomena. Historically, because family violence tends to happen behind closed doors, it has been ignored and neglected. But with the recent body of research in this area, we are beginning to recognize that the American family can be as violent as if not more violent than practically every other American institution.

Murder in the family takes a variety of different forms. It can involve the killing of children by their parents, the killing of parents by their children, and the killing of siblings by their siblings. Most well known, however, is *intimate partner homicide,* which can include any of the following relationships: husband—wife, common-law husband—wife, ex-husband—ex-wife, boyfriend—girlfriend, and intimate partners in homosexual relationships.

INTIMATE PARTNER HOMICIDE

The case of Lisa Bianco is most often cited as the catalyst for changing the way in which the criminal justice system responded to intimate partner violence in this country. Unfortunately, it still epitomizes the response that many victims of intimate partner violence experience from the police; therefore, it is worth describing.

Lisa Bianco was married to Alan Matheney in 1978. After years of abuse and battering, she fled to an Indiana battered women's shelter with her face beaten almost beyond recognition and her clothes in tatters. With the help of counselors from the shelter, Lisa was able to obtain a divorce from Alan and was granted custody of their two children. These legal barriers, however, did not stop Alan from stalking and intimidating Lisa. Lisa repeatedly complained to the police about Alan's stalking and threats. Only after he broke into her home and physically and sexually assaulted Lisa, did the police respond, and then only grudgingly.

After the attack, Alan made a plea agreement with prosecutors for the physical assault charge, and as a result, the rape charges were dropped. Although Alan was sentenced to serve prison time, he was released on furlough within two years. Because Alan was dangerous, the authorities were supposed to warn Lisa of his impending release, but she was not notified. Within hours of his release, Lisa was dead. Her children watched as she ran screaming from her house. They watched along with horrified neighbors as Alan knocked Lisa to the ground and, with the butt of a shotgun, beat her in the head until her skull was shattered. She died at the scene.

The details of this case are indeed heinous and gruesome, but they are no more grisly than many other intimate partner homicides. What makes the case noteworthy, however, is that it marked the first time in our nation's history that the criminal justice system was held accountable for not protecting a victim of intimate partner violence. The state of Indiana awarded a financial settlement to Lisa's two children for the criminal justice system's failure to protect their mother.

Unfortunately, this scenario is still far too common in the United States. In 1998, for example, Zipporah Mack was one of at least 14 Washington, D.C., area women who were killed as they sought to separate from or divorce their partners. When Mack left the home she shared with the father of her child, George Bobbitt, she asked for a police escort because she was afraid he would follow through on his threats to kill her. When Bobbitt began to stalk her, she applied for an order of protection that would keep him away. Despite the fact that Bobbitt violated the protection order on several occasions, he was never arrested. In November of 1998, the police tried to serve a warrant to Bobbitt after he kidnapped Mack from a Greenbelt, Maryland, Metro station at knife point and then assaulted her, but Prince George's County sheriff's deputies said they were unable to find him. A month later, on December 15, 1998, Bobbitt shot Mack to death as she ran screaming from her car toward her grandparents' home.[5]

If you haven't heard of Lisa Bianco or Zipporah Mack, you must certainly have heard of Nicole Brown Simpson. All these women called the police for help to protect them against abusive and violent partners on several occasions before the final call had to be made for them—to the coroner. Each case illustrates the stages of abuse that all too often lead to murder. Although the U.S. criminal justice system has improved its response to victims of intimate partner violence over the past 20 years, these cases are a tragic reminder how often the system is still unable to adequately protect many women. Although most abusers are dissuaded from violence by orders of protection, those intent on killing their partner are not deterred from their lethal goals.[6]

Incidence Rates and Trends
in Intimate Partner Homicide

In 1998, nearly three out of four of the 1,830 victims of intimate partner homicide were women.[7] In terms of the specifics of the relationship, 836 victims were killed by their spouses, 63 by their ex-spouses, and 743 by their boyfriends or girlfriends.[8] Of the more than 1,600 people who were killed by their intimate partners in 1999, 1,218 were women and 424 were men.

These numbers, though horrific, actually represent something of a decline, albeit more for male than for female victims of intimate homicide. Between 1976 and 1993, the number of women killed by intimates remained relatively stable. Between 1993 and 1997, however, the number of women murdered by intimates declined by 23%, although between 1997 and 1998, the number increased again by 8%. The number of male victims of intimate murder decreased 60% during the same time period.[9]

Overwhelmingly, women are the victims of intimate killings in the United States. A woman is much more likely to be killed by male intimates than by any other type of attacker.[10] Just as women are more likely to experience nonlethal forms of violence from their intimate partners, women are also significantly more likely to be killed by their intimate partners than men.[11] Neil Webs-

Exhibit 5.1 Average Annual Intimate Partner Homicide Victimization Rates per 100,000 by Victim Race and Sex, 1998–1999

Race	Men	Women
White	0.3	1.5
African-American	2.8	3.9

SOURCE: James A. Fox and Marianne W. Zawitz, *Homicide Trends in the United States* (Washington, D.C.: Bureau of Justice Statistics, U.S. Department of Justice, 2001).

dale's research on intimate violence and killing has led him to conclude that it is largely a sex-specific phenomenon.[12] Not only is the majority of the violence perpetrated by men against women, but the very nature of the violence is different. Typically, men kill intimates as a lethal culmination of an ever-increasing cycle of violence, whereas women typically kill their intimates in self-defense or in a preemptive attempt to prevent further violence against themselves.[13] Dobash and Dobash echo this when they write, "When the woman dies, it is usually the final and most extreme form of violence at the hands of her male partner. When the man dies, it is rarely the final act in a relationship in which she has repeatedly beaten him."[14] These characterizations are supported by a variety of research. One such study found that two thirds of the women incarcerated for killing their intimates reported having been the victim of previous physical violence from the intimate whom they subsequently killed.[15] Other studies have found a range of 40% to more than 90% of incarcerated female murderers who killed in response to abuse.[16]

Average annual victimization rates per 100,000 of intimate partner homicide for 1998 and 1999 are displayed in Exhibit 5.1. These victimization rates illustrate that both White and African-American women are much more at risk of being killed than their male counterparts. In fact, White women are almost five times more likely to be killed by their intimate partners than White men, whereas African-American women are one and a half times more likely than African-American men to be killed by their intimates. Clearly, however, African-American men and women are both at greater risk of being killed by their intimates than either White men or women. Because individuals who live in households with lower family incomes experience intimate partner violence at significantly higher rates than households with higher family incomes, this differential is undoubtedly related to the fact that African-Americans are disproportionately more likely to live in economically deprived environments.[17] Some have also argued that the passive or even nonexistent policing of many African-American communities so prevalent until recently has also contributed to the higher rates of fatal intimate violence, as it has allowed battering relationships to progress to their more lethal stages.[18]

Since the Lisa Bianco case, our society has become more knowledgeable about the reality of intimate partner violence. Beginning in the 1970s, significant lobbying efforts by victim's rights groups in general and by women's rights groups in particular have worked to erode the antiquated notion that intimate partner violence against women should remain behind closed doors. After extensive lobbying efforts by these groups and empirical research that demonstrated the utility of arrest as a deterrent against future incidents of intimate partner violence, the criminal justice system has finally begun to treat intimate partner violence as a criminal matter appropriate for police and prosecutorial concern. Today, virtually all states and the District of Columbia have mandatory arrest policies for felony domestic assaults and warrantless arrest for an unwitnessed domestic violence–related misdemeanor assault. Mandatory arrest policies require police to detain a perpetrator when there is probable cause that an assault or battery has occurred or that a restraining order has been violated, regardless of a victim's consent or protestations.[19] It is important to remember, however, that as recently as 30 years ago, many jurisdictions viewed violence that occurred between intimates as a private matter, and a few even required victims of spousal assault to pay prosecutors a fee to adjudicate their batterer.[20]

Much of the push toward mandatory arrest policies was derived from the well-known Minneapolis experiment, in which arrest was found to have a significant deterrent effect on batterers.[21] Subsequent attempts at replication, however, have failed to show a deterrent effect in other cities such as Milwaukee, Colorado Springs, Miami, and Omaha. Based on this series of studies, the evidence suggests that arrest deters only batterers who have a lot to lose, whereas arrest may well increase the risk of battering for abusers who have little to lose, such as men who are unemployed.[22] Others argue that arrest by itself does not deter but, when combined with prosecution and incarceration or treatment, indeed dissuades batterers from further acts of abuse.[23]

Has this increased societal awareness of intimate partner violence had an impact on the incidence of intimate partner homicides? Exhibits 5.2 and 5.3 display the rates of intimate partner homicide per 100,000 population for White and African-American male and female victims from 1980 to 1999. Comparing the graphs clearly shows that the decline in intimate murder has been more significant in African-American populations than for Whites. In fact, the per capita rate of African-American intimate murders was 11 times that of Whites in 1980 but less than four times that of Whites in 1999. The sharpest decrease in intimate homicide occurred among African-American male victims. The rate of intimate partner homicide decreased for Whites as well; however, the decline was not nearly as steep as for African-Americans, and as with African-Americans, the rate of decrease was more evident for White men than for White women.

Why have the rates of female-perpetrated homicide against their intimate partners dropped more in recent decades than the rates of male-perpetrated intimate homicide? Because a great deal of research has indicated that the killing of an intimate male partner by a woman often results from a culmination of ongoing violence against her, scholars have investigated whether factors that facilitate a woman's escape from an abusive relationship are related to this decline. James Allen Fox and Jack Levin point out that the liberalization of divorce laws and the diminishment of the stigma associated with being a battered wife have

**Exhibit 5.2 Intimate Partner Homicide Rates
for White Men and Women, 1980–1999**

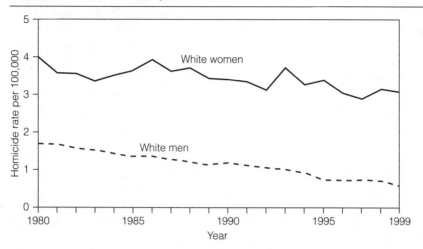

SOURCE: Adapted from James A. Fox and Marianne W. Zawitz, *Homicide Trends in the United States* (Washington, D.C.: Bureau of Justice Statistics, U.S. Department of Justice, 2001).

**Exhibit 5.3 Intimate Partner Homicide Rates
for Black Men and Women, 1980–1999**

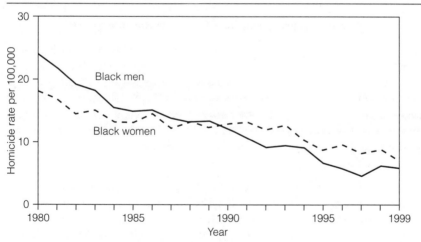

SOURCE: Adapted from James A. Fox and Marianne W. Zawitz, *Homicide Trends in the United States* (Washington, D.C.: Bureau of Justice Statistics, U.S. Department of Justice, 2001).

allowed women to more easily escape battering relationships.[24] Along the same lines, Angela Browne and Kirk Williams have discovered that states with more resources for abused women, such as shelters and other services, had significantly lower rates of female-perpetrated partner homicide against men. They assert that "by offering threatened women protection, escape, and aid, such resources can engender an awareness that there are alternatives to remaining at risk for further violent interactions."[25] These findings were replicated by Dugan, Nagin, and Rosenfeld, who found that cities that offered domestic violence services—particularly legal advocacy programs to help battered women navigate the court system—had significantly lower rates of female-perpetrated homicide against male partners.[26]

So why do these services serve more often to protect men, when they were designed to protect women? Well, the majority of domestic violence resources are aimed at helping women to leave an abusive relationship before they must use deadly force to defend themselves, so it is logical that these services would serve to decrease the fatality rate for men more than for women. As illustrated in the cases cited earlier in this chapter, men who kill more often act out of rage or a desire to maintain control over their female partners. Murder is simply the final act of brutality after years of abuse. Programs and services that help a woman escape an abusive situation may inflame the insecurities of abusive men and trigger a last-ditch effort at control. The bottom line is that today, as throughout our nation's history, women are significantly more likely to be killed by their partners than men. In 1999, there were 1,218 women killed by their intimate partners, compared to only 424 men.[27]

A Note on Men who Kill Their Intimate Partners

Men who kill their intimates, as we have pointed out, almost invariably do so as the fatal culmination of a sustained pattern of violence and abuse. Much of this violence seems to arise from a deep-seated need to control and dominate their partners. In many ways, battering is about perceptions of power and dominance. This is one reason why divorces and separations are especially dangerous times for battered women, because the abuser sees this as a threat to his control over the woman. This is illustrated by the words of a violent man who killed his wife:

> I was out of town, and I called my wife one night to check on what was going on at home. She told me that she had seen an attorney and was filing papers to divorce me. I asked her to hold off until I got back home and could sit down and talk it over with her, but she said, "No, this time I really mean it." After she told me that, I blew up and said, "You better not do that to me. If you do, you'll be sorry for it." She said, "I had a restraining order placed on you, so if you come around here bothering me, the police will get you." I said, "If I really want to get you, the police can't save you." I thought that telling her that would scare her, but it didn't. She just acted calm and confident, like she had everything all planned out. That got me madder. I knew then that it was no use raising

any more hell over the phone since it wasn't intimidating her. I figured that I had to get home and confront her face to face. I just felt plain mad. I hung up the phone and headed straight for home. I wanted to see if she would talk as brave about a divorce to me when I got home as she did over the phone.

When I did get home three hours later, she was in bed, asleep. I woke her up and told her to get up, that I wanted to talk. I told her if she stopped with the divorce that I would promise to act better . . . but she wouldn't buy any of it. I got angrier and angrier. Then she came out and said, "Look, please do me this favor and give me a divorce." At that moment I felt cold hatred for her inside me. I told myself that I better leave before I exploded on her, but then I decided the hell with it, and I looked her straight in the face and said, "Well, X, you better start thinking about those poor kids of ours." She said, "I don't care about them; I just want a divorce."

My hate for her exploded then and I said, "You dirty, no-good bitch," and started pounding her in the face with my fist. She put her arms up and covered her face, so I ran and got my rifle and pointed it at her. I said, "Bitch, you better change your mind fast or I'm going to kill you." She looked up and said in a smart-ass way, "Go ahead, then; shoot me." I got so mad and felt so much hate for her that I just started shooting her again and again.[28]

Clearly, this man felt that he was losing control and believed that the only way to retain power over his wife was to kill her. In fact, a common element to domestic homicides is a batterer who has explicitly threatened that "if I can't have you, no one will," or words to that effect.[29]

In recent years, various scholars have attempted to identify the warning signs or precursors of intimate homicide. Neil Websdale's extensive work in reviewing intimate fatalities using crime scene investigations, newspaper reports, follow-up investigative reports, details of prior protection orders, criminal histories of victims and perpetrators, medical examiner's reports, and statements from witnesses has led him to delineate several common antecedents to potential intimate homicides. Exhibit 5.4 summarizes these risk factors.

Examining these qualities, it is quickly evident that most men who kill their partners exhibit a great number of warning behaviors that should raise alarms of their potential lethality. However, these elements are not necessarily predictors of lethal behavior, nor does the absence of these qualities guarantee a woman's safety. Nevertheless, these elements are typically present among men who murder their intimates.

A Note on Women Who Kill Their Intimate Partners

As we have seen, women are significantly less likely to commit murder than men. When they do kill, it is often in self-defense. In fact, in one of the first systematic studies of homicide, Marvin Wolfgang noted that 60% of the husbands killed by their wives from his data precipitated their own deaths by be-

Exhibit 5.4 High Risk Factors for Intimate Homicide

1. Prior History of Domestic Violence
   - escalation of violence
   - past homicide attempts: choking
   - rape and sexual violence
   - violence toward pets
   - violence during pregnancy
2. Escaping Violent Relationships
   - marital estrangement
3. Obsessive Possessiveness
   - extreme jealousy
   - stalking
   - obsessiveness about the relationship
   - suicide attempts or threats
4. Prior Police Involvement
5. Prior Criminal History of the Perpetrator
6. Threats to Kill
7. Alcohol or Drug Problems
8. Protection Orders
9. Acute Perceptions of Betrayal
10. Child Custody Disputes
    - past attempts to kill or abduct children
    - severe abuse of children
    - sexual abuse of children
11. Mental Illness of Perpetrator (Paranoia, Schizophrenia, Depression)
    - severe abuse as child
12. Hostage Taking
13. Children Are Hers, Not His
14. Change in Circumstances
    - unemployment
15. Her Fear

SOURCE: Janet A. Johnson, Victoria L. Lutz, and Neil Websdale, "Death by Intimacy: Risk Factors for Domestic Violence," *Pace Law Review*, 20(2), 263–296 (2000). Reprinted with permission of *Pace Law Review*. All rights reserved.

ing the first to use physical force or threaten their wives with weapons. In contrast, victim precipitation was involved in only 9% of the cases in which wives were killed by their husbands.[30] Many studies have replicated this finding. In fact, one government commission estimated that homicides committed by women in general were seven times as likely to be in self-defense as homicides committed by men.[31] Angela Browne notes that most battered women do not kill and are themselves more likely to be murdered than their abusive partners. Browne's work suggests that there is no substantial difference between battered women who kill and those who do not. The important variable, she believes, lies in the male batterers. In her study, male batterers who were killed by their wives were more abusive and threatening, used more extreme forms of assault, including sexual assault, and were much more likely to have threatened the children.[32]

Since the 1970s, many defense attorneys have used the battered woman syndrome as a defense for their clients' killing their abusive partners. Coined by Lenore Walker, the term *battered woman syndrome* describes a pattern of psychological and behavioral symptoms found in many women living in battering relationships.[33] There are four general characteristics of the syndrome:

1. A woman believes that the violence was her fault.
2. A woman has an inability to place the responsibility for the violence elsewhere.
3. A woman fears for her life or her children's lives.
4. A woman has an irrational belief that the abuser is omnipresent and omniscient.

Essentially, the rationale underlying this defense is that battered women are suffering from *post-traumatic stress disorder* (PTSD).[34] Even with this kind of justification, the battered woman syndrome defense may sway a jury only to convict a woman on a lesser charge, such as involuntary manslaughter; rarely does it persuade a jury to acquit her. Historically, in fact, battered women were often not even allowed to use self-defense as a legal defense but had to rely on other defenses such as temporary insanity.[35] Of course, not all women who murder their intimate partners do so in self-defense. However, it is certain that many women who kill their intimate partners have done so after a long history of abuse.

PARENTS WHO KILL THEIR CHILDREN

As we pointed out in chapter 1, the intentional killing of a small child is sometimes incorrectly classified as accidental or undetermined. Therefore, the incidence of *filicide,* the killing of a child by a parent, and *infanticide,* the killing of a child by anyone, is somewhat difficult to determine. Questionable infant deaths are among the most difficult to investigate for several reasons. First, there are rarely any witnesses. Second, compared to adult homicides, in which the majority of victims is killed by a gun or a knife, it is often difficult to determine whether a small infant's injuries were accidental or intentional. Because of these problems, the number of young murder victims estimated by the FBI is undoubtedly an underestimate.

Exhibit 5.5 displays the number of murder victims under the age of five by age of the victim from 1980 through 1999. As can be seen, the number of very young children killed increased in the early 1990s but has generally decreased since that time. The number of three- and four-year-olds killed has remained relatively constant over this time period.

Despite this decline, a staggering number of children under the age of five are still murdered in the United States every year. An average of 650 children under the age of five were murdered every year during the 1990s, which aver-

Exhibit 5.5 Young Homicide Victims by Age Group, 1980–1999

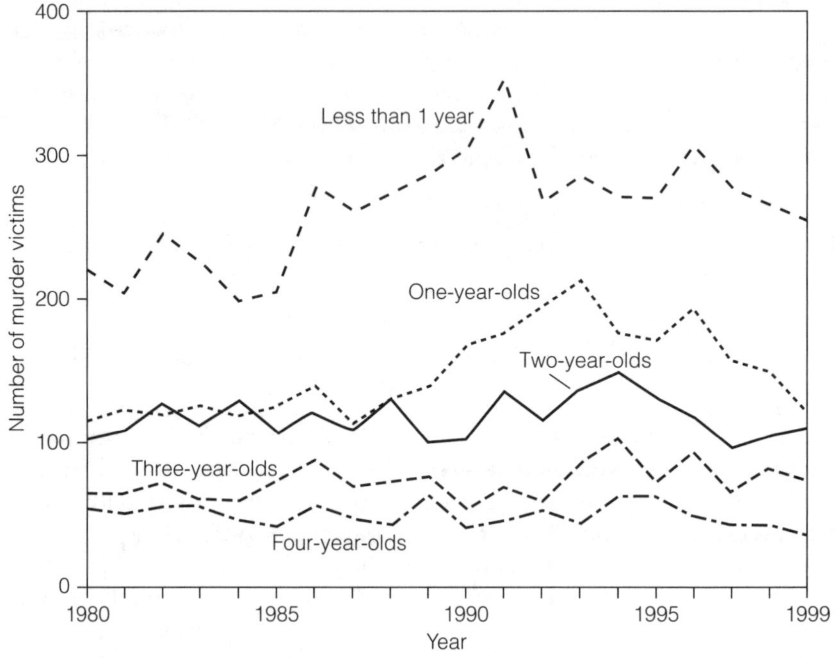

SOURCE: Adapted from James A. Fox and Marianne W. Zawitz, *Homicide Trends in the United States* (Washington, D.C.: Bureau of Justice Statistics, U.S. Department of Justice, 2001).

ages out to almost two young children murdered daily during this decade. The majority of young murder victims under the age of five are younger than one. In fact, in 1999, 42% of young children who were murdered were under the age of one, 20% were one-year-olds, 19% were two-year-olds, 13% were three-year-olds, and only 7% were four-year-olds.[36]

Parents are most often the killers in cases of infanticide. In 1999, 57% of young murder victims were killed by their parents. Mothers were just as likely to kill their children as fathers. A recent case has brought this fact horrifically to our attention. On June 20, 2001, Andrea Yates, who was suffering from a severe case of postpartum depression, drowned her five small children in a bathtub. The children ranged in age from six months to seven years. In approximately 30% of infanticide cases, other offenders were identified as the killers: 8% were killed by other family members and 23% by friends and acquaintances. Only 2% of young children murdered in 1999 were known to have been killed by strangers. Of those children killed by someone other than their parents, the majority were killed by men.[37]

Another specific type of infanticide is *neonaticide*, which is defined as the killing of an infant within 24 hours of his or her birth.[38] In the majority of neonaticide cases, the mother slays her child in secret.[39] In 1996, a case of neonaticide so shocked the nation that it captivated the media's attention for more than two years—the Baby Grossberg case.

Amy Grossberg and Brian Peterson Jr. were both first-year students in upstanding universities in the fall of 1996. They were both from upper-middle-class backgrounds and had no history of violence, delinquency, or other school-related problems. Although Amy's friends and family were not aware of it, she was seven months pregnant when she entered the University of Delaware as a first-year student in September of 1996.

On November 12, 1996, Brian helped Amy give birth to a six-pound baby boy at a roadside Comfort Inn in Newark, Delaware. According to prosecutors, after the birth, the infant was beaten about the head, shaken, stuffed into a gray garbage bag with yellow drawstrings, and deposited in a dumpster outside the motel. It was only because heavy bleeding and discomfort forced Grossberg to go to an area emergency room that the pregnancy was brought to the attention of the authorities. After the attending physicians realized that she had given birth to a baby that was nowhere to be found, they called the police. Questioned by the police, Grossberg admitted that Peterson was the father of the infant and had been with her that evening at the time of the boy's birth.

Police soon located the infant's body in the hotel dumpster. Autopsy reports indicated that the baby had been a healthy infant who was alive after a full-term nine-month pregnancy. Though still denying that they had murdered their infant, Grossberg and Peterson pled guilty to manslaughter in the spring of 1998. Both were fined $5,000 and sentenced to eight years in prison, although five and a half years of Grossberg's and six years of Peterson's prison sentences were suspended because they had cooperated with prosecutors.[40]

In more typical cases of filicide, the child's death is often the final outcome of a history of abuse, as illustrated by the death of Kevin Mikell. Kevin and his sisters had been placed in foster care because both of their parents were in drug treatment programs. After he had completed his treatment program, their father, Anthony Mikell, was given custody of the children. In February of 1996, Mikell was allegedly toilet training his two-year-old son Kevin. One strategy Mikell used involved forcing Kevin to sit on a toilet for more than 12 hours, alternately beating him and feeding him. A neighbor who heard screams from the Mikell apartment summoned 911, but it was too late. Paramedics found Kevin unresponsive and bruised, with a dislocated arm and cigarette burns on his body. He appeared to have been dead about four hours. An autopsy revealed that the toddler died from blows that caused a brain hemorrhage and ripped his intestines.[41]

Another act that often results in severe injury and death to an infant is shaking. Shaken baby syndrome was first described in 1972 by a pediatrician named John Caffey. The syndrome made national headlines in 1997 when Louise Woodward, an au pair from England, shook a Boston couple's infant son to death while caring for him. Woodward was convicted of second-degree murder but only sentenced to the time she had served in prison before and during her trial (279 days).[42] Matthew Eappen, the eight-month-old infant who was killed by Woodward, had suffered head injuries characteristic of shaken baby syndrome. When a baby is shaken so vigorously that his or her head is repeatedly jerked from front to back, it can cause internal bleeding and swelling in the brain, brain stem, or spinal cord. Whereas the results of such injuries are more often nonfatal and include the loss of hearing and sight, paralysis, cerebral palsy, or mental retardation, more than one in four of these babies dies.[43] Matthew Eappen was only one of many such deaths in 1997.

Although some parents premeditate to kill their children for insurance money or some other profit, most child killings are the result of cruel acts administered for corporal punishment or other discipline. As Charles Ewing explains, "most child abuse killings seem to result from misguided, albeit sometimes brutal, efforts to discipline, punish, or quiet children. The parent tries to discipline the child physically, loses control, and ends up beating the child to death."[44]

CHILDREN WHO KILL THEIR PARENTS

Although the exact legal definition varies by state, the general definition of *parricide* is the killing of parents or stepparents by their children. This type of homicide represents a small fraction of all homicides committed annually in the United States, usually less than 3%. However, this low rate still translates into an average of 300 parents per year being killed by their children.[45]

The case of parricide to receive the most media attention in recent years was that of Eric and Lyle Menendez. On August 20, 1989, Lyle Menendez placed a 911 call to the Beverly Hills police. He frantically told the operator that someone had killed his parents. At the residence, the police discovered the bodies of Jose and Kitty Menendez in the television room. Jose was found slumped on the sofa, apparently shot in his sleep. Kitty was found on the floor, her face blown away by a point-blank shot to her left cheek. Both bodies had been ripped apart by gunshots, about 12 shots altogether. Both Jose and Kitty had gunshot wounds close to the knee, a wound similar to the gruesome calling card of a Mafia group in the Beverly Hills area. Because of these wounds, rumors flew throughout the media of a Mafia connection with the murders.

Police had no suspects in the case for months after the murders. However, immediately after their parents' death, Lyle and Eric began a lavish spending spree. They bought a Porsche sports car, Rolex watches, and real estate, and they took expensive vacations. Furthermore, Eric confessed to his best friend, a boy named Craig, that he and Lyle had killed his parents. Because there had been no leads in the case, by November of 1990, the police began interviewing everyone who knew the family, including Craig, who told the police about Eric's confession. In March of 1991, the police got another break. The girlfriend of Lyle and Eric's psychologist confessed that she had overheard a therapy session with Eric, in which Eric admitted to killing his parents. (Before the murders, Eric and Lyle had been sent to counseling by their parents after the brothers had been arrested and convicted of burgling several homes in their affluent neighborhood.) There was much legal wrangling over the admissibility of these confessions, but nearly three years later, the boys were both indicted and sent to trial for the murder of their parents.

Just days before Eric's trial was to begin, his defense attorney told reporters that they were going to use a plea of self-defense, based on the claim that both brothers had lived a life of abuse at the hands of their parents and felt themselves to be in imminent danger from their parents at the time they killed them. After months of testimony in the trials of Eric and Lyle, juries deadlocked in both cases, and in December of 1993, the judge ruled a mistrial for both cases. Another two years passed before a retrial began. Both Lyle and Eric were eventually convicted on two counts of first degree murder for killing their parents and were sentenced to life in prison.

So how could two teenage boys from an affluent family and community come to murder their parents? Because parricide is relatively rare, it has not been studied as much as other types of killings; what we know about it comes primarily from case studies. For example, we know that the Menendez brothers are typical of children who murder their parents; they are usually White, male, middle-class adolescents with above-average intelligence.[46] After examining the FBI's *Supplementary Homicide Reports,* Kathleen Heide identified three categories of children who kill their parents: abused children (the Menendez brothers claimed abuse), mentally ill children, and antisocial children. Heide noted that abused children were the most frequently encountered type of adolescent parricide offender.[47]

Elderly individuals being cared for by their adult children are also at risk of parricide. The murder of 85-year-old Handy Morrow by his daughter Edna Zehnder was vividly recorded on a tape Morrow was using to record a religious broadcast at the time of his death. Apparently, Morrow had been recording a religious sermon on his tape player and became upset at his daughter for playing her television too loudly in the next room. Verbal negotiations collapsed between Morrow and his daughter, and Morrow went to the fuse box and turned off the electricity to Zehnder's room, after which yelling could be heard on the tape, in addition to "several thwacks." Several groans from the man were then heard on the tape, followed by these exclamations from Zehnder: "Shut your face! I don't want to hear you! I don't want to see you!" The thwacks were later discovered to be the sounds of Zehnder beating her father with a tire iron. Morrow was found four days after this incident by his grandson. Lying in his own waste, he was grotesquely bruised, had one broken arm, and had not been fed or given any fluids since the attack. He died 24 days later.[48]

OTHER FAMILY HOMICIDES

Fratricide and *sororicide* are homicides that occur between siblings. Similar to homicides between friends and acquaintances, fratricides and sororicides are often the result of a conflict over a trivial event getting out of control. Pat Langan examined more than 8,000 murder cases from a sample of large urban counties and found that more than 80% of the perpetrators and victims in killings involving siblings were above the age of 19 and that the majority (85%) of sibling murders were committed by men.

In some cases, sibling killings are committed when a family member goes on a killing spree and kills the entire family. This is termed *familicide*. For example, in October of 1993, Gerard McCra, who was then 15 years old, shot his parents and his 11-year-old sister to death. Apparently, the young McCra had been arguing with his parents because they refused to allow him to sleep with his girlfriend in the McCra family home. Gerard had no prior criminal record or history of violence.[49]

More often, however, acts of familicide in which entire families are killed are perpetrated by the male patriarch of the family. Perhaps the worst familicide in U.S. history was committed by Ronald Gene Simmons after the Christmas holiday of 1987 in a small town in Arkansas. Simmons was apprehended after a shooting rampage in which he had killed two people and wounded four others in three area businesses, two of which he had formerly been employed in. During his interrogation by the police, Simmons did not answer questions about his family. When the police went to the rural site where his house was located, they discovered that his murderous rampage had not begun at the businesses. Within sight of the decorated Christmas tree and wrapped presents at the Simmons home, they found five dead bodies: Simmons's son and daughter, their spouses, and his six-year-old granddaughter. The four adults had been shot to death, and the granddaughter had been smothered. After searching the premises, the police also found a shallow grave with seven bodies: Simmons's wife, two of his sons, three of his daughters, and another three-year-old granddaughter. Nearby in the trunks of two junked cars were the bodies of two more grandsons, neither of whom had reached their second birthday. All adults had been shot to death, and the children had been either smothered or strangled. Gene Simmons did have a criminal record; in fact, he had fled from the police with his family to Arkansas after he was convicted of having sexual intercourse with and impregnating his then 15-year-old daughter in New Mexico. In this remote location in Arkansas, he kept his wife and family as isolated from the outside as possible. In June of 1995, after presenting no defense at his trials and refusing to appeal his convictions and sentences, Gene Simmons was executed by lethal injection.[50]

Often, the male patriarch who takes the lives of his family also kills himself, resulting in a murder–suicide. Typically, a combination of marital, social, and economic pressures precedes such mass killings. Charles Ewing explains, "Faced with overwhelming threats to their roles as providers, controllers, and central figures in the lives of their families, . . . the man who kills his family and then himself is, first and foremost, generally a deeply distressed and depressed individual who is at the end of his emotional rope. . . . Ultimately, he convinces himself that familicide followed by suicide is not just the only way out but the honorable and right thing to do."[51]

EXPLANATIONS OF FAMILY AND
INTIMATE PARTNER HOMICIDE

Similar to the connection between assault and homicide, there is also a close relationship between nonlethal forms of intimate and family violence and incidents that result in death. Many of the theories used to explain lethal violence in general can also be applied to violence and murder in the family. However, other factors are also related to the prevalence of intimate and family homicide.

More than three decades of research on family violence have uncovered several broad social and cultural factors related to an increased risk of violence in families. Foremost of these is the character of the family unit itself. Family members spend a great deal of time together in a range of activities, and their involvement with one another is emotionally intense. As a result, families have many potential sources of conflict. Inevitably, the goals of individual family members will conflict on occasion, and arguments and disagreements will arise, particularly between intimate partners. Physical violence is one possible outcome of this conflict. Unfortunately, the privacy of the family situation often serves to shield family members from outside help and intervention.[52]

Feminist Theories

The unequal power relationships that are traditionally inherent in families in particular and in society in general have also been used to explain the high rate of lethal and nonlethal violence against women. Feminist theories incorporate these historical and structural aspects of inequality between the sexes to explain violence against women. For example, in our society, men and women are taught culturally appropriate gender roles, and these roles are inextricably linked to the laws and practices that tacitly approve of male dominance.

Feminist theories explore the relationships and the process through which male violence against women occurs—namely, the *patriarchal* organization of society. Patriarchy constitutes the constellation of social relations and institutions that award men greater status, power, and privilege than women. Violence against women, according to feminist theorists, is a natural product of the system of unequal relations between men and women that is a historical heritage of all Western societies. Thus, the beating and killing of a woman by her male intimate is not simply an individual or a family problem; it is a manifestation of the system of male domination of women that has existed historically in this country. Using international data and interviews with battered women, R. Emerson Dobash and Russell Dobash have empirically demonstrated how the role of a wife has developed into that of an appropriate victim of assault: "Men who assault their wives are actually living up to cultural prescriptions that are cherished in Western society—aggressiveness, male dominance, and female subordination—and they are using physical force as a means to enforce that dominance."[53] Thus, feminist scholars place violence against women in context by focusing on the patriarchal social structure inherent in Western society.

Situational Factors such as Stress, Poverty, and Alcohol

Research has also found a relationship between several situational contexts and family and intimate partner violence. Stress and economic deprivation have both been linked to an increased incidence of family violence. For example, several large-scale surveys, such as the National Crime Victimization Survey, have found that individuals in families with lower incomes have higher rates of intimate partner violence than individuals from families with higher incomes. Others, however, have contended that violence in low-income families is simply more visible because of the limited options available to the victims apart from contacting the police.[54]

Alcohol use is another situational factor thought to be related to violence in the family. The correlations found between heavy alcohol use and intimate partner violence are very consistent. For example, the Violence Against Women Survey conducted in Canada found that women who were married to or living with heavy drinkers were five times as likely to be assaulted by these men than women who lived with nondrinkers.[55] According to Glenda Kaufman Kantor and Murray Straus, however, it is not just heavy drinking but the combination of drinking with a low occupational status and approval of violence against one's partner that is associated with the greatest probability of violence. Kantor and Straus found that men with these characteristics had a rate of spouse abuse eight times higher than other men.[56]

Social Learning Theory

Many researchers have found a strong relationship between individuals' experiencing violence as a child and becoming violent toward their own partners or children as adults. Social learning theory is the foundation on which the association between childhood maltreatment and later delinquency and criminal offending is based. Researchers have referred to this relationship with different terms, including the *intergenerational transmission of violence* and the *cycle of violence*. In general, it is believed that children will learn aggressive approaches to resolving conflicts if they have been exposed to violence at home—either personally or through observation—and see a greater benefit from using these strategies than from using nonviolent means. In fact, some scholars contend that the physical punishment of children is a fundamental mechanism through which violence is promoted in the family, because it teaches children that love is associated with violence and that those who love you also have the right to hurt you.[57]

The majority of studies that have examined the empirical relationship between childhood victimization and later violent offending, however, are retrospective in nature. That is, they typically rely on samples of offenders, asking them about their victimization experiences as children. Few studies have actually tracked abused children over time to determine if they are more likely to become violent offenders than nonabused children. The most extensive study of this kind was conducted by Cathy Spatz Widom, who has found that child abuse victims generally are more likely to engage in a number of maladaptive behaviors, including violence, than their nonabused peers.[58]

SUMMARY

In this chapter, we have examined patterns and trends in murders that occur in the context of the family and other intimate relationships, including intimate partner homicide, infanticide, filicide and neonaticide, parricide, fratricide and sororicide, and familicide. We have learned that the family is not the mythologized safe haven it was once thought to be. In fact, many kinds of people, including very young children and women, are more likely to be killed by a family member they love and trust than by anyone else. The extreme levels of family homicide that exist in our society are undoubtedly related to the high levels of violence we tolerate in general.

A common thread that runs through all the types of family homicide discussed in this chapter is that many incidents were preceded by other, nonlethal forms of violence. Therefore, it is clear that many more resources are needed for programs to identify this violence in its early stages. As Charles Ewing so eloquently states, "individuals identified as victims of [family] violence should always be considered potential homicide victims. As such, their plight should always be taken extremely seriously, and they should be entitled to our utmost efforts to protect them."[59]

NOTES

1. Jim Struve, "Dancing with Patriarchy: The Politics of Sexual Abuse," in *The Sexually Abused Male,* ed. Mic Hunter (New York: Lexington Books, 1990).

2. See, for example, Neil Websdale, *Understanding Domestic Homicide,* ed. Claire Renzetti, *The Northeastern Series on Gender, Crime, and Law* (Boston: Northeastern University Press, 1999).

3. C. H. Kempe et al., "The Battered-Child Syndrome," *Journal of the American Medical Association,* 181 (1962), 17–24.

4. Murray A. Straus, Richard J. Gelles, and S. K. Steinmetz, *Behind Closed Doors: Violence in the American Family* (Anchor Press, 1980), p. 3.

5. Brooke A. Masters and Leef Smith, "In Some Domestic Cases, Legal System Falls Short," *Washington Post,* January 27, 1999, p. B01.

6. See, for example, Websdale, *Understanding Domestic Homicide.*

7. Callie Marie Rennison and Sarah Welchans, *Intimate Partner Violence* (Washington, D.C.: U.S. Department of Justice, Bureau of Justice Statistics, 2000).

8. James Alan Fox and Marianne W. Zawitz, *Homicide Trends in the United States: 1998 Update* (Washington, D.C.: Bureau of Justice Statistics, Department of Justice, 2000).

9. Rennison and Welchans, *Intimate Partner Violence.*

10. See, for example, Angela Browne and Kirk R. Williams, "Exploring the Effect of Resource Availability and the Likelihood of Female Perpetrated Homicides," *Law and Society Review,* 23, 75–94 (1989); A. L. Kellermann and J. A. Mercy, "Men, Women, and Murder: Gender-Specific

Differences in Rates of Fatal Violence and Victimization," *Journal of Trauma,* 33, 1–5 (1992); M. I. Wilson, H. Johnson, and M. Daly, "Lethal and Nonlethal Violence against Wives," *Canadian Journal of Criminology,* 37, 331–361 (1995).

11. Ronet Bachman and Linda Saltzman, *Violence against Women: Estimates from the Redesigned Survey* (Washington, D.C.: Bureau of Justice Statistics, U.S. Department of Justice, 1995); Rennison and Welchans, *Intimate Partner Violence.*

12. Neil Websdale, *Rural Woman Battering and the Justice System,* ed. Claire Renzetti and Jeffrey L. Edleson, *Sage Series on Violence against Women* (Thousand Oaks, Calif.: Sage, 1998); Websdale, *Understanding Domestic Homicide.*

13. Websdale, *Understanding Domestic Homicide.*

14. R. E. Dobash and R. Dobash, *Women, Violence, and Social Change* (New York: Routledge, 1992), p. 6.

15. D. Hall et al., *Homicide by Women* (New York: New York State Division of Criminal Justice Services, 1996).

16. K. Lindsey, "When Battered Women Strike Back: Murder or Self-Defense," *Viva,* September, 1978, pp. 58–59, 66–74; J. Totman, *The Murderess: A Psychosocial Study of Criminal Homicide* (San Francisco: R & E Research, 1978).

17. Bachman and Saltzman, *Violence against Women;* Rennison and Welchans, *Intimate Partner Violence.*

18. Darnell F. Hawkins, "Devalued Lives and Racial Stereotypes: Ideological Barriers to the Prevention of Family Violence among Blacks," in *Violence in the Black Family,* ed. Robert L. Hampton (Lexington, Mass.: Lexington Books, 1987); Websdale, *Understanding Domestic Homicide.*

19. L. G. Mills, "Mandatory Arrest and Prosecution Policies for Domestic Violence: A Critical Literature Review and the Call for More Research to Test Victim Empowerment Approaches," *Criminal Justice and Behavior,* 25, 306–318 (1998).

20. Zorza, J., "Symposium on Domestic Violence: Criminal Law: The Criminal Law of Misdemeanor Domestic Violence,

1970–1990," *Journal of Criminal Law and Criminology,* 83, 46–72 (1992).

21. Lawrence W. Sherman and R. A. Berk, "The Minneapolis Domestic Violence Experiment," *Police Foundation Reports,* no. 1 (1984).

22. For a thorough discussion of these issues, see Lawrence W. Sherman, *Policing Domestic Violence: Experiments and Dilemmas* (New York: Free Press, 1992); Websdale, *Rural Woman Battering and the Justice System.*

23. See D. G. Duttorn, "The Outcome of Court-Mandated Treatment for Wife Assault: A Quasi-Experimental Evaluation," *Violence and Victims,* 1(3), 163–175 (1987); E. Stark, "Mandatory Arrest of Batterers: A Reply to the Critics," *American Behavioral Scientist,* 36, 651–680 (1994).

24. James Alan Fox and Jack Levin, *The Will to Kill: Making Sense of Senseless Murder* (Boston: Allyn & Bacon, 2001).

25. Browne and Williams, "Exploring the Effect of Resource Availability."

26. L. Dugan, D. Nagin, and R. Rosenfeld, "Explaining the Decline in Intimate Partner Homicide: The Effects of Changing Domesticity, Women's Status, and Domestic Violence Resources," *Homicide Studies,* 3, 187–214 (1999).

27. James Alan Fox and Marianne W. Zawitz, *Homicide Trends in the United States* (Washington, D.C.: Bureau of Justice Statistics, Department of Justice, 2001).

28. Quoted in Lonnie Athens, *Violent Criminal Acts and Actors Revisited* (Urbana: University of Illinois Press, 1997), pp. 63–64.

29. Janet A. Johnson, Victoria L. Lutz, and Neil Websdale, "Death by Intimacy: Risk Factors for Domestic Violence," *Pace Law Review,* 20(2), 263–296 (2000).

30. Marvin E. Wolfgang, "A Sociological Analysis of Criminal Homicide," in *Studies in Homicide,* ed. Marvin E. Wolfgang (New York: Harper & Row, 1967).

31. *Crimes of Violence: A Staff Report to the National Commission on the Causes and Prevention of Violence* (Washington, D.C.: U.S. Government Printing Office, 1969).

32. Angela Browne, *When Battered Women Kill* (New York: Free Press, 1987).

33. Lenore Walker, *The Battered Woman* (New York: Harper Perennial, 1979).

34. Carl P. Malmquist, *Homicide: A Psychiatric Perspective* (Washington, D.C.: American Psychiatric Press, 1996).

35. Cynthia Gillespie, *Justifiable Homicide: Battered Women, Self-Defense, and the Law* (Columbus: Ohio State University Press, 1989).

36. Average annual number estimated from table listing homicides of children under age five by race of victim, 1976–1999. Percentage of victims by age was taken from chart listing infanticide by victim age, 1976–1999. Data from Fox and Zawitz, *Homicide Trends in the United States*. These national distributions are consistent with other research performed at other levels of aggregation. For example, see Arthur R. Copeland, "Homicide in Childhood: The Metro-Dade County Experience from 1956–1982," *American Journal of Forensic Medicine and Pathology* 6(1), 21–24 (1985); Fox and Zawitz, *Homicide Trends in the United States;* George A. Gellert et al., "Fatalities Assessed by the Orange County Child Death Review Team, 1989 to 1991," *Child Abuse and Neglect,* 7, 875–883 (1995).

37. Almost 11% of the victim–offender relationships in homicides involving children under the age of five in 1999 could not be identified, however. See Fox and Zawitz, *Homicide Trends in the United States*.

38. N. P. Unnithan, "Children as Victims of Homicide: Making Claims, Formulating Categories, and Constructing Social Problems," *Deviant Behavior,* 15(1), 63–83 (1994).

39. Paul Duggan, "Mother Charged in Slayings of 5 Children in Houston," *Washington Post,* June 21, 2001, p. A09.

40. Michael D. Kelleher, *When Good Kids Kill* (Westport, Conn.: Praeger, 1998).

41. Ibid.

42. "The Au Pair Outcome," *Washington Post,* November 12, 1997, p. A22.

43. Charles P. Ewing, *Fatal Families: The Dynamics of Intrafamilial Homicide* (Thousand Oaks, Calif.: Sage, 1997).

44. Ibid., p. 97.

45. Ewing, *Fatal Families*.

46. Kelleher, *When Good Kids Kill*.

47. For other accounts of children killing their parents, see Kathleen M. Heide, *Why Kids Kill Parents: Child Abuse and Adolescent Homicide* (Columbus: Ohio State University Press, 1992); Paul Mones, *When a Child Kills: Abused Children Who Kill Their Parents* (New York: Pocket Books, 1991).

48. "Tape of Sermon Picked up Argument and Beating," *Detroit Free Press,* December 2, 1992, section NWS, p. 1b.

49. Kelleher, *When Good Kids Kill*.

50. "Alleged Mass Killer Asks Swift Execution," *Washington Post,* May 12, 1988, p. A3; Ewing, *Fatal Families;* "Nine Victims Found at Killing Site," *Washington Post,* December 30, 1987, p. A1; "Slain Wife Weighed Leaving Mass-Murder Suspect," *Washington Post,* January 4, 1988, p. A10.

51. Ewing, *Fatal Families,* p. 136.

52. For a discussion of the characteristics of modern families that make them vulnerable to violence, see Richard J. Gelles and Murray A. Straus, *Intimate Violence: The Causes and Consequences of Abuse in the American Family* (New York: Simon & Schuster, 1980).

53. R. Emerson Dobash and Russell P. Dobash, *Violence against Wives: A Case against Patriarchy* (New York: Free Press, 1980), p. 24.

54. Holly Johnson, *Dangerous Domains: Violence against Women in Canada* (Toronto: Nelson Canada and ITP, 1996).

55. Ibid.

56. G. Kantor and M. Straus, "The 'Drunken Bum' theory of wife beating," in *Physical Violence in American Families: Risk Factors and Adaptations to Violence,* ed. Murray A. Straus and Richard J. Gelles. (New Brunswick, N.J.: Transaction, 1990); G. K. Kantor and M. A. Straus, "Substance Abuse as a Precipitant of Wife Abuse Victimizations," *American Journal of*

Drug and Alcohol Abuse, 15, 173–189 (1989).

57. See, for example, Murray A. Straus, "Social Stress and Marital Violence in a National Sample of American Families," in *Physical Violence in American Families: Risk Factors and Adaptations to Violence,* ed. Murray A. Straus and Richard J. Gelles

(New Brunswick, N.J.: Transaction, 1990).

58. See Cathy Spatz Widom, "Does Violence Beget Violence? A Critical Examination of the Literature," *Psychological Bulletin,* 106(1), 3–28 (1989).

59. Ewing, *Fatal Families,* p. 156.

6

When There Are Multiple Victims

Mass, Spree, and Serial Murders

Please dad I need you now. I've reached an agreement with the doctors
that I am not well. I'm sure that you must realize that I'm no cold
blooded killer. Rather, there is a problem with my mind.

DAVID BERKOWITZ[1]

It was just an impulse thing that if I wanted to kill somebody, I'd go
and kill 'em. I wouldn't plan it, how I was gonna do that. Then I
would sit and plan how to get rid of the body.

HENRY LEE LUCAS[2]

I'm full of hate and I love it.

ERIC DAVID HARRIS[3]

INTRODUCTION

In recent years, Americans have become fascinated by multiple murders and
their perpetrators. Many bookstores have sections devoted to true crime stories,
which are often dominated by accounts of serial killers and mass murderers. In
fact, our fascination with the topic appears to be increasing. Writing about se-

rial murder, Philip Jenkins points out that "both in fiction and in true crime, there were considerably more publications in the three years from 1991 through 1993 than in the 1960s and 1970s combined."[4] Echoing this theme, Eric Hickey traced the number of films about serial murder and found that from the 1960s to the 1990s, the number of films on the subject of serial murder more than quadrupled.[5] This appeal is undoubtedly fueled by media accounts that focus on serial and mass murders in all of their sensational and gory details and by films that glamorize these violent acts and their perpetrators. One has only to think of Anthony Hopkins as Hannibal Lecter in *Silence of the Lambs* or Christian Bale in *American Psycho* to recognize this. Ted Bundy even had a song written about him, in which some lyrics went, "So let's salute the mighty Bundy, here on Friday, gone on Monday. . . . It's hard to keep a good man down."[6] The press even comes up with catchy nicknames for the killers, such as the Boston Strangler, the Nightstalker, and the Coed Killer, to name just a few examples. Some serial killers have been interviewed on prime-time television, and Charles Manson had his own line of clothing for sale. Although much of the interest in this phenomenon seems voyeuristic and base, there remains a legitimate need to understand the dynamics and motivations of these kinds of crimes.

Multicide or multiple murder is the killing of more than one person. Beyond this, scholars tend to disagree about various types of multicide. In fact, there is disagreement about the definition of the most commonly known type of multicide, *serial murder.* Is serial murder when one person kills several people at a single moment in time, or does it have to involve killings over a period of time? If so, how much time must pass between the killings? One week? One month? One year? How many people must one kill to be labeled a serial killer? Some argue that only two murders are necessary to qualify an individual as a serial killer,[7] others argue that there must be at least three victims,[8] and still others require at least four killings to qualify the killer as a serial murderer.[9] Even with these difficulties, however, it is still possible to generically distinguish between different types of multicide.

Broadly speaking, there are three primary types of multicide: mass murder, spree murder, and serial murder.[10] Although these terms are often used interchangeably, these homicides can be quite distinctive and are generally distinguished by the number of victims, the time frame of the killings, and sometimes by the geography of the killings. John Douglas defines them this way:

- *Mass murder:* When someone kills four or more victims in one location in one incident. The location may be a building with numerous rooms, and the incident may stretch over a period of minutes or hours, but the killings are all part of the same emotional experience.

- *Serial murder:* when someone has murdered on at least three occasions, with what can be called an emotional cooling-off period between each incident. This cooling-off period can be days, weeks, months, or even years; occasionally, it is only hours. The important consideration, however, is that each event is emotionally distinct and separate.

- *Spree murder:* When someone murders at two or more separate locations but with no emotional cooling-off period between the homicides. Therefore, the killings tend to take place over a shorter period of time. However, if a serial killer's cooling-off period is short enough, he might even work faster than a spree killer.[11]

Douglas's definitions specifically recognize that each type of killing has certain distinctive patterns that set it apart from the others. The defining characteristics concern the emotional connection or disconnection between types of killing. For Douglas, the emotional content is more important than the absolute quality of time. Sadly, none of the three types is lacking in examples for us to discuss.

MASS MURDER

To reiterate, mass murder is the killing of several victims in one place at one point in time. However, it is important to note that there is some disagreement over this definition. For example, some scholars have suggested a minimum of either three or four victims for an event to be considered mass murder.[12] Moreover, some researchers only include killings that take place over a period of hours as mass murder. Mass murders also take place within a restricted geographic range and, in fact, may all take place at one location. For example, James Huberty killed 20 people and wounded 19 others when he opened fire with automatic weapons at a McDonald's in San Ysidro, California. Other times, however, the killings are perpetrated in several separate locales. Charles Whitman, for example, first killed his mother in her house, then his wife in their apartment, before going to the clock tower at the University of Texas, from which he opened fire, killing another 13 people and wounding 31 others.[13] Each of these killings, however, is still considered to be part of the same mass murder. In both cases, the killings are limited to one or a couple of distinct locations within a small geographic area, as opposed to serial killing, which may occur from one end of the country to the other over a period of years. Another distinction between mass murderers and spree and serial killers is that mass murderers often kill themselves after they have completed their deadly rampage. This is not typically the case for serial or spree murders. Other mass murderers are killed by the police, but many of these may be perceived as "suicide by cop" incidents, because the murderers manipulate the situation in such a way that their own death is almost inevitable.[14]

Most mass murderers tend to be White, middle-age men. Prior to their rampage, these men have often been perceived by others as extremely frustrated or angry. In many ways, mass murders are symbolic statements—a means of lashing out at those who the murderers believe have hurt or maltreated them.[15] Frequently, mass murderers have a history of written complaints about those who they feel have wronged them. One study found that 99% of workplace murderers had made threats, whereas 100% of mass murder cases in school also had a history of previous grievances.[16] Prospective mass murderers may have expressed this hatred in journal form.[17] For example, several months before Matthew Beck went on a deadly rampage in which he killed four of his superiors at the Connecticut State Lottery, he had filed a grievance contending that he was being assigned jobs outside of his work classification and that he deserved a raise of $2 an hour. Just days before his killings, he spoke angrily of suing the Lottery.

Because many mass murderers have a problem with anger management and conflict, some scholars believe that these acts of violence could be decreased if more social and personal support systems were available in our society. For example, Levin and Fox state quite emphatically, "The real culprit in explaining mass murder can be found in society itself and in a trend that has affected almost everyone. During recent years, there has been an eclipse of community, a dwindling of the social relationships—family ties and neighborliness—that had protected former generations of Americans from succumbing to disaster. . . . For too many Americans who suffer, their misery has no company." [18]

The easy availability of high-powered and semiautomatic weaponry in our society must also be related to the high number of deaths that have characterized recent mass murders. Individuals who see themselves as relatively defenseless victims of injustice may feel drawn to the perceived aura of power surrounding such weapons, which they find lacking in their own lives. [19] Mass murders in America typically occur in one of three places: the home, the workplace, or the school.

Mass Murder in the Home

In the town of Westfield, New Jersey, the police made a gruesome discovery on December 7, 1971. On that day, in the home of John and Helen List, the police found the decaying bodies of Helen List and her three children. They had been dead since November, but it was only when a neighbor began to get suspicious that the police were notified. In the attic, the body of 85-year-old Alma List, John List's ailing mother, was also discovered. All had been shot to death. The only person missing was 46-year-old John List, and after a thorough search of the house, the police discovered not only the firearms used to kill the family but a letter in which John List confessed to the murders. Complaining of increasing debts and of how his wife and daughter were turning away from God, List asserted that he was killing his family for their own good and that they would now be safe and at peace in heaven. His car was found at John F. Kennedy International Airport in nearby New York City, but nothing more was heard about him until almost two decades had passed. In 1989, the television show *America's Most Wanted* aired a segment about John List that featured a clay bust showing List's appearance as he might have aged. A woman in Colorado believed that the description and the bust matched her former neighbor. She called the hot line with the address of this man, who called himself Bob Clark. [20] When FBI agents confronted him, he denied being John List, but a fingerprint test quickly identified him as the man who had killed his family in New Jersey all those years ago.

John List is a mass murderer who best fits the type that has been termed a *family annihilator.* According to Ronald and Stephen Holmes, the family annihilator is someone who feels "alone, anomic, and helpless, this killer launches a campaign of violence typically against those who share his home. Because of the despair in his own life, the killer wishes to change the situation, and reacts in this bizarre fashion."[21] John List felt that his life was out of control, and the only way to fix things was to kill his family and start over. He had a history of losing jobs and was financially overextended. His wife had stopped going to church and was often confrontational and hostile to him. His mother, who lived with them, was suffering from various medical problems, and his children, especially his oldest daughter, were somewhat rebellious of his strict discipline. For a time, his hobbies distracted him and provided a refuge. These hobbies consisted mainly of reading about crime, war, and weapons. Ultimately, however, he decided that starting over was his best option, and he did this by killing his entire family. He justified the murders to himself and others by asserting that he had spared his family having to live in poverty and that he had saved their souls by his actions. Years later, when confronted by his murdered wife's sister who asked him for an explanation, his answer was, "Because there was no other way."[22]

Mass Murder in the Workplace

It is a sad commentary on modern American life that the term "going postal" has entered our common lexicon. The term originated on August 20, 1986, when Patrick Sherrill went to the Edmond, Oklahoma, post office where he worked and killed his supervisor and 14 other employees before finally killing himself.[23] Interesting enough, although the term has gained wide currency, postal workers are approximately two and a half times less likely to be killed while at work than the average worker, who appears to be increasingly at risk.[24] According to the Bureau of Labor Statistics, violence in the workplace is increasing, and homicide has become the second leading cause of death while on the job.[25] However, not all of this increasing violence in the workplace is the result of employees running amok and killing their supervisors and coworkers.[26] Most of the victims of workplace homicides are working in retail businesses and are victims of robbery homicides, which are typically perpetrated by strangers rather than by coworkers. In fact, retail salespeople have a greater annual number of violent victimizations than law enforcement personnel, although law enforcement as a profession still has a higher victimization rate. As with violent victimization in general, the most common type of workplace violence is simple assault. Approximately 1.5 million simple assaults occur every year, compared to about a thousand workplace murders.[27]

Murder is the second leading cause of death on the job, following fatal accidents. Approximately one out of every six deaths in the workplace is the result of murder.[28] Most of the victims are White men, and more than 80% of the victims are killed with firearms. As indicated earlier, the vast majority of these are employees working in retail stores who are killed by armed robbers. Workers are killed by their fellow employees far less frequently, although when they are, the consequences can be devastating. Robert Simon asserts that workplace violence usually occurs in one of five categories: (1) a disgruntled employee or former employee kills or injures other employees; (2) angry spouses or relatives stalk employees at work; (3) violence is committed during a criminal act such as robbery; (4) violence is committed against people in dangerous jobs, such as law enforcement personnel; and (5) acts of terrorism or hate crimes are committed against the workplace, as with the World Trade Center attack in New York or Oklahoma City's bombing of a federal building.[29] Regarding the last category, the year 2001 saw perhaps the single most destructive example of mass murder in American history, with the attacks on the Pentagon and the destruction of the twin towers of the World Trade Center by operatives of the Al Qaeda terrorist organization.[30]

When an employee or ex-employee mounts an assault against the people at their place of employment, the number of victims is often very high. For example, in 1987, a commuter plane crashed while flying from Los Angeles to San Francisco, killing all 45 people aboard. The details are somewhat speculative because there were no survivors, but the crash was probably caused by a disgruntled airline employee who forced the plane to crash.[31] Having just lost his job for theft, David Augustus Burke apparently snapped and decided to get revenge on his supervisor, who was on the flight. In the process, a large number of innocent people were also killed. Investigators at the crash site found a note on a burned airsickness bag that read, "Hi, Ray, I think it's sort of ironical that we end up like this. I asked for some leniency for my family, remember. Well, I got none and you'll get none."[32] They also found a .44 Magnum in the wreckage. Air traffic controllers reported that the pilots had radioed that they had heard gunshots from the passenger cabin, and the flight recorder indicated that someone had entered the cockpit and fired shots, after which the plane went into a dive. This evidence strongly suggests that Burke passed the note to his former supervisor, shot him, and then shot one or more of the pilots, causing the plane to crash. Burke's act of violence was by all indications a suicidal form of vengeance and a highly public statement of his outrage—all classic characteristics of mass murderers. These individuals feel that they have nothing to lose and expect to be killed by the police or to kill themselves. Because in their own eyes, their lives are lost or forfeit, they have no compunction about taking any number of other people with them.

Other, more recent examples of similar mass murders abound. In 1999 alone, for example, the nation experienced a number of these deadly attacks. In Fort Worth, Texas, a lone gunman named Larry Gene Ashbrook opened fire in a Baptist church, killing seven people and wounding seven more before killing himself. In Atlanta, Georgia, another gunman went to the brokerage offices where he worked and killed nine coworkers and wounded another 13 before he committed suicide. Immediately prior to this massacre, he had killed his wife and two young children. In Pelham, Alabama, a man shot and killed two fellow employees, before driving to a former place of employment and killing again.[33] More recently, on December 26, 2000, Michael McDermott drove to his job in Wakefield, Massachusetts, and shot and killed seven people at the software firm where he worked. The trigger seems to have been financial in origin, as his company had agreed to garnish his wages for the IRS. And on February 5, 2001, 66-year-old William Baker entered an engine plant in suburban Chicago where he had worked for 40 years and opened fire. He had brought with him an AK–47 assault rifle, a .38–caliber revolver, a shotgun, and a hunting rifle. Before it was all over, he had killed four people, wounded another four, and ended the massacre by shooting himself. This happened on the day before he was scheduled to start a five-month prison term for stealing company property.[34]

These cases all exhibit the classic symptoms of the workplace mass murderer. The killers feel acutely what they perceive as a pattern of wrongs inflicted on them. They create violent fantasies of retaliation with themselves in the role of avenger. Their violence, at least in their own eyes, is perceived as a chance to strike back at those who have wronged them or as a way to highlight or call attention to the injustices they have endured. Combining this with the paranoia and depression that many of them suffer can prove lethal.[35] Although they may specifically target management or supervisors, they also typically kill any coworkers they come across. In this way, they tend to kill indiscriminately. Although these massacres were often in the news during the 1990s, they were largely overshadowed by another type of mass murder: school killings.

Mass Murder in Schools

April 20, 1999, marks the date of one of the most notorious mass murders in modern American history. On that day, Dylan Klebold and Eric Harris went on a shooting and bombing rampage in their high school that resulted in the death of 13 of their fellow students before they ended the ordeal by killing themselves.

This event was not a spontaneous act of rage; rather, it was planned and carried out with chilling precision. Klebold and Harris left behind several videotapes in which they had discussed their plans, displayed their weapons, and philosophized about killing. Chillingly, they pointed out that they had been planning this for months and that they realized their families and friends would be devastated.[36] Investigators subsequently discovered several itineraries that detailed their preparations.

On April 20, 1999, Klebold and Harris arrived at the school a little bit after 11 a.m. and, after a couple of minutes, went into the school cafeteria and left two 20-pound propane bombs in two duffel bags. The bombs were set to go off at a time when the cafeteria would have been crowded with students. Luckily, the bombs never went off. After placing several more bombs in the parking lot, Klebold and Harris mounted some steps that gave them a vantage point over part of the Columbine campus, readied their firearms, and opened fire. Both were armed with a shotgun each, and Klebold carried an Intratec TEC-DC9, a 9-mm semiautomatic handgun, whereas Harris carried a Hi-Point 9-mm carbine in addition to the shotgun. These firearms had been bought for them by several different friends. Although they did not use them, both carried an assortment of knives as well.

Within seconds of opening fire, they shot numerous students, although some were only wounded. Methodically, Dylan went down the stairs and shot some of the wounded students again in an effort to finish them off. During this time, they reportedly also threw various homemade explosives around. One of them was heard to yell, "This is what we always wanted to do. This is awesome!"[37]

After a deputy arrived at the scene and exchanged gunfire with the two boys, Klebold and Harris went inside the school and continued their deadly rampage. Witnesses later reported that they were often laughing and joking as they were shooting and tossing pipe bombs. They even took the time to drink from water bottles. They also encouraged each other as they ruthlessly hunted down various students. In one instance, they asked a female student if she believed in God, and when she answered in the affirmative, they killed her.[38] Their shooting spree lasted until shortly after 12 noon, when they went back into the library and shot themselves in the head, thus ending the worst school shooting in American history. During their rampage, they fired 188 shots, killed 13 people, and wounded 21 others. Countless other survivors, families, and neighbors will be scarred forever by this tragedy.

Why did they engage in this rampage? Why didn't their parents or teachers or friends do something to prevent this atrocity? Because Dylan Klebold and Eric Harris killed themselves, we will never know with certainty what they hoped to accomplish. However, they left behind enough clues to illuminate the answers to some of these questions.

Both boys appeared to be typical and relatively ordinary middle-class students, but a closer examination reveals an undercurrent of anger and hatred flowing through them both. In that way, at least, Dylan and Eric fit the classic profile of mass murderers. Both were very angry at the world and wanted revenge for perceived injustices against them. The violence was a means of lashing out at those who had wronged them. For example, both Klebold and Harris belonged to a loose-knit affiliation of students sometimes referred to as the Trenchcoat Mafia, after the style of dress they affected. Evidently, the members of this group were often harassed by some student athletes or "jocks," as they were known.

Students who perpetrate these massacres often feel "picked upon" by other students. For example, Kip Kinkel, the perpetrator of another school massacre, also felt angry at other students for teasing him. On May 21, 1998, Kipland "Kip" Kinkel, a 15-year-old living in Springfield, Oregon, killed both of his parents before going to school and killing two students and wounding 23 others. His apparent motivation was anger and revenge. He wanted to get back at his parents for confiscating his guns, at the school for expelling him, and at his classmates for teasing him.[39] In another case, after subduing a 16-year-old who had just finished killing a number of fellow students, the vice-principal of the school asked the student why he had done it, and this teen murderer replied that "the world has wronged me, and I couldn't take it any more."[40]

These youthful killers often suffer from depression and other psychiatric problems that may contribute to their anger, frustration, and violence. Eric Harris, for example, had recently suffered a form of rejection when his application to the Marine Corps was turned down because he was taking antidepressant medication. On his personal Web site, he described his hatred and desire to lash out when he wrote, "God, I can't wait until I can kill you people. . . . I'll just go to some downtown area in some big (expletive) city and blow up and shoot everything I can."[41] There were other warning signs. As part of a

Exhibit 6.1 Characteristics of Selected School Shootings

Perpetrator(s)	Age	Date	Location	Victims
Gary Pennington	17	1/18/93	Grayson, Ky.	1 teacher killed 1 janitor killed
John Sirola	13	1/23/95	Redlands, Calif.	1 principal wounded
Toby Sincino	16	10/12/95	Blackville, S.C.	1 teacher killed
Jamie Rouse	17	11/15/95	Lynnville, Tenn.	1 teacher killed 1 teacher wounded 1 student killed
Barry Loukaitis	14	2/2/96	Moses Lake, Wash.	1 teacher killed 2 students killed 1 student wounded
Evan Ramsey	16	2/19/97	Bethel, Alaska	1 principal killed 1 student killed 2 students wounded
Luke Woodham	16	10/1/97	Pearl, Miss.	Mother killed 2 students killed 7 wounded
Michael Carneal	14	12/1/97	West Paducah, Ky.	3 students killed 5 wounded
Joseph Todd	14	12/15/97	Stamps, Ark.	2 students wounded
Andrew Golden Mitchell Johnson	11 13	3/24/98	Jonesboro, Ark.	1 teacher killed 4 students killed 10 wounded
Andrew Wurst	14	4/24/98	Edinboro, Pa.	1 teacher killed 1 teacher wounded 2 students wounded
Kipland Kinkel	15	5/21/98	Springfield, Ore.	Mother and father killed 2 students killed 20 wounded
Eric Harris Dylan Klebold	18 17	4/20/99	Littleton, Colo.	1 teacher killed 12 students killed 23 wounded
Thomas Solomon	15	5/20/99	Conyers, Ga.	6 students wounded

SOURCE: John Nicoletti, Kelly Zinna, and Sally Spencer-Thomas, *Violence Goes to School: Lessons Learned from Columbine* (Lakewood, Colo.: Nicoletti-Flater Associates, 1999).

school project, Harris and Klebold made a video that showed them shooting their way through the school.

Sadly, the Columbine incident was not the only example of school shootings in recent years. Exhibit 6.1 reviews several school shootings that have occurred in this country in recent years. It is important to remember, however, that these school shootings occurred at a time when overall, violence among our nation's young was decreasing. These school shootings indicated a change in the nature of violence within our schools, but they did not reverse the trend of diminishing violence within the adolescent population in general and within our schools in particular. As shown in Exhibit 6.2, homicides at school were decreasing during the 1990s.

Exhibit 6.2 Annual Number of Homicides at School, 1992–1999

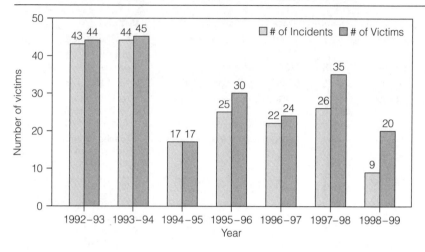

SOURCE: *School Associated Violent Deaths* (Westlake Village, Calif.: National School Safety Center, 2002).

Although the 1990s focused students' fear in schools on their fellow class-mates, in the 1980s, the danger was perceived to come from the outside. Mass murderers who turned their fire on schoolyards in that decade were more likely to be middle-age adults. For example, in 1989, 25-year-old Patrick Purdy went on a rampage in an elementary schoolyard in Stockton, California, killing five Southeast Asian children as they played at recess, before killing himself with a handgun.[42]

SPREE MURDER

Spree murder is perhaps the least common of the three types of multicide. This type of killing occurs when one or more individuals go on a binge of killing and destruction. The trigger for the violence can often seem fairly minor, but once begun, spree killers only stop when they are killed or captured. Their violence seems fairly directionless and unplanned. Many of the victims of spree killers are truly innocents who happen to be in the wrong place at the wrong time.

Perhaps the most infamous case of spree murder in the United States hap-pened in the winter of 1958 in Nebraska, when Charles Starkweather and his girlfriend Caril Fugate went on a week-long killing spree. Starkweather's first murder actually occurred a number of weeks earlier when, after holding up a gas station, he forced the attendant into his car, drove him to an isolated loca-tion, and killed him with a 12-gauge shotgun. His total haul from the robbery was $108. This killing seems to have been motivated by nothing more than want-ing to eliminate a witness.[43]

The Starkweather killing spree began six weeks later, after Charles got into an argument with Caril's mother at her home and was forced to leave the house. Returning later that afternoon, he took up the argument again, this time with Caril's stepfather. This time, however, he didn't leave. Instead, he retrieved a .22 rifle and shot the man in the head, after which he shot Caril's mother. He used the butt of the rifle to finish his attack against the mother and also to kill Caril's two-and-a-half-year-old little sister. Because the stepfather was still showing signs of life, Starkweather used a knife to finally kill him. Caril and Charles then moved the bodies out of the way and sat down to watch television. For six days, they stayed in the house, until they could no longer ward off curious friends and relatives. Then they drove off with a vague plan to go to Washington state. After killing a nearby farmer and stealing his money, they abandoned their car and were picked up by two high school students, who were also murdered. In Lincoln, they broke into the home of a wealthy industrialist and ended up killing him, his wife, and their maid. Heading west again, they killed a traveling salesman for his car but were discovered in the act. After a high-speed chase, Starkweather was eventually stopped and arrested. Ultimately, both were convicted of first degree murder. Charles Starkweather received the death penalty and was executed on June 25, 1959, whereas Caril received a life sentence and was paroled in June of 1976.[44] Their violent escapade bears all the classic hallmarks of the typical killing spree: a short but violent killing rampage that doesn't seem to have much rhyme or reason.

A more recent example that made headlines is the case of Andrew Cunanan, who embarked on a similarly senseless and ultimately self-destructive killing binge.[45] A young man with a taste for the good life, Andrew Cunanan enjoyed the attentions of older and successful men, who gave him credit cards and bought things for him in return for relationships and sexual favors. However, in 1997, at age 28, he found that his wealthy patrons were no longer interested in him. Furthermore, two of his lovers, Jeffrey Trail and David Madson, began dating each other. Seething with jealousy, Cunanan traveled to Minneapolis where he confronted the two men. Enraged, he bludgeoned Trail to death with a hammer. Perhaps Cunanan realized that after this killing, there was no going back. He and Madson stayed in the apartment with the body for several days, until the manager discovered Trail's body. Cunanan and Madson then left town, but the trip for Madson didn't last long; Cunanan shot and killed him just north of Minneapolis. From there, Cunanan traveled to Chicago, where he tortured and killed a man he had never met before, a 72-year-old realtor named Lee Miglin. Continuing his killing spree, Cunanan eluded law enforcement and, in New Jersey, killed a cemetery caretaker named William Reese to steal his pickup truck. Heading south, Cunanan traveled to Miami Beach, Florida, where he hid out for several months. Then, on July 15, 1997, he murdered the clothes designer Gianni Versace on the steps of Versace's mansion. As the police closed in on him, Cunanan committed suicide on the houseboat where he had been hiding.

Although his murder spree lasted several months, longer than most spree events, in other ways it follows the basic pattern. After the killing began, his rampage continued without real rhyme or reason. There was no plan to his actions. Cunanan had reached the end of his rope and embarked on a destructive orgy of violence. In fact, the evidence indicates that he was very careless in his behavior during his several-month spree and was numerous times extremely lucky that he was not captured.

It should be noted here that some scholars set a time limit on killing sprees. For example, Holmes and Holmes define a killing spree as the slaying of three or more people within 30 days.[46] To qualify as a spree killing, then, the first and last homicides must have been committed within a 30-day time period. Although in many ways he fits the profile of a spree killer, according to this definition, Andrew Cunanan would not have been classified as a spree killer but as a serial killer.

SERIAL MURDER

Of the three types of multicide, serial murder most often captures the imagination and interest of the public. Perhaps the most comprehensive definition of serial murder has been developed by Steven Egger who asserts that

1. serial murder occurs when one or more individuals (in many cases, men) commit a second murder or subsequent murder;
2. there is generally no prior relationship between the victim and the attacker (if there is a prior relationship, such a relationship will place the victim in a subjugated role to the killer);
3. subsequent murders are at different times and have no apparent connection to the initial murder;
4. subsequent murders are usually committed in a different geographical location;
5. the motive is usually not material gain but the murderer's desire to have power or dominance over his victims;
6. the victims may have symbolic value for the murderer or are perceived to be prestigeless and, in most instances, are unable to defend themselves or alert others to their plight, or they are perceived as powerless given their situation in time, place, or status within their immediate surroundings;
7. examples of typical victims include vagrants, homeless people, prostitutes, migrant workers, homosexuals, missing children, single women (out by themselves), elderly women, college students, and hospital patients.[47]

Although some media portrayals of serial killers tend to suggest that they are a new and uniquely American phenomenon, neither is the case. Serial murders have been documented since the earliest written accounts of murder and crime in general. David Lester has delineated a long history of serial murder that dates back to the fifteenth century. Among the most notable serial killers are Gilles de Rais, a Frenchman who was convicted of sexually abusing and murdering

140 children; Vincent Verzeni, who killed and sucked the blood out of the bodies of several women in Italy in the mid-1860s; Peter Kurten, known as the Vampire of Düsseldorf, who was responsible for nearly 80 murders or attempted murders in Germany during the early 1900s; and Jack the Ripper, who terrorized London in the late nineteenth century, killing and disemboweling at least five women.[48]

Because the United States is a relatively new country, our history of serial killing is well established. Holmes and Holmes have documented instances of serial killing in the United States as early as the mid–nineteenth century. One such killer was a farmer from Northern California named Joseph Briggen. Briggen had a pen of prize Yorkshire pigs, who were apparently the envy of his neighbors. Briggen claimed that his pigs prospered because of the special feed he prepared for them; he did not, however, reveal his recipe. It was eventually discovered that Briggen frequently traveled to San Francisco, where he cruised the Embarcadero district and, under the ruse of employment, picked up homeless and transient men. Once at Briggen's farm, the men worked for room and board. However, when they pressed Briggen for real wages, he simply killed them, ground the bodies up, and fed the mash to his pigs. Although the total body count is not known, Briggen was convicted of 12 homicides and sent to San Quentin.[49]

There are other noteworthy serial killers in our history. In the 1890s, Herman Mudgett turned a three-story row of connected buildings into a torture chamber, where he reputedly killed between 20 and 100 men, women, and children. Between 1834 and 1867, Sally Skull, later referred to as the Black Widow, married five men who either disappeared or met with unfortunate accidents. And the Jeffrey Dahmer of his day was Albert Fish. In the 1920s, Fish murdered and cannibalized between 8 and 15 children. The list could go on, but it is apparent that serial killing is not a recent nor a uniquely American phenomenon.[50]

How Often Do Serial Killings Occur?

It would be useful to provide a number or rate at which people are killed by serial killers annually, but this figure is difficult if not impossible to determine. The primary difficulty, of course, is in defining exactly what is meant by serial killing. Some scholars, for example, exclude killings that were committed for financial gain, whereas others omit killings where there was some prior relationship between the victim and the offender. Do we classify a mob contract killer who kills for money in the same category as an individual who kills and mutilates because of some internal motivation?

Even if there was a consensus on the definition, however, many other problems would still exist in estimating the prevalence rates of serial murder. Neither the FBI nor the Centers for Disease Control and Prevention keep separate records for serial killings. In fact, the only federal agency that attempts to count the number of serial killings in the United States is the FBI's Behavioral Sciences and Investigative Support Unit at the National Center for the Analysis of Violent Crime. This group does not rely on official homicide data, however. Instead, it estimates rates of serial killing using reports from newspaper wire services. As one might imagine, these estimates have been shown to be very unreliable.[51]

Why is it so difficult to estimate rates of serial killing? The major barrier in estimation is related to the difficulty of identifying serial killings in the first place. Discovering similarities in the way that several murders were committed requires the police to overcome several impediments. For example, unless an individual kills in a distinctive manner or leaves a unique signature at the crime scene, such as neatly folding the victim's clothes or leaving a common object, a killing may not even be suspected as being serial. This problem is compounded when serial killings occur in another city or even in another state. Suspecting that one unsolved murder is part of a pattern is more difficult when the killings occur across several different jurisdictions. Steven Egger uses the term *linkage blindness* to describe the poor communication about unsolved murders or missing persons across law enforcement jurisdictions.[52] Another problem that hinders this communication is that law enforcement personnel tend to be somewhat secretive and reluctant to share information about cases even with other law enforcement officials. The bottom line is that it is difficult to estimate the number of serial killings primarily because many are never identified as such. For example, every year, many unidentified homicide victims are discovered in shallow graves, in garbage dumps, and in ditches alongside roads. It is not illogical to assume that some of these—along with a proportion of the thousands of children and other individuals who are reported missing each year—may have been victims of serial killers. Determining how many, however, is impossible.

In addition to the communication problems that exist across jurisdictions, another obstacle to the identification of serial murders is financial. It is extremely expensive to conduct a long-term criminal investigation of several murders, particularly when they have occurred in different jurisdictions. The costs of labor, forensic analysis, experts, overtime, and travel can be prohibitive to an already overburdened law enforcement budget. For example, in King County, Washington, beginning in July of 1982, a number of bodies of prostitutes and young teenagers were discovered and assumed to be the work of a serial killer. This assumed killer was nicknamed the Green River Killer. A task force to investigate the crimes was established and, at one time, included nearly 100 law enforcement officials, investigators, and experts who investigated some 200 suspects at an approximate cost of $2 million a year. By 1998, however, the killer had still not been caught, and the task force had been reduced to one investigator.[53]

Despite the obstacles to estimation, several scholars have attempted to calculate the number of serial murderers active in the United States in a given year. These estimates, however, vary widely. Several of the leading research teams in this area place the estimate at approximately 35 active serial killers in a given year.[54] Others, however, have placed the number much higher.[55]

Is serial murder increasing? Although popular films such as *Silence of the Lambs* and other horror flicks may lead us to conclude that serial murder is on the rise, the crude data that are available suggest that it is actually media attention that is increasing, not serial killing itself. In fact, Holmes and Holmes could not identify any upward trend in the number of serial killers operating in the United States in the last four decades.[56] It is important to keep in mind that although multicide in general and serial killings in particular are a staple of books and movies, these killings represent only a small fraction of all murders that occur in the United States in a typical year.

Characteristics of Serial Murderers

Although there are many different types of serial killers, as we shall discuss shortly, research indicates that like mass murderers, most serial killers are White men in their twenties and thirties.[57] There are some notable exceptions, such as Wayne Williams, an African-American man who was convicted of killing two young African-American boys in Atlanta, Georgia, in the late 1970s and who was suspected in the deaths of at least 20 other missing young African-American boys. However, according to research by Eric Hickey, only about 20% of serial killers are African-Americans.[58]

The majority of serial killers are men; however, there are also cases of women committing serial murder. Female serial killers tend to be far less violent and brutal in their crimes than men. In fact, among the more than 100 female serial murderers documented by Kerry Segrave, no female counterparts could be found to a Ted Bundy or a John Wayne Gacy, to whom sex or sexual violence was a part of the murder pattern. Segrave states that "there are no women who desecrate the body afterward by cutting off parts or ripping it open and eating the insides, and so on."[59] Eric Hickey classified female serial killers as either *quiet,* because they killed their spouses or partners, or as *angels of death,* because they killed the patients under their care.[60] For example, Genene Jones, a nurse at a pediatric clinic in Kerrville, Texas, was convicted of injecting a drug into a 14-month-old girl, causing her death. Although Jones was charged with and convicted of this one murder, she was suspected by the authorities of having caused the deaths of at least 13 other children while she worked at the Bexar County Hospital during 1981 and 1982.[61]

The nature of the victims also distinguishes serial killing from other types of murder. Most serial killers tend to kill strangers.[62] Targeting strangers may be a strategy designed to provide anonymity for the perpetrators, making it less likely that they will be identified. Killing strangers may also make it easier to dehumanize the victims. How does a serial killer target a particular stranger? It appears that the main criterion has to do with vulnerability. For example, serial killers often choose young women who are susceptible to their advances. Prostitutes, waitresses, female hitchhikers, women looking for jobs, nurses, models, and female students walking alone are among the more common targets of serial killers.[63] In this sense, serial killers are very logical, because they pick victims who are relatively easy to isolate and dominate—who are least able to protect and defend themselves. Prostitutes, for example, are used to getting into vehicles with total strangers and driving to secluded areas. This behavior, of course, makes them very vulnerable to victimizations of many kinds, including serial killing. According to Egger, "From the killer's view these women are simply available in an area that provides anonymity, comfort from easy detection, and adequate time in which to make a viable selection. It is highly probable that the serial killer selects prostitutes most frequently because they are easy to lure and control during the initial stages of what becomes an abduction. Potential witnesses of this abduction see only a pickup and transaction prior to paying for sex."[64] Other common victims of serial killers are children who are alone, travelers, homeless people and transients, homosexuals, and elderly people who live alone.[65]

Two other similarities among serial murderers deserve mention. First, they tend to work alone. There are instances of pairs of serial killers who work in tandem, such as Kenneth Bianchi and Angelo Buono, the Hillside Stranglers, but most serial killers act on their own without help or accomplices. Second, many apprehended serial killers also have previous criminal records. For example, John Gacy had been previously convicted of having sex with minor boys, and Ted Bundy had a history of shoplifting and juvenile car theft.

Despite the many similarities between serial killings, there are also differences that some scholars have characterized into typologies. For example, Holmes and Holmes distinguish six types of serial killers, based on the explicit or implicit motives of the killers:

The *hedonistic lust killer* is the first of three subtypes of hedonistic serial killers. Hedonistic lust killers are distinguished by their effort to obtain sexual pleasure from killing. The lust killer derives direct sexual satisfaction from murdering his victims or satisfies his sexual desires by having sex with the corpse or by mutilating or cutting off sex organs. For example, the Ukrainian serial killer Andrei Chikatilo represents this type, as he claimed to achieve sexual satisfaction only by torturing and killing his male and female victims. He also cannibalized his victims' body parts, particularly their sexual organs. Jerry Brudos, from the United States, can also be characterized as a hedonistic lust killer. Brudos removed body parts from his victims, had sex with their corpses, and in one case, removed the breasts from a victim and made an epoxy mold of them, which he kept as a memento.

The *thrill killer* is the second subtype of hedonistic killer. Thrill killers also derive sexual satisfaction from their murders, but they require a live victim for sexual satisfaction. In contrast to the lust killer, thrill killers receive sexual pleasure from torturing, dominating, terrorizing, and humiliating their victims while they are alive. Kenneth Bianchi and Angelo Buono, known as the Hillside Stranglers, were thrill killers. After abducting female victims, the two cousins would take them to Buono's house, where the victims were repeatedly tortured until they became unconscious. When the victims eventually died, their bodies were disposed of, and new victims were sought.

The *comfort killer* is the third subtype of hedonistic serial killer. As the name implies, this type of killer murders for creature comfort, such as financial gain. Examples include Fay and Ray Copeland, elderly Missouri ranchers who asked their farmhands to purchase cattle on their own credit, with a promise of reimbursement from the ranch's later proceeds. Once the cattle were purchased, however, the farmhands disappeared. The Copelands were linked with five such murders.

The *power/control killer* murders to obtain a sense of domination and total control over the victim. Although sex is sometimes involved, the pleasure is not derived from the sex act itself (as with lust or thrill killers) but from the complete control that the offender has over the victim. Ted Bundy was a power/control killer. Bundy openly admitted seeking out victims whom he thought were particularly vulnerable, trusting, and weak (usually young college women), and he told his interviewers that his pleasure came from possessing and controlling his victims, not from any violence or sexual act.

The *mission killer* murders because he is on a mission to rid the world of a group of people he perceives as unworthy or inferior in some way. The mission serial killer restricts his killing to those identified group members. Peter Sutcliffe, nicknamed the Yorkshire Ripper, and his namesake Jack the Ripper are examples of mission killers. Both targeted prostitutes. More recent mission serial killers include Joel Rifkin, who murdered approximately 17 prostitutes in New York City from 1980 through 1983.

The *visionary killer* is the least common type of serial killer and is characterized by a severe break with reality. Such murderers are frequently driven by voices or images that command them to kill, and they may even be possessed by multiple personalities. This psychotic killer generally leaves a graphic, chaotic, and brutally vivid crime scene. Joseph Kallinger represents this form of killer. Kallinger experienced visions of a floating head he named Charlie, who demanded that he kill everyone in the world. Kallinger responded by killing his own son, another youth who lived in the neighborhood, and a nurse.[66]

Because there are so many motives that characterize serial killings, it is difficult to explain this type of murder. As one can imagine, different scholars offer different explanations. In the next section, we will summarize some of the most popular explanations for serial murder.

How Can Someone Do Such a Thing?

We are constantly amazed and baffled at the bizarre and horrible crimes that some human beings can inflict on others. Because their behavior is so extreme, we instinctively want to characterize these individuals as monsters or demons. Part of this reaction is the belief that they must be crazy to commit these heinous crimes. By definition, we want to believe that anyone who can kill, mutilate, and perhaps eat other human beings must be crazy. This is a natural reaction, but it does not help us further our understanding of how and why these individuals do what they do. Moreover, this conception of serial killers as crazy is not accurate. Most serial killers are not found to suffer from a psychosis and can typically distinguish right from wrong.[67] As James Fox and Jack Levin put it, "They know right from wrong, know exactly what they are doing, and can control their desire to kill—but choose not to. They are more cruel than crazy. Their crimes may be sickening, but their minds are not necessarily sick. Most apparently do not suffer from hallucinations, a profound thought disorder, or major depression. Indeed, those assailants who are deeply confused or disoriented are generally not capable of the level of planning and organization necessary to conceal their identity from the authorities and, therefore, do not amass a large victim count."[68]

Others have argued, however, that some violent offenders—serial killers included—may have a biological or at least a biosocial predisposition to violence. Brain trauma is seen as one type of predisposing biological event.[69] Research in this area suggests that children who receive blows to their heads can suffer brain damage that affects their thinking processes and their impulse control. Others have noted that because of constitutional defects, such as a dysfunctional autonomic nervous system, the serial killer has an unusual need for stimulation, thrills, and excitement.[70] As one scholar suggests, however, "the neuropsychiatric problems alone don't make you violent. Probably the environmental factors in and of themselves don't make you a violent person. But when you put them together, you create a very dangerous character."[71]

Psychological explanations of serial killing also abound in the literature. Although most serial killers do not suffer from psychoses, several have been diagnosed with a specific type of personality disorder, still widely known as sociopathy or psychopathy,[72] although these terms have largely been superseded by the use of the term *antisocial personality disorder.* The current edition of the *Diagnostic and Statistical Manual of Mental Disorders* (DSM-IV), for example, now relies on this term.[73] The characteristics of this disorder include insincerity, a lack of shame or remorse, an inability to love, extreme selfishness and self-centeredness, and the lack of a conscience.[74] People suffering from this disorder are often perceived to be aggressive, charismatic, and intelligent, but they also suffer from chronic feelings of emptiness and isolation.[75] To these individuals, other human beings are there to be used and exploited. Because they lack a conscience, the suffering of others does not affect them in the way that most people might empathize and sympathize with another person's pain. Moreover, they are unable to defer their drives and need for immediate gratification.[76] They also often experience a need to be dominant and in control, which may in part explain their crimes of violence. They may perceive the act of killing as offering them a chance, however temporary, of having absolute power over someone else. Because of this, they are often drawn toward careers believed to convey the power that they crave, such as law enforcement. John Wayne Gacy, for example, was fascinated with the idea of being a police officer from childhood through adulthood and was described by his wife as a "police freak."[77] Edmund Kemper also wanted to become a law enforcement officer, and after his excessive height precluded this career, he began driving vehicles that resembled police vehicles. At one point in his life, he frequented a bar patronized by off-duty police officers and discussed gun types and ammunition with them.[78]

How does this disorder arise? Robert Simon summarizes the issue well when he writes,

> Important factors in the development of the disorder are maternal deprivation during the child's first 5 years, which leads to insufficient nurturing and socialization, and having an antisocial or alcoholic father, even if he is not in residence. It should be noted, however, that other studies show that adequate discipline can decrease the risk in children whose parents are antisocial. More moderate correlations between adult antisocial behavior and certain other childhood factors have been found. These in-

clude early-onset conduct disorder (before age 10 years) with or without accompanying hyperactivity, attention-deficit/hyperactivity disorder, and mild signs of neurologic deficit. Emerging evidence indicates that the brains of psychopaths do not process feelings and emotions properly. Neuroimaging studies show that psychopaths use different areas of their brain than do normal individuals in regulating emotions. Twin and adoption studies also indicate a possible genetic factor. The most plausible model for causation involves many factors, with a combination of genetic, developmental, and environmental factors all interacting to produce an antisocial personality.[79]

It should be noted that this disorder is not necessarily evident to others. Most people who have an antisocial personality disorder also have jobs and careers, may be married, and may even have children. For example, Ted Bundy was described by a coworker in this way: "Ted had control of what he was doing. He was really poised. He was friendly. He was always smiling. He was terribly charismatic. Obviously he was someone who had a great deal of compassion in dealing with other people." Similarly, one former girlfriend said of him that "if you know him, you can't help but have a great deal of affection for him as a human being."[80] A neighbor said of a serial killer by the name of Westley Allan Dodd that "Wes seemed so harmless, such an all-around, basic good citizen."[81] These individuals are often active in their local community and belong to various civic and church groups.[82] In short, individuals with this disorder may appear normal, healthy, friendly, and affectionate. However, this is only a front put on to disguise their true nature. Fundamentally, individuals who have this personality type are incapable of truly caring about other people. One psychiatrist who assessed a serial killer with this disorder described him in this way: "This man seems not to know what love and affection are, as though he has never experienced such feelings. In describing his relationship with his sister, the best he could do was say, "We didn't hate each other." It is striking that this intelligent man could not describe either parent. He seems so separated from emotional experiences as to suggest some sort of chronic dissociative process. I suspect that he is dimly aware of this defect or lack in himself, and, in part, the homicides were an attempt to experience strong emotions."[83]

In short, other people's feelings, emotions, and pain are meaningless to individuals with antisocial personality disorder. The American Psychiatric Association suggests that 3% of all men in American society have this disorder. Of course, most of these individuals are not serial killers or even criminals.

Because not all people with antisocial personality disorder are killers, Giannangelo has proposed a new type of disorder to be added to the DSM-IV, which he calls *homicidal pattern disorder,* consisting of the following qualities:

1. Commits deliberate and purposeful murder or attempts at murder of strangers on more than one occasion.

2. Experiences tension or affective arousal at some time before the act.

3. Experiences pleasure, gratification, or relief in the commission of or reflection on the acts.

4. Displays personality traits consistent with a diagnosis of at least one cluster B personality disorder (antisocial, borderline, histrionic, narcissistic).

5. Understands the illegality of actions and continues to avoid apprehension.

6. Does not murder for monetary gain, to conceal criminal activity, to express anger or vengeance, in response to a delusion or hallucination, or as a result of impaired judgment (as in dementia, mental retardation, or substance intoxication).[84]

The inclusion of this classification into the DSM-IV would serve to differentiate between nonviolent sociopaths and serial predators. However, although it is tempting, we cannot use this personality disorder to fully explain the meaning of and motivation for serial killing. In other words, other factors may play a role in the creation of these dangerous offenders.

Another condition common to many serial killers is a history of abuse and neglect by their parents or caregivers.[85] Leibman, for example, found that the serial murderers she studied had all been rejected by their parents, and most had experienced severe violence at the hands of their parents.[86] Others have found a similar pattern of parental neglect and abuse in the histories of serial killers.[87] One possible theoretical process compatible with this explanation is *social learning theory*.[88] Within this general theory, one form of learning is imitative—a person learns by watching others and copying their behavior. Abused children, therefore, learn through imitation and modeling that violence is a tool they can use in their relationships with others. Adult serial killers may be imitating the violence committed against them or the violence they witnessed as children. There is empirical confirmation of this notion. For example, Cathy Spatz Widom has documented a strong relationship between experiencing and witnessing violence as a child and committing violent acts as an adult. She suggests that this relationship may arise because those victimized as children learn destructive coping mechanisms, including skills in manipulation and denial as well as violent behavior.[89]

Similarly, David Lester suggests that abused children may act violently as adults out of a tremendous sense of anger and rage.[90] Especially important to this process is the role that the mother plays in perpetrating the abuse, which creates what Leyton terms "mother rage."[91] Robert Ressler and Tom Schachtman sum up the importance of the mother–child relationship as follows: "From birth to age six or seven, studies have shown, the most important adult figure in a child's life is the mother, and it is in this time period that the child learns what love is. Relationships between our subjects and their mothers were uniformly cool, distant, unloving, or neglectful. There was very little touching, emotional warmth, or training in the ways in which normal human beings cherish one another and demonstrate their affection and interdependence."[92] This is not to suggest that all serial killers are symbolically killing their mothers, although some in fact are. Edmund Kemper, for example, had a tremendous amount of anger for his mother that he graphically described, "I had this love–hate complex with my mother that was very hard for me to handle and I was very withdrawn—withdrawn from reality because of it. I couldn't handle the hate, and the love was actually forced upon me, you know. It was a very strong family-tie type love. There was a constant battle inside me that was the major thing of my whole life."[93] After killing a number of young women, Edmund Kemper killed his mother while she slept, bludgeoning her, slicing her throat, and ultimately decapitating her. Because of the constant verbal abuse he had suffered from her, he cut out her larynx and tried to flush it down the garbage disposal. Although hatred of his mother was not the only motivating force for his killings, it certainly was an important factor. Similarly, David Berkowitz, the infamous Son of Sam, admitted in an interview that he had killed women because he hated his mother and because he was unable to develop meaningful relationships with women.[94] Henry Lee Lucas also blamed his hatred of women on his mother and, in fact, stabbed her to death.[95]

Another interesting commonality between many serial killers is known as the *homicidal triad:* bed-wetting past an appropriate age, cruelty to animals, and fire setting.[96] Any one of these behaviors alone is not particularly significant but, according to John Douglas, most serial offenders he studied displayed at least two of these three qualities in their childhood. According to psychologist David Lester, this triad suggests a high amount of frustration and aggression and a lack of impulse control.[97] For example, bed-wetting at a relatively late age, or *enuresis* as it is known, may reflect emotional or psychological disturbances. Fire-setting behavior has been linked with certain violent themes of destruction and power and with hyperactive excitement and anger, whereas cruelty to animals indicates a high level of sadism and viciousness. Each of these behaviors in and of themselves are not necessarily indicative of a potential for future violence but, when combined with each other, their significance changes drastically.

Cruelty to animals, the last component of the homicidal triad, may be particularly significant as a warning sign. As a child, Edmund Kemper buried the family cat alive in the yard and, after its death, decapitated it and put its head on a spindle. Another time, he sliced off the top of another cat's skull and then tortured it while it convulsed.[98] Similarly, by age nine, Henry Lee Lucas reportedly tortured and killed animals and then had sex with the bodies.[99] David Berkowitz also reportedly tormented and dispatched small animals when he was a child.[100] It is unclear whether or not Jeffrey Dahmer killed animals himself, but he was fascinated by dead animals and would sometimes dissect the bodies of road-killed animals, and once he even mounted the head of a dog on a stake. It seems that before they graduate to human victims, many serial killers develop their skills on animals.

Despite these explanations, very little is actually known about serial killing. As with all forms of violence, there will probably never be any *one* causal factor that can help us explain and predict all serial murderers. As Huesmann and his colleagues conclude, "it is doubtful if any one explanation will suffice to account for exceptionally hostile, repetitive, violent acts, like those committed by serial killers."[101]

SUMMARY

In this chapter, we have explored the great variety of multicidal killings, and we have found that they occur in a number of different settings and with a wide range of motivations. However, it is important to point out that for all of their inherent sensationalism, these types of killing are not the norm when it comes to murder in this country. Although the lion's share of media attention continues to focus on these highly dramatic and sensational crimes, they occur very infrequently relative to the more common types of one-on-one homicide.

NOTES

1. Quoted in Elliott Leyton, *Hunting Humans: The Rise of the Modern Multiple Murderer* (Toronto: McClelland and Stewart, 1986), p. 167.

2. Quoted in Steven A. Egger, *The Killers among Us: An Examination of Serial Murder and Its Investigation* (Upper Saddle River, N.J.: Prentice Hall, 1998), p. 123.

3. John P. Stone and John A. Dunaway, *Columbine Report* (Jefferson County, Colo., Sheriff's Department, 2000). http://abcnews.go.com/sections/us/columbine/toc.htm (retrieved June 16, 2000).

4. Philip Jenkins, *Using Murder: The Social Construction of Serial Homicide* (New York: Aldine de Gruyter, 1994), p. 2.

5. Eric W. Hickey, *Serial Murderers and Their Victims,* ed. Todd Clear, 2nd edition, *Wadsworth Contemporary Issues in Crime and Justice* (Belmont, Calif.: Wadsworth, 1997), p. 4.

6. Quoted in David Lester, *Serial Killers: The Insatiable Passion* (Philadelphia: Charles Press, 1995), p. 41.

7. Egger, *The Killers among Us;* Steven A. Egger, *Serial Murder: An Elusive Phenomenon* (Westport, Conn.: Praeger, 1990).

8. Hickey, *Serial Murderers and Their Victims;* Ronald M. Holmes and James De Burger, *Serial Murder* (Newbury Park, Calif.: Sage, 1988); Lester, *Serial Killers.*

9. R. R. Hazelwood and John E. Douglas, "The Lust Murderer," *FBI Law Enforcement Bulletin* (1980).

10. It is beyond the scope of this book to examine *all* the different types of multicide that exist, which can include murder for hire, state terrorism and revolutionary terrorism, and genocide. Instead, this chapter focuses exclusively on mass, spree, and serial killing.

11. John Douglas and Mark Olshaker, *The Anatomy of Motive* (New York: Lisa Drew, 1999), pp. 190–191.

12. See, for example, Park Dietz, "Mass, Serial and Sensational Homicides," *Bulletin of the New York Academy of Medicine, 62,* 477–491 (1986); Hickey, *Serial Murderers and Their Victims;* Holmes and De Burger, *Serial Murder.*

13. Ronald M. Holmes and Stephen T. Holmes, *Murder in America* (Thousand Oaks, Calif.: Sage, 1994).

14. Douglas and Olshaker, *The Anatomy of Motive.*

15. Ibid.

16. Kelly A. Zinna, *After Columbine: A Schoolplace Violence Prevention Manual* (Silverthorne, Colo.: Spectra, 1999).

17. Douglas and Olshaker, *The Anatomy of Motive.*

18. James Alan Fox and Jack Levin, *The Will to Kill: Making Sense of Senseless Murder* (Boston: Allyn & Bacon, 2001), p. 44.

19. John Nicolletti, Kelly Zinna, and Sally Spencer-Thomas, *Violence Goes to School: Lessons Learned from Columbine* Lakewood, Colo.: Nicolletti-Flater, 1999).

20. Katherine Ramsland, *John List*. http://www.crimelibrary.com/classics/ list/index.htm (retrieved February 29, 2000).

21. Holmes and Holmes, *Murder in America*, p. 85.

22. Ramsland, *John List*.

23. Nicolletti et al., *Violence Goes to School*.

24. Barry Glassner, *The Culture of Fear* (New York: Basic Books, 1999), p. 27.

25. Ronet Bachman, *Violence and Theft in the Workplace* (Washington, D.C.: U.S. Department of Justice, Bureau of Justice Statistics, 1994).

26. Robert J. Meadows, *Understanding Violence and Victimization* (Upper Saddle River, N.J.: Prentice Hall, 1998), p. 113.

27. Greg Warchol, *Workplace Violence, 1992–96* (Washington D.C.: U.S. Department of Justice, 1998).

28. Ibid.

29. Robert I. Simon, *Bad Men Do What Good Men Dream: A Forensic Psychiatrist Illuminates the Darker Side of Human Behavior* (Washington, D.C.: American Psychiatric Press, 1996).

30. As important as these attacks were, a detailed discussion of terrorism is beyond the scope of this book. Although the terrorism of September 11, 2001, has dramatically affected American political and social life, we have chosen not to discuss this type of violence in this chapter. Political and collective acts of violence such as terrorism are not only distinct from the types of violence that this book focuses on, but they are also so complex and nuanced that to adequately discuss them, one needs much more space than one chapter or even one book can provide.

31. Douglas and Olshaker, *The Anatomy of Motive*.

32. Ibid., p. 147.

33. CNN.com, *Multiple Shootings in 1999*. http://www9.cnn.com/US/9911/02/ multiple.shootings.02/index.html (retrieved June 25, 2000).

34. CNN.com, *Former Chicago-Area Factory Worker Kills 4, Self, Police Say*. http:// www.cnn.com/2001/US/02/05/plant .shooting.04/index.html (retrieved February 9, 2001).

35. Simon, *Bad Men Do What Good Men Dream*.

36. Stone and Dunaway, *Columbine Report*.

37. Ibid.

38. Zinna, *After Columbine*.

39. Nicolletti et al., *Violence Goes to School*.

40. Quoted in Douglas and Olshaker, *The Anatomy of Motive*, p. 157.

41. Fiona Steel, *Calm before the Storm: The Littleton School Massacre*. http://www .crimelibrary.com/serial14/littleton/ index.htm (retrieved February 29, 2000).

42. James A. Fox and Jack Levin, *The Will to Kill: Making Sense of Senseless Murder*. (Boston: Allyn & Bacon, 2001).

43. Leyton, *Hunting Humans*.

44. Marilyn Bardsley, *Charles Starkweather and Caril Fugate*. http://www.crimelibrary .com/starkweather/starmain.htm (retrieved February 29, 2000).

45. Douglas and Olshaker, *The Anatomy of Motive*.

46. Ronald M. Holmes and Stephen T. Holmes, *Serial Murder* (Thousand Oaks, Calif.: Sage, 1998).

47. Egger, *The Killers among Us*, pp. 5–6.

48. Lester, *Serial Killers*.

49. Holmes and Holmes, *Serial Murder*.

50. S. Giannangelo, *The Psychopathology of Serial Murder: A Theory of Violence* (Westport, Conn.: Praeger, 1996); Holmes and Holmes, *Serial Murder*; Robert K. Ressler and Tom Schachtman, *I Have Lived in the Monster* (New York: St. Martin's Press, 1997).

51. Egger, *The Killers among Us*.

52. Ibid., p. 180.

53. Holmes and Holmes, *Serial Murder*; Lester, *Serial Killers*.

54. Holmes and Holmes, *Serial Murder*.

55. For an excellent review, see Egger, *The Killers among Us*.

56. Holmes and Holmes, *Serial Murder*.

57. See, for example, Holmes and Holmes, *Serial Murder;* F. H. Leibman, "Serial Murderers," *Federal Probation,* 53(4), 41–45 (1989).

58. Hickey, *Serial Murderers and Their Victims;* Michael D. Kelleher and C. L. Kelleher, *Murder Most Rare: The Female Serial Killer* (Westport, Conn.: Praeger, 1998).

59. Kerry Segrave, *Women Serial and Mass Murderers: A World-Wide Reference, 1580 through 1990* (Jefferson, N.C.: McFarland, 1992).

60. Hickey, *Serial Murderers and Their Victims.*

61. Egger, *The Killers among Us.*

62. Hickey, *Serial Murderers and Their Victims;* Holmes and Holmes, *Serial Murder.*

63. Hickey, *Serial Murderers and Their Victims.*

64. Egger, *The Killers among Us,* p. 79.

65. Hickey, *Serial Murderers and Their Victims.*

66. Holmes and Holmes, *Serial Murder.* Other have categorized serial killers in other ways. For example, Dietz argues for five different types: (1) the psychopathic sexual sadist, (2) the crime spree killer, (3) the organized crime killer, (4) the custodial poisoner or asphyxiator, and (5) the supposed psychotic. Dietz, "Mass, Serial and Sensational Homicides."

67. See also Hickey, *Serial Murderers and Their Victims;* Jack Levin and James Alan Fox, *Mass Murder: America's Growing Menace* (New York: Plenum, 1985); Leyton, *Hunting Humans.*

68. James Alan Fox and Jack Levin, "Serial Murder: Popular Myths and Empirical Realities," in *Homicide: A Sourcebook of Social Research,* ed. M. Dwayne Smith and Margaret A. Zahn (Thousand Oaks, Calif.: Sage, 1999), p. 168.

69. See also Egger, *The Killers among Us;* Dorothy O. Lewis, J. H. Pincus, M. Feldman, L. Jackson, and B. Bard, "Psychiatric, Neurological, and Psychoeducational Characteristics of 15 Death Row Inmates in the United States," *American Journal of Psychiatry,* 143, 838–845 (1986); Joel

Norris, *Serial Killers: The Growing Menace* (New York: Doubleday, 1988).

70. D. Sears, *To Kill Again* (Wilmington, Del.: Scholarly Resources, 1991).

71. Quoted in Fox and Levin, "Serial Murder," p. 170.

72. Originally, the term *psychopath* was used to refer to all personality disorders, but over time, it was narrowed down considerably, until in 1968 the DSM-II changed over to the term *sociopath.* See Simon, *Bad Men Do What Good Men Dream.*

73. The terms *psychopath* and *sociopath* were replaced in the third edition of the *Diagnostic and Statistical Manual of Mental Disorders* (DSM-III) with the term *antisocial personality disorder.* American Psychiatric Association, *Diagnostic and Statistical Manual of Mental Disorders,* 4th edition (Washington, D.C.: American Psychiatric Association, 1994).

74. Hickey, *Serial Murderers and Their Victims.*

75. Simon, *Bad Men Do What Good Men Dream.*

76. Egger, *The Killers among Us.*

77. Ibid., 96.

78. Marlee Macleod, *Edmund Kemper III.* http://www.crimelibrary.com/serials/ kemper/kempermain.htm (retrieved June 25, 2000).

79. Simon, *Bad Men Do What Good Men Dream,* pp. 33–34.

80. R. W. Larsen, *Bundy: The Deliberate Stranger* (Upper Saddle River, N.J.: Prentice Hall, 1980), p. 5.

81. Neighbor quoted in Egger, *The Killers among Us,* p. 44.

82. Fox and Levin, "Serial Murder."

83. Quoted in Robert K. Ressler and Tom Schachtman, *Whoever Fights Monsters* (New York: St. Martin's Press, 1992), p. 122.

84. Giannangelo, *The Psychopathology of Serial Murder.*

85. See, for example, Douglas and Olshaker, *The Anatomy of Motive;* Egger, *The Killers among Us;* A. Ellis and J. Gullo, *Murder and Assassination* (New York: Lyle Stuart, 1971); Hazelwood and Douglas,

"The Lust Murderer"; Hickey, *Serial Murderers and Their Victims;* Leyton, *Hunting Humans;* W. S. Willie, *Citizens Who Commit Murder: A Psychiatric Study* (St. Louis, Mo.: Warren H. Green, 1975).

86. Leibman, "Serial Murderers."

87. Holmes and Holmes, *Serial Murder.*

88. Ronald L. Akers, *Social Learning and Social Structure: A General Theory of Crime and Deviance* (Boston: Northeastern University Press, 1998); Albert Bandura, *Aggression: A Social Learning Analysis* (Englewood Cliffs, N.J.: Prentice Hall, 1973); Albert Bandura, *Social Learning Theory* (Englewood Cliffs, N.J.: Prentice Hall, 1977).

89. Cathy Spatz Widom, "Does violence beget violence? A critical examination of the literature," *Psychological Bulletin,* 106(1), 3–28 (1989); Cathy Spatz Widom, *The Cycle of Violence* (Washington, D.C.: National Institute of Justice, U.S. Department of Justice, 1992).

90. Lester, *Serial Killers.*

91. Leyton, *Hunting Humans,* p. 59.

92. Ressler and Schachtman, *Whoever Fights Monsters,* p. 83.

93. Leyton, *Hunting Humans,* p. 61.

94. Ressler and Schachtman, *Whoever Fights Monsters,* p. 77.

95. Michael Newton, *The Encyclopedia of Serial Killers: A Study of the Chilling Criminal Phenomenon from the "Angels of Death" to the "Zodiac" Killer* (New York: Checkmark Books, 2000).

96. Douglas and Olshaker, *The Anatomy of Motive,* p. 40.

97. Lester, *Serial Killers,* p. 99.

98. Leyton, *Hunting Humans,* p. 45.

99. Egger, *The Killers among Us;* Lester, *Serial Killers.*

100. Ressler and Schachtman, *Whoever Fights Monsters.*

101. L. R. Huesmann, J. F. Moise, and C. L. Podolski, "The Effects of Media Violence on the Development of Antisocial Behavior," in *Handbook of Antisocial Behavior,* ed. D. M. Stoff, J. Breiling, and J. D. Maser (New York: John Wiley, 1997), pp. 181–193.

7

Tools of Death

Firearms, Drugs, and Alcohol

I'm scared if I'm sober. I wouldn't talk this shit . . . but since I drunk,
I kill that fat son of a bitch. Understand? Ah' kill that motherfucker!

CAESAR [1]

Whenever I want to buy my boys something nice,
I buy 'em a gun. Give a boy a gun and you're makin' a man.

CLAUDE LAFAYETTE DALLAS SR. [2]

INTRODUCTION

In February of 2000, Natasha Williams and her boyfriend Andre Wallace at-
tended a basketball game at Wilson High School in Washington, D.C. Both
were high school seniors with good grades, part-time jobs, and college plans. Sitting beside them were Carlton Blount and Jermaine Johnson. Andre was a popular student and star football player at the high school with no history of violence, so bystanders were shocked to see him fistfighting with Carlton after a
disagreement that had apparently escalated into blows. Students witnessing the
incident intervened to break up the brawl, and Carlton supposedly said, "I'm
going to get my hammer," and left with Jermaine. After the game, Natasha and

Andre went to the grocery store to pick up a few items for Natasha's mother and then returned to the Williams home. As they were walking up the sidewalk to the front door, Carlton and Jermaine drove up, and Carlton confronted the couple with a 9-mm handgun. Natasha pleaded with him, but Carlton ignored her. He raised the gun to Andre, lowered it, then raised it again and shot—first Andre, then Natasha. While they lay dying on the ground, he stood over them and pumped more bullets into their bodies. When asked why he did it, Carlton said, "Because they kept playing me like that." According to Carlton's "crew," a man is not supposed to be humiliated in public. A man can't let someone like Andre Wallace give him a "beat down" in front of a high school gym full of people and not come back and make a statement. Twenty years ago, the disagreement might have ended with a few bloody noses, but with firearms so easily available today, it ended two young lives.[3]

Any discussion concerning the nature and patterns of murder in the United States must address not only the issue of firearms but also those of alcohol and illegal drugs. At least one of these issues is usually pivotal in increasing the likelihood that a particular conflict will result in murder. Americans kill each other in ways that are sometimes distinct from the murders typically found in other societies. As this chapter reveals, the peculiar dynamics of American criminal homicide are greatly influenced by the use of firearms and alcohol and by the use, business, and prohibition of other drugs.

FIREARMS

As discussed earlier, most murders in America are perpetrated with firearms. More specifically, they are committed with handguns. Exhibit 7.1 shows the weapons most commonly used in criminal homicides and reveals that during the 1980s, 60.2% of all murders were perpetrated with firearms. During the 1990s, this increased to just over 67%. For some specific groups, this percentage is even higher. In 1994, for example, almost 90% of murder victims between the ages of 15 and 19 were murdered with firearms. The large increase in homicide rates during the 1980s and early 1990s was in large part created by an increase in African-American homicides committed with handguns.[4] Another population at high risk during this time period were gang members. One study found that 75% of gang members studied had been threatened with a gun, and 40% had been shot at.[5] Another study of gang members found that their homicide victimization rate was 60 times higher than that of the general population.[6] To sum up, the risk of being killed by a firearm has not been distributed equally throughout society.

After firearms, the most commonly used weapons are cutting and stabbing instruments such as knives. These instruments, however, were used less than half as often as guns: 20.2% during the 1980s, and 13.8% during the 1990s. Firearms are by far the weapon of choice for most homicide offenders.

Examining Exhibit 7.1 a bit more closely, we find that of all the different types of firearms available, the most prevalent type to be used in murders are

Exhibit 7.1 Percentage of Murders by Weapon Used, 1980–1989 and 1990–1998

	MURDER (MEAN %)	
Weapon	1980–1989	1990–1998
Total Firearms	60.2	67.4
Handguns	44.6	55.9
Rifles	4.6	3.5
Shotguns	6.8	4.7
Other Guns	.2	.2
Firearms not specified	4.1	5
Cutting/Stabbing	20.2	13.8
Blunt Objects	5.6	4.8
Personal Objects	6.3	5.9
Poison	.1	.1
Explosives	.1	.1
Fire	1.3	1
Narcotics	.1	.2
Drowning	.3	.2
Strangulation	1.9	1.4
Asphyxiation	.6	.6
Other	3.4	5

Note: Percentages may not add up to 100% due to rounding.

SOURCE: Federal Bureau of Investigation, *Uniform Crime Reports: Crime in the United States, 1980–1995.*

handguns (44% during the 1980s, and 55.9% from 1990 through 1998). In other words, the well-known linkage between firearms and murder largely concerns handguns, including revolvers, manual and semiautomatic pistols, and derringers.[7] Compared to handguns, rifles and shotguns are not frequently used in criminal homicides. In part, this is a result of the high availability of handguns, combined with the small size and portability of handguns relative to the larger and more cumbersome long guns. We should also note that the greater reliance on handguns may well reflect the rationale for purchasing handguns relative to rifles and shotguns. For example, most handguns are purchased for self-defense, whereas many long firearms are purchased for other reasons such as sport, hunting, and collection. Buying a weapon for the explicit purpose of protecting oneself from others may well indicate a greater willingness to use that weapon against people. As rifles and long guns are primarily intended for hunting, it may require a greater psychological adjustment for the weapon to be used against another human being.

It is important to note that firearms are also used in crimes and acts of violence other than murder. For example, approximately 25% of all the victims of nonlethal violent crimes such as rape and sexual assault, robbery, or aggravated assault report that the perpetrator had a firearm, almost always a handgun.[8] In 1998, 670,500 people who were victims of significant violent crimes reported that their attacker had a gun.[9] As discussed in chapter 4, the presence of a gun in these situations is important because it tends to alter the interactional pattern between the victim and the perpetrator. In robberies, for example, the presence of a gun means that violence is less likely to occur. Perhaps the victim is more intimidated by the firearm and, therefore, less likely to resist. Perhaps the robber feels more confident and in control with a gun and, therefore, less likely to act out of nervousness or fear. Violence typically occurs when the interaction seems to get out of control or when assailants feel the need to back up their threat with physical intimidation, which occurs less often with a gun.[10] However, it is also true that if violence does occur in spite of the gun's presence, someone—usually the robbery victim—is much more likely to end up dead. The rate of fatality for gun robberies is three times higher than for robberies perpetrated with knives and 10 times higher than for robberies using other weapons.[11] Put another way, Zimring and Hawkins point out that "firearms are responsible for 40% of robberies and 73% of all robbery killings so that the apparent death rate from gun robbery nationwide is four times that of nongun robberies in the aggregate."[12]

The incidence of noncriminal death from firearms is also high in the United States. For example, according to the Centers for Disease Control and Prevention, there were more than 17,800 firearm-caused homicides, more than 18,700 firearm suicides, and 1,300 unintentional deaths from firearms in 1994.[13] It should also be pointed out that there are estimated to be about three nonfatal gun injuries for every fatality.[14] Young people are even more vulnerable to death from firearms. Firearm injuries are the second leading cause of death for individuals between 10 and 24 years old and the third leading cause for 25- to 34-year-olds.[15]

In short, the human cost of firearms in the United States in terms of death and suffering is tremendous. In addition to the pain and suffering, the monetary cost of these shootings is also significant. One study estimated that in 1992, the cost of every lethal gunshot wound in America was $21,700; $28,000 for every nonfatal gunshot wound requiring hospitalization; and $6,500 for every nonfatal gunshot wound without hospitalization.[16] This calculation includes expenditures for medical care, mental health care, emergency transportation, police assistance, and the administration of insurance policies and settlements. The combined annual cost of gun killings and woundings was a resounding $63.4 billion. Anywhere from half to 80% of these costs seem to devolve on the taxpaying public.[17]

So what is the special relationship between Americans and firearms? Why are firearms so much more a part of our life and death than for people in other industrialized nations? There are four primary reasons why guns are used so often in American murders: culture, availability, lethality, and ease.

Culture

The first factor that relates to the prevalent use of guns in American society concerns the fact that firearms enjoy a unique and privileged cultural status in the United States. Some people fervently believe that the cornerstone of this privilege comes directly from the Second Amendment to the Constitution. In its entirety, this amendment states that "A well regulated Militia, being necessary to the security of a free State, the right of the people to keep and bear Arms, shall not be infringed." Anti–gun control activists, including many National Rifle Association members, interpret this amendment in its widest possible sense, believing that it gives Americans the freedom to own any type and any quantity of weapons they desire. Gun control activists, on the other hand, interpret the amendment in the context for which it was written—that is, in terms of a well-regulated militia. Regardless of which perspective one subscribes to, it is clear that guns represent much more than just a piece of hardware to many Americans.

Historically, firearms have not only been tools but also highly charged symbols. Guns are representative in many ways of whom we believe ourselves to be. This symbolism is as alive and well today as it was in colonial times. According to Tom Diaz, the entertainment media, gun advocacy groups, and firearm manufacturers have "helped create and maintain the unique U.S. gun culture, within which the firearm is less a utilitarian tool than an icon, so laden with implicit value that its hold over its devotees approaches the mystical."[18] How has this image emerged to have such a hold on the American consciousness?

For many, gun ownership is part and parcel of being an American. Guns evoke a history replete with images of minutemen, pioneers, settlers, gunslingers, and desperados. For example, we have enshrined the image of the noble colonists, with guns in hand, standing against the redcoated forces of tyranny at Concord bridge in 1776. In a similar vein, the image of the western pioneer as a tough and resolute individual who was able and willing to protect himself and his family is a staple of popular culture. Firearms are, of course, integral to these characterizations. The importance of guns to this image is exemplified by the Colt .45 revolver being known variously as the "peacemaker" and "the gun that won the West." In short, gun ownership is not just about owning a means of self-defense or a tool for sport, but it is also a highly tangible link to a past replete with heroic figures defending distinctly American values armed with guns. As a result, America has more guns per capita than any other nation in the world. This leads us to the second reason for guns' prominent role in murder: their availability.

Availability

If we remember that many homicides occur during conflict situations, it makes sense that the easy availability of a weapon can be a crucial factor in the lethality of a conflict resolution. During heated arguments, when participants intend to escalate their actions from words to blows and try to arm themselves, people choose the weapons that are most available. Research has indicated that when a violent interaction occurs in a home, a gun in the household greatly increases the risk of a homicide.[19] One must recognize that in the United States, many handguns are readily obtainable. In fact, as one commentator noted, "the United States is the world's greatest market for civilian firearms."[20]

The number of guns in private hands has skyrocketed during the past 20 years. According to the Bureau of Alcohol, Tobacco, and Firearms, from

1899 to 1993 about 223 million guns came into circulation; 79 million of these were rifles, 77 million were handguns, and 66 million were shotguns. The great majority of these have been acquired by private citizens since the 1970s.[21] In short, fewer and fewer people own more and more guns. The average number of guns among private households is now up to 4.4, which constitutes a significant increase over the last 20 years.[22]

Although most gun ownership has traditionally involved rifles and shotguns, the possession of handguns has been increasing in recent years. For example, handguns once accounted for only a third of all new gun sales. Today, however, they account for nearly half of all new gun sales.[23] This is an important trend because most firearm violence involves handguns. Whereas rifles and shotguns are mostly owned for sporting and hunting purposes, handguns are primarily purchased for self-defense. The increase in handgun sales is primarily related to two factors: the increased levels of fear that many Americans have of crime and a change in the marketing strategies employed by firearm manufacturers in the United States.[24]

Firearms in general, and handguns in particular, are also easily available outside of the home. For example, approximately 9% of American adults reported carrying a handgun outside the home in 1998.[25] Of those 9%, 22% reported taking their guns with them almost daily, and 11% did so several times a week. One study of high school students found that one in six had carried a firearm in the preceding month, whereas another study found that 8% had carried a gun within the previous month.[26] This means that arguments away from home can escalate into gunplay, because a nontrivial percentage of people have access to a gun on their person or in a nearby vehicle.

This easy availability of guns translates directly into their use in criminal homicides. This contention is supported by a body of research suggesting that the more guns in circulation, the higher the rate of their usage. Philip J. Cook, for example, conducted a city-level analysis of gun availability and found that increases in gun density resulted in more robberies with guns and more robbery homicides.[27] Similarly, David McDowall found that higher amounts of gun density increased the danger of homicides in the city of Detroit.[28] Thus, when gun ownership is high in the population, gun violence also tends to be high. These studies have been replicated by other research that also lends empirical support to this connection.[29]

Does this mean that controlling the availability of guns would decrease the rate of murder? The empirical evidence regarding this issue remains inconclusive. On the other side of this issue are those who point out that various societies have high rates of gun ownership and yet have very low rates of criminal homicide.[30] This indicates the need to examine gun availability within the particular contexts in which the violence occurs. In other words, one has to look not only at gun availability but also at culture, class and inequality, and race and ethnicity. We must also remember that here in the United States, the gun control debate remains largely ideological. As Philip Cook and Mark Moore contend, "In a debate driven by strongly held beliefs and values, empirical facts matter little."[31]

Other scholars, such as John Lott and Gary Kleck, suggest that the private ownership and use of guns may actually prevent crime by providing some crime victims with self-protection.[32] Essentially, these scholars contend that when private citizens carry concealed weapons or have firearms in their homes, predatory criminals are less likely to target them. Moreover, they estimate that many attempted crimes are unsuccessful because these armed citizens brandish, display, and perhaps even use their guns to prevent the crime from being completed. For example, based on survey data, Gary Kleck and Mark Gertz found that guns were used more commonly in self-defense than in crime. Using the same data along with data from other surveys, however, other researchers have found that the use of guns for criminal acts is far higher than that for self-protection purposes. The reason for these different estimates is primarily methodological. For example, one of the main difficulties that researchers have in estimating the relative efficacy of gun use in preventing crime is that estimates of self-defensive use are largely based on conjecture and, therefore, remain speculative at best. Furthermore, authors such as Cook contend that Kleck's estimates of self-defense are actually overestimates because many acts of supposed self-defense may not be justifiable as such. For example, many felons carry guns for reasons of self-defense, as do many juveniles convicted of serious crimes.[33] Zimring and Hawkins highlight this perceptual issue well: "*Each* party to an argument that turned violent is likely to regard the other party as a criminal aggressor, and to think that his own use of force was permissible self-defense." In fact, one survey of convicted felons in prison found that the most common reason they offered for carrying a gun was self-defense.[34]

Regardless of this debate, however, much of the prevailing evidence indicates that the easy availability of guns does result in higher rates of criminal homicide and has created a lethal environment on the streets and in homes across America. As one man, when asked why guns were so common in his community, asserted, "because you never know what's going to happen out there in the street. You get in an argument—just like myself—I don't carry nothing. I get in an argument with a guy, I'm ready to hold my fists. He pulls out a gun, and I could be totaled. If he blasts me, I'm finished. He's probably feeling the same way, he don't know what I got."[35]

Lethality

It might seem like stating the obvious, but the third factor that places firearms at the forefront of murder statistics is their lethality. All firearms are deadly weapons. Guns are far more deadly than other available tools such as knives or blunt instruments. From the largest to the smallest and the oldest to the newest, all functioning guns have the capacity to kill. When guns are used in a conflict or felony situation, the likelihood of someone dying increases dramatically. In domestic situations, guns are three times more likely to result in a fatality than knives and 23 times more likely than all other assaults together.[36]

Of course, not everyone who is shot dies. In fact, estimates suggest that for every gunshot fatality, there are perhaps three to six nonfatal shootings, not counting shots that completely miss their targets.[37] In 1997, for example, there were 39,400 nonfatal assaults that involved firearm injuries, compared to the 13,252 homicides committed with firearms.[38] Despite the fact that guns do not always cause death, they are typically far more lethal than most other weapons. There are several specific reasons for this.

First, guns allow multiple attacks. In other words, a person can be shot numerous times during an incident. A revolver typically has six bullets in the chamber, whereas a semiautomatic handgun may have nine or more bullets in the clip. Moreover, from 1973 to 1993 the production of handguns has moved away from revolvers to semiautomatic weapons; semiautomatic handguns now account for 80% of all handguns produced.[39] These kinds of guns may have up to 15 rounds in the magazine, all of which can be fired in the space of a few seconds. This, of course, increases the odds that a person will receive multiple wounds. Not surprisingly, the percentage of individuals who have been shot two or more times has increased from about 26% before 1987 to 43% from 1988 through 1990.[40] This increase undoubtedly accounts for the increase in gunshot mortality noted by researchers. In Tom Diaz's words, "pistols began killing more people than revolvers had, and their enhanced firepower (especially more rounds) was directly reflected in more lethal injuries on U.S. streets."[41] As one trauma surgeon succinctly noted, "it seems like we never see just one shot anymore."[42] Obviously, the more wounds a person receives, the more damage inflicted. This further increases the likelihood that a vital organ or artery may be hit, thereby increasing the likelihood that the attack will result in death.[43] As a result, the overall improvement of emergency medical services during the 1980s and 1990s did not help gunshot victims, because the percentage of victims who died at the scene rose from 5% to 34%, primarily because of more severe and more numerous wounds.[44]

A second factor associated with the lethality of guns is the tremendous damage they can inflict on the body. Ammunition rounds come in a variety of configurations that involve the diameter and speed of the bullet as well as its impact characteristics. Larger caliber bullets, for example, can cause massive damage as they plough through soft tissue and bone. It is no wonder that criminals prefer large caliber handguns.[45] Since the mid-1980s, the production of large caliber handguns has also increased substantially.[46]

The types of bullets manufactured have also become more destructive, as manufacturers continue to search for ammunition with greater stopping power. Often referred to as *defensive ammunition,* certain bullets are designed to expand or mushroom after hitting their target. Many of these rounds have hollowed-out tips that are filled with very soft lead that enlarges on impact, thus causing greater damage to the body.[47] Other bullets are designed to break apart on impact and send bullet fragments into various parts of the body, whereas still others are designed to tumble after they hit and can travel incredible distances through the body, bouncing off bones and slicing through flesh, arteries, and organs. The nature of these bullets, combined with the type of handguns now widely available, results in more and deadlier injuries.

Ease

The final reason for the large role that firearms, and especially handguns, play in murder is that they are relatively easy to use. Out of arm's reach, safe from immediate harm, all the attacker has to do is point the weapon and squeeze the trigger. The trigger of most firearms only requires the application of a few pounds of pressure to fire them. Mustering up the strength for this does not require a strenuous effort. Aiming the firearm takes a bit more effort, especially in a tense conflict situation, when adrenaline is pumping through the body and nerves are taut. This explains why more people who are involved in gun incidents are wounded than are killed and why more people are missed than are wounded. Of course, shootings that occur at relatively close range increase the likelihood of actually hitting a target—especially when we consider that handguns allow multiple rounds to be shot at a target relatively quickly.

Handguns also allow an offender to be somewhat distant from the target of the attack and correspondingly safer. A knife attack, on the other hand, requires some physical prowess, because one must be within arm's reach of the intended victim, who can and usually will fight back. Knives are also generally less deadly than guns, meaning that an individual intending to kill another must usually inflict multiple stabbings or slashings in their attempt to kill. Again, in these situations, the victim is generally capable of reacting fairly vigorously—and potentially capable of turning the offender into the victim. Admittedly, this last is also true for handguns but, because the gun wielder can be some distance from the intended victim and because handguns can be quickly lethal, this scenario is less likely than with knives.

Ease of use also relates to the use of handguns versus long guns. It is true that rifles and shotguns can be more deadly than handguns, but they are also potentially more cumbersome and awkward in the close confines of a house or apartment. They are also much more difficult to transport and to conceal. Compared to all other weapons, handguns are perhaps the easiest to use.

It should be clear by now that there is a strong correlation between the use of firearms and lethal violence in the United States. But guns are not the only things that play a strong role in shaping patterns of American murder. Another typical element in the homicide equation is alcohol.

ALCOHOL

A recent study released by the U.S. Department of Justice brought media attention to the fact that the use of alcohol is linked to a large percentage of criminal offenses. In fact, the study found that almost four out of ten violent crimes involved alcohol according to reports by crime victims and self-reports of attribution by criminal offenders.[48] This report confirmed the wide body of academic literature that has documented the association between alcohol consumption and interpersonal violence—both lethal and nonlethal—in adults.[49]

The relationship between alcohol and violence is certainly not a new phenomenon. Alcohol has had a long and troubled relationship with violence and homicide in this country. In our not so distant past, alcohol was considered a staple of life and was thought to provide strength for working men. In fact, some believed that it was healthier than water.[50]

Historical annals are replete with examples illustrating that from colonial times on, men drank a great deal of hard liquor, typically with violent results. For example, the historian Robert Utley writes, "Everywhere on the frontier nearly all men drank nearly all the time, which made nearly all men more or less drunk most of the time. Drink enhanced self-importance, impaired judgment, generated heedless courage, and encouraged unreasoning resort to violence."[51] Although this statement may be somewhat exaggerated, it is based on a real relationship between alcohol and violence. The image of the cowboy riding into town for a night of drinking and carousing is based largely on reality. Saloons were ubiquitous in the old West. It was the norm for cowboys to come into town after a cattle drive or a payday and spend their earnings on a drinking and gambling binge that often culminated in lethal violence; the high homicide rates in many western cattle-driving towns are testimony to this fact. The following narrative of a cowboy from this era graphically illustrates an event typical of what occurred on the frontier by mixing the volatile ingredients of alcohol, guns, and insecure machismo:

> I was really dangerous. A kid is more dangerous than a man because he's so sensitive about his personal courage. He's just itching to shoot somebody in order to prove himself. I did shoot a man once. I was only sixteen, and drunk. A bunch of us left town on a dead run, shooting at the gas lamps. I was in the lead and the town marshal was right in front of me with his gun in his hand calling, "Halt! Halt! Throw 'em up!" And I throwed 'em up all right, right in his face. I always had that idea in my head—"shoot your way out." I did not go into town for a long time afterwards, but he never knew who shot him, because it was dark enough so he could not see. He was a saloon man's marshal anyway and they wanted our trade, so did not do much about it. That was how us cowboys got away with a lot of such stunts.[52]

This description, though dated in its references, still applies to the attitudes exhibited by many young men who find that alcohol, youth, and firearms provide a lethal catalyst in interpersonal relations.

In perhaps the largest research undertaking of its kind to look specifically at the violence–alcohol connection, Kai Pernanen analyzed data from a probability sample of men and women over the age of 20 and from a comparison sample of violent crimes based on police records. In more than half the incidents of violence in the community sample and in 42% of the violent crimes in the police reports, either the victim, the assailant, or both had been drinking. This study led Pernanen to conclude that alcohol is abundantly present in day-to-day violent confrontations.[53] Another important contribution of Pernanen's work is its demonstration that alcohol was more pervasive within particular subsets of violent incidents. For example, alcohol involvement was present in more than half of all episodes of male-perpetrated violence but in only 27% of female-perpetrated violence. Alcohol involvement also varied by the victim–offender relationship; more than three quarters of the incidents involving strangers and nearly half the incidents of spouse assault involved drinking by either the victim or the assailant. The high prevalence of alcohol involvement in intimate partner violence has been confirmed by other research as well.[54]

Not surprisingly, when homicide is specifically examined, we find that alcohol overwhelmingly is the substance most frequently used by homicide offenders and victims. For example, in 1991, 41.4% of the offenders serving time for murder had been drinking alcohol at the time of the killing.[55] The evidence for a homicide–alcohol nexus is nothing new. In 1958, Marvin Wolfgang's famous study of murder in Philadelphia found that 55% of the offenders had been drinking alcohol.[56] A few years later, Voss and Hepburn found that 53% of Chicago murders involved alcohol. More recently, a study of regional homicide patterns in the United States noted that reported alcohol involvement for offenders ranged from a low of 28% to a high of 86%.[57] Recent research even suggests that rates of homicide and rates of alcohol use are closely related. That is, when people drink less they also kill each other less.[58] This linkage between alcohol and homicide is not unique to the United States; studies in Russia, Finland, Germany, Iceland, Denmark, Scotland, Canada, Rhodesia, and France have all found that alcohol is a significant contributory factor to homicides in these countries.[59]

None of these correlational studies, of course, establish a causal relationship between the use of alcohol and intentional violence. Experimental studies do, however, illuminate the possibility that alcohol consumption may have a distinct causal influence on subsequent violent behavior. A large proportion of experimental studies investigating the relationship between alcohol ingestion and violence have measured aggression using the Taylor paradigm.[60] In this methodology, aggression is typically operationalized using a version of the Taylor competitive reaction time task, which involves shocking a bogus opponent (measure of aggression) as well as receiving shocks from a bogus opponent (provocation). In general, these studies have found that intoxicated participants give a greater number of markedly higher shocks than sober participants, particularly under conditions of frustration and provocation. Unlike the correlational studies discussed earlier, these experimental studies have the advantage of permitting inferences about the causal link between alcohol and violence. However, due to the artificiality of the drinking situation and the operationalization of aggression (shocks instead of real aggression in everyday life), these studies have limited generalizability outside the laboratory setting.[61] Other research has found that the presence of an audience, the participant's being young and male, and the presence of alcohol in the bloodstream all make it more likely that an insult will be answered and escalated into violence.[62]

Why does this relationship between alcohol and violence exist? Knowing that there is a connection is one thing, but understanding how that relationship works is another. The first point to make is that alcohol in and of itself does not cause violence. Although alcohol affects individuals differently and although those effects are mediated by the context, it is safe to say that alcohol can dramatically affect the central nervous system and is both a depressant and a stimulant. Not only can it serve to tranquilize an individual, but in small amounts alcohol can also act as a stimulant, because it triggers the release of a neurotransmitter called dopamine.[63] It also quickly affects the parts of the brain that control inhibitions, lowering or reducing them.[64] This is why after drinking many people experience strong emotions, become aggressive, unruly, or simply talkative. In short, they lose the self-control that is normally such a strong part of their conscious persona, and they may say or do things they normally would not. They may also feel invulnerable or especially tough. As one individual remarked, "when you put that alcohol in your system, an S grows on your chest like Superman. Liquor makes you get bigger than what you are. You feel like you can whip the world."[65]

Although alcohol is both a stimulant and a depressant, its effects are largely mediated by the social context within which it is used. People react to alcohol as they have been conditioned or expect to react.[66] MacAndrew and Edgerton were two of the first scholars to historically document the socially learned response that American Indians had to alcohol. Through a content analysis of the diaries of missionaries and fur traders, these researchers documented how many American Indians' first contact with alcohol did not result in drunken brawls and mayhem but rather in fear or passivity. By watching the White settlers, however, American Indians soon learned that alcohol *should* produce drunken brawls and mayhem, and their own drunken behavior consequently began to mirror this perception.

The link between alcohol and violence continues to dominate the expectations we have about the effects of alcohol on individual behavior, especially when drinking alcohol is also closely tied with notions of masculinity and toughness for young men. When these expectations are combined with the disinhibiting effects of alcohol, the probability of violence is likely to increase. Alcohol, however, is not the only drug that has been linked to violent acts, as we will see in the next section.

ILLICIT DRUGS

The relationship between illegal drugs and violence is much more complex than one would suspect based on popular perceptions of drugs and the public discourse on drug policy. In fact, a strong case can be made that our understanding of the relationship between homicide and illicit drugs is based more on hype and rhetoric than on empirical facts. Unfortunately, public policy is also more often controlled by the myths about drugs than by the reality. Henry Brownstein makes the same point when he writes that "the connection [of drugs] to violence was more firmly grounded in politics than science."[67]

Generally speaking, the violence that results from illicit drugs falls into four categories: (1) violence that is a consequence of the drug's psychoactive effects; (2) violence that results from attempts to support drug addictions through economic crimes; (3) violence deriving from the illegal business of drugs; and (4) violence that is a direct effect of the war on drugs.[68] We next describe the empirical literature that investigates the drugs and violence relationship within each of these realms.

Psychoactive Effects

As with the relationship between alcohol and violence, the pathways that link illicit drugs to violence are not always direct. However, some substances do directly affect the cognitive processes in the brain, and some researchers contend that these effects serve to increase the likelihood of aggressive behavior. One well-known example concerns *phencyclidine,* also known as PCP (peace pill), angel dust, ozone, whack, and rocket fuel. An artificially created white chemical powder, this drug can be ingested in liquid, tablet, capsule, or powder form and can result in mood disorders, extreme unease, paranoia, feelings of invulnerability, and aggression.[69] To these formidable symptoms can be added heightened levels of strength, brought about by a PCP-induced release of stress hormones. Because of these chemical effects, some researchers believe that users of phencyclidine are at a tremendous risk of engaging in acts of violence. This conclusion, however, is based almost exclusively on case studies of individuals with psychiatric disturbances.[70] Official crime statistics do not show conclusive evidence for a direct link between PCP use and violent crime.

The media have also implanted in the public mind the notion that other drugs, such as heroin and cocaine—particularly crack cocaine—are related to an increased risk of aggression and violence. However, because of methodological inconsistencies across studies, there is no conclusive evidence that any illicit drug directly increases an individual's propensity to become violent. On the contrary, the data suggest that most illicit drugs are not involved in the perpetration of violence. For example, victims of violence who report their victimizations to the National Crime Victimization Survey are far more likely to perceive their attackers as being under the influence of alcohol (more than one fourth) than under the influence of other, illicit drugs (less than 10%). Urinalysis arrest data also indicate that only a very small percentage (generally less than 7%) of violent offenders arrested are under the influence of illicit drugs at the time of their offense.[71]

Moreover, as we saw in the last section, correlation does not mean causation. Even if a person has used drugs before engaging in violence, this does not necessarily mean that the ingestion of the drugs caused the violence. In fact, some research has indicated that whereas some criminals began ingesting drugs before beginning to commit crimes, many began their criminal behavior *before* they started using drugs, and still others began doing both simultaneously.[72] In other words, illegal drug use and criminal behavior appear to operate independently of each other for most individuals. It may be that drug use and violent or criminal behavior are both part of a certain lifestyle but are not causally linked to each other. Many armed robbers, for example, use alcohol prior to their stickups as an enabler.[73] The alcohol, however, does not cause the robbery; it is merely another tool that helps facilitate the perpetration.

Although many murderers under the influence of drugs and alcohol initially blame the murder on their inebriation, some in-depth interview data reveal a more complex scenario. For example, after interviewing a murderer who confessed to having been high on cocaine during the homicide, Henry Brownstein reports that the murderer also asserted that the cocaine did not *cause* him to perpetrate the killing. Rather, it was just one of a number of ingredients that also included saving face and image, peer pressure, and other environmental conditions. Significantly, the offender maintained that the killing could easily have happened without drugs being involved.[74]

In sum, the image presented in the media of the junkie on a violent, drug-induced rampage is far from supported by the empirical literature. As Robert Nash Parker and Kathleen Auerhahn state, "our review of the literature finds a great deal of evidence that the social environment is a much more powerful contributor to the outcome of violent behavior than are pharmacological factors associated with any of the substances reviewed here [including PCP, heroin, and crack]."[75]

Maintaining Addictions

Certain drugs are known to be highly addictive. Their use creates a craving within the individual for further consumption of that substance, and its use becomes more a matter of need than of choice. Dennis Donovan defines *addiction* as a "progressive behavior pattern having biological, psychological, sociological, and behavioral components. What sets this behavior apart from others is the individual's overwhelmingly pathological involvement in or attachment to it, subjective compulsion to continue it, and reduced ability to exert personal control over it."[76]

Substances such as heroin, cocaine, and crack cocaine are highly addictive. When deprived of these substances after having developed a habit, individuals become physiologically depressed and may suffer extreme withdrawal symptoms as their bodies attempt to adjust. These symptoms may include watery eyes, a runny nose, a loss of appetite, cramping, nausea, chills and sweats, and in extreme cases, coma and possibly death.[77] Obviously, an individual who is suffering from these symptoms craves the substances that will reduce or eliminate the discomfort. However, research indicates that most of these individuals do not commit crimes to sustain their addictions, even though illegal drugs are often expensive.

One study found that approximately 50% of those studied maintained legitimate jobs while addicted, and about 20% received public assistance. Other addicts may well engage in the business of selling and distributing drugs as a means of further supporting their habits. Although this criminal behavior may well necessitate violence, it may not involve the dealer in perpetrating predatory street crimes in order to keep a personal supply of drugs coming in. Others may turn to prostitution as a means to get the money to buy drugs. When drug addicts do engage in predatory crime, most are purely economic in orientation rather than violent. Crimes such as burglary, larceny theft, auto theft, forgery, fraud, fencing stolen goods, and embezzlement are typically the crimes of choice.[78] The object of these activities obviously is to acquire property that can easily be converted to cash, which is then used to purchase the coveted substances. Robbery—a crime of violence—is another possibility for the addict. However, there are evidently many avenues other than violence open to the drug-dependent user.

Thus, the media portrayal that drug users become addicted and then go on to commit crimes in order to support those addictions is inaccurate. In fact, when we examine drug use in the United States, it quickly becomes evident that many people have experimented with drugs, sometimes often, and do not go on to become addicts and perpetrate further criminality. As one criminologist put it, "most drug use is casual and recreational and does not have serious antisocial consequences."[79]

Even those who do become addicted to certain drugs do not necessarily go on to commit acts of crime and violence. One study of heroin addicts, for example, found that the vast majority of them did not regularly engage in violent behavior.[80] They were largely able to support their habits nonviolently. In 1989, for example, approximately a third of all jail inmates convicted of property offenses indicated that they were under the influence of drugs or alcohol when they committed the offense. Less than one out of four of these, however, asserted that their motivation was to support a habit.[81] This is not to say that drug addicts do not commit crimes or that they never engage in violence. Rather, the risk that these individuals pose is often overblown by the simplistic imagery that is a staple of popular perceptions of drug use. The reality is a bit more complex. The business of drug dealing, however, is another matter.

The Business of Drugs

Of all the possible pathways that connect illicit drugs and homicide, the distribution and sale of illicit drugs is perhaps the most conspicuous. For example, one study of murder in New York found that more than half the murders during the period under study had drugs or alcohol as a primary cause and that the murders related to drugs were principally related to trafficking. Most of these murders occurred at or near sites where drugs were sold, giving further credence to the significance of violence for the distribution of drugs. Studies in Washington, D.C., and Miami found that a significant proportion of the murders in those cities was similarly drug related.[82]

Drug trafficking is by all accounts an extremely violent business enterprise, in large part due to the illegal nature of the venture. Legal businesses have a variety of methods for dealing with competition, disagreements, and bad or troublesome employees. When dealing in criminal operations, however, these methods are obviously not available, and violence consequently becomes one of the few available options. As Corman and her colleagues point out, "many believe that violence associated with drugs is primarily due to the illegality of the market. Drug producers and sellers have no other recourse to settling dis-

**Exhibit 7.2 Sources of Utilitarian Violence
in the Illegal Drug Business**

- Guarding drug-producing crops during harvest season
- Territorial disputes between rival drug dealers
- Enforcing normative codes within dealing hierarchies
- Robberies of drug dealers, and their violent retaliation
- Elimination of drug informers
- Punishment for selling poor quality, adulterated, or phony drugs
- Punishment for failing to pay debts
- Punishment for stealing, tampering with, or not sharing drug supplies
- Retaliation for stealing, using without permission, or not sharing drug paraphernalia

SOURCE: Bureau of Justice Statistics, *Drugs, Crime, and the Justice System: A National Report from the Bureau of Justice Statistics* (Washington, D.C.: U.S. Department of Justice, 1992).

putes and force is a typical method in obtaining market power."[83] This violence is typically very utilitarian, serving a specific end within the illegal drug distribution industry. Exhibit 7.2 illustrates some of the primary rationales for the use of violence in the drug trafficking business.

As is evident from an examination of Exhibit 7.2, participants often perceive that violence and killing in their business are quite rational. Of course, this is not to say that their murders are justified—rather that they do not simply occur randomly or without a reason. If an organization that is engaged in legitimate business, for example, is victimized by some sort of theft, that business can call on law enforcement to seek help in finding and punishing those responsible. They can also contact insurance companies to receive compensation for their losses. Drug dealers, on the other hand, have no such recourse. Instead, they arm themselves for protection or to seek restitution and punishment. One man in the illegal drug business put it this way: "Drug-trafficking is automatic trouble. Right from jump street. If you're trafficking and use drugs, that's trouble right off the bat. Because now at that time, you either set yourself up for a rip-off . . . somebody's trying to rip you off . . . or you're selling to undercover cops. It's trouble—either way, it's trouble. But besides the violence, you have to protect yourself. People will try to rip you off. There's violence there. A lot of people have been getting shot and killed. The trafficking or the selling or the buying, all of it, none of it's good."[84]

This reliance on violence as a way of solving business problems results in an industry where acts of violence and murder are perennial elements of the job. In fact, for some, the violence may be so routine that it is not even defined as such. As one individual in the business remarked, "if somebody messes with your property, then they need to be checked. I don't call that violence, that's just tightening your business up."[85] Closely related to the systemic violence that arises from the business of drugs is the violence that arises out of the war on drugs.

The War on Drugs

The law of unintended consequences suggests that our actions sometimes have results that are not anticipated and, in fact, can be counterproductive. The war on drugs that the United States has engaged in over the past 20 years is a prime example of this effect. Ostensibly designed to make our society safer, the war on drugs has in the view of many scholars contributed substantially to violence and homicide since its inception. How has this happened?

First, a primary strategy of the drug war has been to severely amplify the legal penalties for trafficking and possession of controlled substances. However, rather than having a deterrent effect, this strategy has mostly served to increase the stakes. As one observer notes, "raising the penalties for drug dealing is equivalent to *lowering* the penalties on other crimes in the course of the illegal drug business. *The result is more intimidation, violence, and lawlessness by drug dealers.*"[86] In other words, the penalties for dealing and using drugs may be so extreme that offenders may become desperate to avoid capture and, thus, more likely to resort to lethal violence. Killing an informer or a police officer in an attempt to avoid detection may be seen as a reasonable alternative to arrest.

Second, the arrest of specific dealers or the targeting of a particular trafficking group has increased the homicide rate by destabilizing specific drug markets. That is, the arrest of various dealers or traffickers creates a vacuum in the market. This vacuum is simply an opportunity for other, rival dealers and organizations to expand their market share. These competitors may then engage in violent conflict to gain control of the territory in dispute. Moreover, the police strategy of cracking down on specific targets or neighborhoods does not result in a decrease in the number of dealers or of drugs available, because it simply displaces the dealers to another community or neighborhood. The arrest of one drug dealer is seen as a job opportunity for another.[87] The net outcome of this is simply to further destabilize the distribution networks. The National Criminal Justice Commission assesses the situation in this way: "After police raid a drug corner, drug dealers usually pick up and move their operation to another block to continue. Police could never really *stop* the drug trade, they could only *displace* it. In the process of that displacement, violence erupted as dealers jockeyed to control market share. Experts who have studied the drug war have concluded that the amount of trafficking, lawlessness, and violence in the United States increased along with the all-out attempt to capture, prosecute, and imprison traffickers and users of illicit drugs." One journalist described this reality succinctly, "All the crackdown does is tear up turf and reshuffle turf and introduce additional chaos to the street, which leads to additional—and essentially gratuitous—violence sanctioned by a society ostensibly dedicated to bringing violence down."[88]

In addition to these unintended consequences, a strong case can be made that the clearly racist nature of the war on drugs is in itself an act of violence that produces further violence. Although drug usage in this country is distributed across all racial and ethnic groups, the efforts to combat the distribution and use of drugs have fallen most heavily on minority communities, primarily African-American ones. As the National Criminal Justice Commission points out, "African-American arrest rates for drugs during the height of the 'drug war' in 1989 were five times higher than arrest rates for Whites *even though Whites and African-Americans were using drugs at the same rate*. African-Americans make up 12% of the U.S. population and constitute 13% of all monthly drug users, but represent 35% of those arrested for drug possession, 55% of those convicted of drug convictions, and 74% of those sentenced to prison for drug possession."[89]

Another example of the racist nature of the war on drugs is the sentence disparities that exist between the two forms of cocaine—crack versus powder. Crack cocaine is made by dissolving powder cocaine in a solution of water and sodium bicarbonate and then boiling it and cutting it into rocks. Back in the late 1980s, crack became the street drug of choice in many urban areas, because it was much cheaper than its powder equivalent and gave users a more intense high. Although research has demonstrated that there are virtually no behavioral outcome differences between the two forms of cocaine, the penalty for trafficking or using crack is 100 times that of the penalty for dealing or using its powder counterpart. That is, under current law, a first-time offender who attempted to sell five grams of crack would receive a five-year mandatory minimum sentence, but it would take 500 grams of powder cocaine—100 times more—to receive the same five-year mandatory sentence. This disparity remains in force despite the U.S. Sentencing Commission's recommendation to Congress that the sentencing disparities should be removed.[90] Because African-Americans are much more likely to use crack, whereas Whites are more likely to use cocaine in powder form, the effect of these sentencing disparities is to condemn African-Americans to more punitive sentences for essentially the same act.

In sum, the war on drugs that has been raging in this nation has done very little to reduce the number of Americans using drugs. In fact, the demand for illicit drugs appears to be as great as ever; new synthetic drugs hit the streets every year, and new versions of older drugs also continue to emerge. For example, whereas heroin was historically stigmatized as a dirty drug because it had to be injected, a new breed of heroin is so potent that inhaling the powder produces the same high. This has served to enhance its appeal among young people. Although the war on drugs has not had the consequences that policy makers envisioned, it has more than quadrupled our nation's prison population. The wars being fought on America's streets for territory to distribute these drugs are similar to the gang wars fought for territory to distribute alcohol during Prohibition in the early part of the twentieth century.

SUMMARY

In this chapter, we have seen that the dynamics of American criminal homicide are greatly influenced by the use of firearms, the ingestion of alcohol, and the use, business, and prohibition of other drugs. Although it remains true that these guns and these substances do not cause murder, they are certainly contributory factors. When these facilitators are linked with certain cultural characteristics that equate masculinity with toughness and a readiness to engage in violence, it is not hard to understand how many seemingly minor conflicts may erupt in lethal violence. This is particularly so for many young men who perceive themselves as victims of an unjust society and who have few legitimate routes to the American Dream of wealth and status.

NOTES

1. Philippe Bourgois, *In Search of Respect: Selling Crack in El Barrio* (Cambridge, U.K.: Cambridge University Press, 1996), p. 26.

2. Claude Dallas Sr.'s son Claude Dallas Jr. was convicted of the murders of two Fish and Game officials. See Jack Olson, *Give a Boy a Gun: A True Story of Law and Disorder in the American West* (New York: Dell, 1985), pp. 207–208.

3. Jennifer Frey, "Broken Connections; a Fistfight, Gunshots and Two Teenage Sweethearts Are Dead. But That's Not Where the Story Ended," *Washington Post,* May 31, 2000, p. C01.

4. Alfred Blumstein, "Disaggregating the Violence Trends," in *The Crime Drop in America,* ed. Alfred Blumstein and Joel Wallman (Cambridge, U.K.: Cambridge University Press, 2000).

5. Scott H. Decker, Susan Pennell, and Ami Caldwell, *Illegal Firearms: Access and Use by Arrestees* (Washington, D.C.: National Institute of Justice, 1997).

6. Beth Bjerregaard and Alan J. Lizotte, "Gun Ownership and Gang Membership," *Journal of Criminal Law and Criminology,* 86, 37–59 (1995).

7. Marianne W. Zawitz, *Guns Used in Crime* (Washington, D.C.: U.S. Department of Justice, 1995).

8. Bureau of Justice Statistics, *Firearms and Crime Statistics.* http://www.ojp.usdoj.gov/bjs/guns.htm (retrieved July 16, 2000); Zawitz, *Guns Used in Crime.*

9. Ibid.

10. Franklin E. Zimring and Gordon Hawkins, *Crime Is Not the Problem: Lethal Violence in America,* ed. Michael Tonry and Norval Morris, *Studies in Crime and Public Policy* (New York: Oxford University Press, 1997).

11. Philip J. Cook and Mark H. Moore, "Guns, Gun Control, and Homicide: A Review of Research and Public Policy," in *Homicide: A Sourcebook of Social Research,* ed. M. Dwayne Smith and Margaret A. Zahn (Thousand Oaks, Calif.: Sage, 1999).

12. Zimring and Hawkins, *Crime Is Not the Problem,* p. 115.

13. National Center for Injury Prevention and Control, National Summary of Injury Mortality Data, 1987–1994 (Atlanta: Centers for Disease Control and Prevention, 1996).

14. J. L. Annest, J. A. Mercy, D. R. Gibson, and G. W. Ryan, "National Estimates of Nonfatal Firearm-Related Injuries: Beyond the Tip of the Iceberg," *Journal of the American Medical Association,* 283, 1749–1754 (1995).

15. National Center for Injury Prevention and Control, National Summary of Injury Mortality Data, 1987–1994.

16. Ted R. Miller and Mark A. Cohen, "Costs of Penetrating Injury," in *Textbook of Penetrating Trauma,* ed. Rao Ivatury and C. Gene Cayten (Philadelphia: Lee and Civiga, 1995).

17. Philip J. Cook et al., "The Medical Costs of Gunshot Injuries in the United States," *Journal of the American Medical Association,* 282, 447–454 (1999); Garen Wintemute and Mona A. Wright, "Initial and Subsequent Hospital Costs of Firearm Injuries," *Journal of Trauma,* 33, 556–560 (1992).

18. Tom Diaz, *Making a Killing: The Business of Guns in America* (New York: New Press, 1999), p. 50.

19. A. L. Kellermann et al., "Gun Ownership as a Risk Factor for Homicide in the Home," 329, 1084–1091 (1993).

20. Diaz, *Making a Killing*, p. 69.

21. Zawitz, *Guns Used in Crime*.

22. P. J. Cook and J. Ludwig, *Guns in America: Results of a Comprehensive National Survey on Firearms Ownership and Use* (Washington, D.C.: Police Foundation, 1996).

23. P. J. Cook, "Notes on the Availability and Prevalence of Firearms," *American Journal of Preventive Medicine*, 9, 33–38 (1993).

24. Diaz, *Making a Killing*.

25. Tom W. Smith, *1998 National Gun Policy Survey of the National Opinion Research Center: Research Findings* (Chicago: National Opinion Research Center, University of Chicago, 1999).

26. Louis Harris, *A Survey of Experiences, Perceptions, and Apprehensions About Guns among Young People in America* (Boston: Harvard University School of Public Health, 1993); Laura Kann et al., "Youth Risk Behavior Surveillance—United States, 1993," *Morbidity and Mortality Weekly Report*, 44, no. SS-1 (1995).

27. Philip J. Cook, "The Effect of Gun Availability on Robbery and Robbery Murder: A Cross-Section Study of 50 Large Cities," in *Policy Studies Review Annual*, ed. Robert H. Haveman and B. Bruce Zellner (Newbury Park, Calif.: Sage, 1979).

28. David McDowall, "Firearm Availability and Homicide Rates in Detroit, 1951–1986," *Social Forces*, 69(4), 1085–1101 (1991).

29. See, for example, Philip J. Cook, "The Effect of Gun Availability on Violent Crime Patterns," *Annals of the American Academy of Political and Social Science*, 445 (1981); Philip J. Cook, "The Technology of Personal Violence," in *Crime and Justice: A Review of Research*, ed. Michael Tonry (Chicago: University of Chicago Press, 1991); Albert J. Reiss, Jeffrey A. Roth, and the National Research Council, *Understanding and Preventing Violence* (Washington, D.C.: National Academy Press, 1993); Garen Wintemute, "Firearms as a Cause of Death in the United States, 1920–1982," *Journal of Trauma*, 27, 556–560 (1987); Zimring and Hawkins, *Crime Is Not the Problem*.

30. David B. Kopel, *The Samurai, the Mountie, and the Cowboy* (Buffalo, N.Y.: Prometheus, 1992).

31. Cook and Moore, "Guns, Gun Control, and Homicide," p. 277.

32. Gary Kleck, *Point Blank: Guns and Violence in America* (New York: Aldine de Gruyter, 1991); John R. Lott Jr., *More Guns, Less Crime*, 2nd edition, ed. William M. Landes and J. Mark Ramseyer, *Studies in Law and Economics* (Chicago: University of Chicago Press, 2000).

33. M. Dwayne Smith, "Sources of Firearm Acquisition among a Sample of Inner-City Youths: Research Results and Policy Implications," *Journal of Criminal Justice*, 24 (1996); James D. Wright and Peter H. Rossi, *Armed and Considered Dangerous* (New York: Aldine de Gruyter, 1986).

34. James D. Wright and Peter H. Rossi, *Armed and Considered Dangerous: A Survey of Felons and Their Firearms*, 2nd edition. (Hawthorne, N.Y.: Aldine de Gruyter, 1994).

35. William Oliver, *The Violent Social World of Black Men* (New York: Lexington Books, 1994), p. 62.

36. Linda Saltzman et al., "Weapon Involvement and Injury Outcomes in Family and Intimate Assaults," *Journal of the American Medical Association*, 267(22), 3043–3047 (1992).

37. P. J. Cook, "The Case of the Missing Victims: Gunshot Woundings in the National Crime Survey," *Journal of Quantitative Criminology*, 1, 91–102 (1985); Marianne W. Zawitz, *Firearm Injury from Crime* (Washington, D.C.: U.S. Department of Justice, 1996).

38. Marianne W. Zawitz and Kevin J. Strom, *Firearm Injury and Death from Crime, 1993–1997* (Washington, D.C.: Bureau of Justice Statistics, U.S. Department of Justice, 2000).

39. Zawitz, *Guns Used in Crime*.

40. Zawitz, *Firearm Injury from Crime*.

41. Diaz, *Making a Killing*, p. 104.

42. Quoted in Ibid., p. 103.

43. Zawitz, *Firearm Injury from Crime*.

44. Michael D. McGonigal et al., "Urban Firearm Deaths: A Five-Year Perspective," *Journal of Trauma,* 35, 532–537 (1993).

45. Wright, *Armed and Considered Dangerous.*

46. Zawitz, *Guns Used in Crime.*

47. See, for example, Diaz, *Making a Killing.*

48. Lawrence A. Greenfeld, *Alcohol and Crime: An Analysis of National Data on the Prevalence of Alcohol Involvement in Crime* (Washington, D.C.: U.S. Department of Justice, 1998).

49. For an extensive review of this literature, see B. J. Bushman and H. M. Cooper, "The Effects of Alcohol on Human Aggression: An Integrative Review," *Psychological Bulletin,* 107, 341–354 (1990); Robert N. Parker and Kathleen Auerhahn, "Alcohol, Drugs, and Violence," *Annual Review of Sociology* 24, 291–311 (1998).

50. Andrew Barr, *Drink: A Social History of America* (New York: Carroll & Graf, 1999).

51. Robert M. Utley, *High Noon in Lincoln: Violence on the Western Frontier* (Albuquerque: University of New Mexico Press, 1987), p. 176.

52. Quoted in David T. Courtwright, *Violent Land: Single Men and Social Disorder from the Frontier to the Inner City* (Cambridge, Mass.: Harvard University Press, 1996), pp. 91–92.

53. K. Pernanen, *Alcohol in Human Violence* (New York: Guilford Press, 1991).

54. Glenda Kaufman Kantor, "Alcohol and Spouse Abuse: Ethnic Differences," in *Recent Developments in Alcoholism: Volume 13, Alcohol and Violence,* ed. Marc Galanter (New York: Plenum Press, 1997). See also an original work documenting this connection in G. K. Kantor and M. A. Straus, "The 'Drunken Bum' Theory of Wife Beating," *Social Problems,* 34(3), 213–230 (1987).

55. Greenfeld, *Alcohol and Crime.*

56. H. L. Voss and J. R. Hepburn, "Patterns in Criminal Homicide in Chicago," *Journal of Criminal Law, Criminology, and Police Science,* 59(4), 499–508 (1968); Marvin Wolfgang, *Patterns of Criminal Homicide* (Philadelphia: University of Pennsylvania Press, 1958).

57. R. Wilson, H. Malin, and C. Lowman, "Uses of Mortality Rates and Mortality Indexes in Planning Alcohol Programs," *Alcohol Health and Research World,* 8(1), 41–53 (1983).

58. Robert Nash Parker and Randi S. Cartmell, "Alcohol and Homicide in the United States 1934–1995 — or One Reason Why U.S. Rates of Violence May Be Going Down," *Journal of Criminal Law and Criminology,* 88, 1369–1398 (1998).

59. See, for example, Gary G. Forrest and Robert H. Gordon, *Substance Abuse, Homicide, and Violent Behavior* (New York: Gardner Press, 1990).

60. S. P. Taylor, "Aggressive Behavior and Physiological Arousal as a Function of Provocation and the Tendency to Inhibit Aggression," *Journal of Personality,* 35, 297–310 (1967).

61. For a review of this literature, see Bushman and Cooper, "The Effects of Alcohol on Human Aggression."

62. For a discussion of this research, see Marcus Felson, *Crime and Everyday Life,* ed. George S. Bridges, Robert D. Crutchfield, and Joseph G. Weis, *The Pine Forge Press Series in Crime and Society* (Thousand Oaks, Calif.: Pine Forge Press, 1998).

63. Oscar Bukstein, David A. Brent, and Yifrah Kaminer, "Comorbidity of Substance Abuse and Other Psychiatric Disorders in Adolescents," *American Journal of Psychiatry,* September, 1131–1141 (1989); Michael Dettling et al., "Dopaminergic Responsivity in Alcoholism: Trait, State, or Residual Marker?" *American Journal of Psychiatry,* 152(9), 1317–1321 (1995).

64. C. Fernando Valenzuela, "Alcohol and Neurotransmitter Interactions," *Alcohol Health and Research World,* 21(2), 144–148 (1997).

65. Oliver, *The Violent Social World of Black Men,* p. 75.

66. Howard Abadinsky, *Drugs: An Introduction,* 4th edition. (Belmont, Calif.: Wadsworth Thomson, 2001).

67. Henry H. Brownstein, *The Social Reality of Violence and Violent Crime* (Boston: Allyn & Bacon, 2000), p. 18.

68. Paul Goldstein uses a similar classification scheme, although he recognizes only three types of drug-related violence: psychopharmacological, economic compulsive, and systemic. See Paul J. Goldstein, "The Drugs/Violence Nexus: A Tripartite Conceptual Framework," *Journal of Drug Issues,* 15(4), 493–506 (1985); Paul J. Goldstein et al., "Crack and Homicide in New York City, 1988: A Conceptually Based Event Analysis," *Contemporary Drug Problems,* 16(4), 651–687 (1990).

69. Abadinsky, *Drugs: An Introduction.*

70. For a review, see Parker and Auerhahn, "Alcohol, Drugs, and Violence."

71. Bureau of Justice Statistics, *Drugs and Crime Facts* (Washington, D.C: U.S. Department of Justice, 1992); Bureau of Justice Statistics, *Drugs, Crime, and the Justice System: A National Report from the Bureau of Justice Statistics* (Washington, D.C.: U.S. Department of Justice, 1992).

72. Samuel Walker, *Sense and Nonsense About Crime and Drugs: A Policy Guide* (Belmont, Calif.: Wadsworth Thomson, 2001).

73. Richard T. Wright and Scott H. Decker, *Armed Robbers in Action: Stickups and Street Culture* (Boston: Northeastern University Press, 1997).

74. Brownstein, *The Social Reality of Violence and Violent Crime,* p. 34.

75. Parker and Auerhahn, "Alcohol, Drugs, and Violence," p. 305.

76. Dennis M. Donovan, "Assessment of Addictive Behaviors: Implications of an Emerging Biophysical Model," in *Assessment of Addictive Behaviors,* ed. Dennis M. Donovan and G. Alan Marlatt (New York: Guilford Press, 1988), p. 6.

77. Abadinsky, *Drugs: An Introduction.*

78. Bureau of Justice Statistics, *Drugs, Crime, and the Justice System.*

79. Walker, *Sense and Nonsense About Crime and Drugs.*

80. David N. Nurco et al., "A Classification of Narcotics Addicts Based on Type, Amount, and Severity of Crime," *Journal of Drug Issues,* 21, 429–448 (1991).

81. Bureau of Justice Statistics, *Drugs, Crime, and the Justice System.*

82. Ibid.

83. Hope Corman, Theodore Joyce, and Naci Mocan, "Homicide and Crack in New York City," in *Searching for Alternatives: Drug-Control Policy in the United States,* ed. Melvyn B. Krauss and Edward P. Lazear (Stanford, Calif.: Hoover Institution Press, 1991).

84. Oliver, *The Violent Social World of Black Men,* p. 67.

85. Quoted in William Weir, *In the Shadow of the Dope Fiend* (North Haven, Conn.: Archon, 1995), p. 181.

86. Daniel K. Benjamin and Roger Leroy Miller, *Undoing Drugs: Beyond Legalization* (New York: Basic Books, 1991), pp. 86–87, 108.

87. See, for example, Steven R. Donziger, ed., *The Real War on Crime: The Report of the National Criminal Justice Commission* (New York: Harper Perennial, 1996); K. D. Harries, *Serious Violence* (Springfield, Ill.: Charles C. Thomas, 1990); Walker, *Sense and Nonsense About Crime and Drugs.*

88. Donziger, ed., *The Real War on Crime,* pp. 119–120.

89. Donziger, ed., *The Real War on Crime,* p. 115.

90. Donziger, ed., *The Real War on Crime.*

8

Capital Punishment

In using the death penalty, . . . the United States finds itself
in the uncomfortable company of such repressive regimes as The
People's Republic of China, Iran, Iraq, Korea, Libya, and South Africa.

RAYMOND PATERNOSTER[1]

Each time a person is executed, the effect upon the public
is infinitely more degrading than deterrent.

AMOS SQUIRE[2]

INTRODUCTION

So far in this book, we have examined forms of illegal killing that are committed by individuals. In this chapter, we are going to examine a type of legal killing. Specifically, the focus of this chapter is on capital punishment—the execution of convicted criminal or political offenders.

We discuss the death penalty for a variety of reasons. In many jurisdictions, the
death penalty is one of the possible penalties for first degree murder. Remember
that murders committed with premeditation and deliberation are considered
the worst type of murder, especially when they are accompanied by certain ac-

tions such as torture or rape. The punishment sometimes mandated for these especially heinous killings is the death penalty. One reason is that many people believe that capital punishment is a *deterrent* to potential murderers.[3] By executing prisoners who have committed murder, it is believed, other possible killers will think twice about killing, knowing that their own life will most likely be forfeit. But is this perception accurate? Does the death penalty truly deter? There are some who suggest the opposite, namely that capital punishment may ultimately contribute to higher criminal homicide rates.[4] This argument is summarized by Bill Bowers, who suggests that "the lesson of the execution, then, may be to devalue life by the example of human sacrifice. Executions demonstrate that it is correct and appropriate to kill those who have gravely offended us."[5] This *brutalization* argument, as Bowers terms it, asserts that the death penalty, by desensitizing society to killing and devaluing human life, increases tolerance toward lethal behavior and, therefore, increases the criminal homicide rate.

The public debate about violence and murder in the United States often centers around the death penalty as one possible solution. This chapter offers an exploration of this type of legal killing and its impact on our society and on criminal homicide.

THE DEATH PENALTY
IN THE UNITED STATES

Capital punishment has a very long history in the United States. In fact, long before the United States came into existence, lawbreakers were being executed. The first known recorded execution occurred in 1608, when Captain George Kendall, one of the original settlers of the Jamestown colony in Virginia, was put to death.[6] Since that time, approximately 15,000 executions have occurred in the United States. This figure is not, of course, an exact number but only an estimate developed by scholars relying on the limited historical evidence about capital punishment. A much better and more accurate estimate can be generated of the number of executions that have taken place in modern times. From 1930 until the end of 1999, there have been more than 4,400 official executions in the United States. We say *official* because this number does not reflect the number of lynchings and other forms of extralegal executions. Many of these lynchings could be described as *semi-official,* because they occurred with either the support or the knowledge of local law enforcement and judicial officials. The figure of more than 4,000 post-1930 executions reflects the number of executions that have occurred under local, state, or federal authority.

One important pattern in modern era executions is that the use of the death penalty has by no means been consistent over time. Exhibit 8.1 presents the annual number of executions recorded in the United States from 1930 until December 31, 1999. You can see that the annual number of executions was highest during the 1930s. In that decade, there were on average 175 executions per

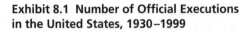

**Exhibit 8.1 Number of Official Executions
in the United States, 1930–1999**

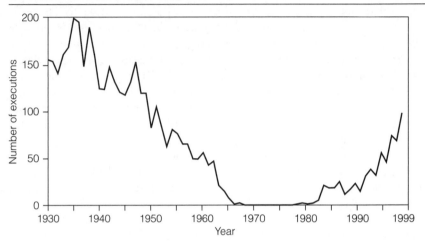

SOURCE: Tracy L. Snell, *Capital Punishment, 1999*. NCJ Report 184795, December 2000 (Washington, D.C.: Bureau of Justice Statistics, U.S. Department of Justice).

year, or about one every other day. There was a slight decline in the number of executions during the 1940s, but the annual average was generally quite stable. Beginning in the 1950s, however, the use of the death penalty steadily declined, from about 150 per year in the early 1950s to about 50 per year at the end of the decade. This steady decline continued during the 1960s, so that by 1968, there were no executions in the United States. This informal moratorium continued until 1977, since then there has been a fairly steady climb in the frequency of executions, although not to the level of the 1930s. Currently, the United States averages approximately 50 executions per year.

One very noticeable thing about the number of executions shown in Exhibit 8.1 is the absence of any executions during the period from 1967 to 1977. During this time, death penalty opponents, led by the Legal Defense Fund of the National Association for the Advancement of Colored People (NAACP), mounted constitutional challenges in federal courts against the states' use of capital punishment.[7] These challenges included the following arguments: (1) that death penalty jurors were selected in such a manner as to produce a jury that was biased in favor of returning a guilty verdict and the penalty of death;[8] (2) that the death penalty was administered disproportionately against minority defendants;[9] (3) that the death penalty was excessive punishment for the offenses of rape and armed robbery when no life was taken and, therefore, could be considered "cruel and unusual";[10] and (4) that the practice of using single verdict juries and standardless juries in capital cases was unconstitutional.[11] During this time, governors of death penalty states were not willing to sign an execution warrant and have anyone put to death so long as these important legal issues remained unresolved. This legal offensive also coincided with a time in which popular support for the death penalty was relatively low.

A resolution of sorts came in 1972, with the landmark United States Supreme Court case *Furman v. Georgia,* which took up the issue of standardless capital juries. In a sharply divided five-to-four decision in which each of the nine justices wrote their own opinion, the court held that the manner in which states administered the death penalty under standardless juries was unconstitutional. The justices did not hold that capital punishment was unconstitutional per se; rather, they objected to the way in which it was being applied. In other words, the methods by which the states imposed this punishment violated the due process rights of defendants. Too much discretion in the hands of capital juries produced an unconstitutional product, the court argued; death sentences were not always imposed on the most deserving and culpable criminals but were instead, in their own words, "arbitrary and capricious." [12] The court feared that there was little to distinguish between those who lived and those sentenced to death—other than bad luck or some impermissible factor such as race. In fact, one judge compared receiving the death penalty to being struck by lightning; both were seemingly random and unpredictable.

The *Furman* decision did not spell the end of capital punishment in the United States, but it did have three important consequences. The first result was a continuance of the moratorium on executions that had begun in mid-1967. The second effect of *Furman* was that all capital defendants then on death row (more than 600 of them) across the United States had their death sentences reduced to life imprisonment. The third major consequence of the *Furman* decision was to motivate states—at least those that wanted to retain capital punishment—to modify their statutes in order to deal with the problem of too much sentencing discretion in the hands of capital juries. State legislators went to work on the problem and devised two solutions. One solution was to eliminate jury sentencing discretion altogether by crafting *mandatory death statutes.* Under a mandatory statute, once a defendant is convicted of some special form of capital murder, the sentence automatically becomes a death sentence. Although juries have discretion as to the *type* of crime they convict a defendant of, that discretion evaporates once the defendant is convicted of capital murder. The second solution was not to eliminate jury discretion but to guide and limit it through what was called a *guided discretion statute.* These sentencing guidelines take the form of statutorily enumerated aggravating and mitigating factors that a capital jury is required to consider before sentencing a defendant to death. Examples of *aggravating factors* include the commission of another felony offense such as kidnapping, rape, or armed robbery, or the murder of a police officer. Examples of possible *mitigating factors* include the youthful age of the defendant, the fact that the defendant was under the influence of an emotional instability (though not sufficient to establish an insanity defense) at the time of the murder, or the lack of a violent criminal record. Some states adopted the mandatory solution to the problem of too much capital jury discretion, whereas others went the route of a guided discretion statute. [13]

In 1975, the United States Supreme Court reviewed the constitutionality of mandatory and guided discretion capital statutes. In a series of cases during that term,[14] the court determined that guided discretion statutes were constitutionally acceptable, because they narrowed the category of murder that would make a defendant eligible for the death penalty (murder plus at least one aggravating factor) but also allowed the sentencing authority to consider the unique culpability of individual defendants (through the consideration of mitigating factors).[15] The court, however, ruled that mandatory statutes were constitutionally unacceptable. The fatal flaw of a mandatory statute was that by its very nature, it did not allow the sentencing authority to consider the individual culpability of murder suspects, treating them instead "as members of a faceless, undifferentiated mass to be subjected to the blind infliction of the death penalty."[16] According to the Supreme Court, a constitutional death statute must allow the sentencing authority to consider each defendant's individual characteristics, attributes, and blameworthiness.

As a result of the decisions of the Supreme Court in 1976, the states were back in the death penalty business. The first execution that occurred after the end of the unofficial moratorium came on January 17, 1977, with the death of Gary Gilmore by firing squad in Utah. From the lifting of the moratorium in 1977 up to July 23, 2001, there have been 725 executions in the United States. Currently, 38 states have capital punishment statutes,[17] although not every state has carried out an execution under the newly reformed laws. Exhibit 8.2 lists the states that have had at least one execution since 1976. Notice that the number of state executions is not evenly distributed; about one third of the executions since 1976 have taken place in the state of Texas, and about two thirds have taken place in only five states (Texas, Virginia, Florida, Missouri, and Oklahoma). Most of these states carry out their executions by lethal injection. Exhibit 8.3 reports the method of execution that each state uses and shows that 34 states allow at least some of the condemned to die by lethal injection.[18]

At the end of 2000, there were more than 3,700 condemned persons on death row in 37 states,[19] and each year about 300 new death sentences are added to this list. Although less than 2% of these inmates are women, this still translates into 50 women on death row. More than half of all inmates on death row had less than an 11-grade education, and approximately 80 of them were arrested when they were 17 years old or younger.[20]

Although the annual number of executions today is nowhere near what it has been in the past, there is little likelihood that the use of the death penalty will disappear in the near future. There seem to be two reasons for this. The first, of course, is that the number of people awaiting their execution on death row across the United States is so large. The second reason why capital punishment will likely remain in the United States in the near future is that there continues to be much popular support for it. This, however, may be changing. Public opinion polls taken since the first post-moratorium execution in 1977 have indicated that a large majority of the United States population has felt some degree of support for the death penalty for criminals who commit murder. In the mid-1990s, this level of support peaked at 80% of the population.

**Exhibit 8.2 Number of Executions Carried out under State
Authority between 1976 and December 21, 2001, by State**

State	Number of Executions	State	Number of Executions
Texas	256	Utah	6
Virginia	83	Mississippi	4
Missouri	53	Washington	4
Florida	51	Maryland	3
Oklahoma	48	Nebraska	3
Georgia	27	Pennsylvania	3
Louisiana	26	Kentucky	2
South Carolina	25	Montana	2
Arkansas	24	Ohio	2
Alabama	23	Oregon	2
Arizona	22	Colorado	1
North Carolina	21	Idaho	1
Delaware	13	New Mexico	1
Illinois	12	Tennessee	1
California	9	Wyoming	1
Nevada	9	Federal	2
Indiana	9		

SOURCE: Death Penalty Information Center, *Number of Executions by State Since 1976.* http://www
.deathpenaltyinfo.org/dpicreg.html (retrieved April 9, 2001).

Support for the death penalty, however, is highly conditional and beginning to
decline. By 1999, support for capital punishment for convicted murderers had
declined to 71%.[21] Furthermore, this support is a little soft, because it declines
even further when respondents are asked if they favor the death penalty over
the punishment of life imprisonment without parole.

THE DEATH PENALTY INTERNATIONALLY

The United States is not alone among the nations of the world to employ the
death penalty either for common criminal offenses or for military or political
crimes. Amnesty International has reported that

- 75 countries have abolished the death penalty for all crimes.
- 12 countries have abolished the death penalty for all criminal offenses but
  retain it for exceptional crimes such as treason and crimes committed
  during wartime.
- 21 countries have abolished the death penalty in practice if not by law.
  They have retained capital punishment in their statutes, but they have not
  carried out an execution in the past 10 years.
- 87 countries both retain and use the death penalty.[22]

Exhibit 8.3 Method of Legal Execution in the United States by State

Lethal Injection	Electrocution	Lethal Gas	Hanging	Firing Squad
Arizona	Alabama	Arizona	Delaware	Idaho
Arkansas	Arkansas	California	New Hampshire	Oklahoma
California	Florida	Missouri	Washington	Utah
Colorado	Georgia	North Carolina		
Connecticut	Kentucky	Wyoming		
Delaware	Nebraska			
Idaho	Ohio			
Illinois	Oklahoma			
Indiana	South Carolina			
Kansas	Tennessee			
Kentucky	Virginia			
Louisiana				
Maryland				
Mississippi				
Missouri				
Montana				
Nevada				
New Hampshire				
New Jersey				
New Mexico				
New York				
North Carolina				
Ohio				
Oklahoma				
Oregon				
Pennsylvania				
South Carolina				
South Dakota				
Tennessee				
Texas				
Utah				
Virginia				
Washington				
Wyoming				

SOURCE: Tracy L. Snell, *Capital Punishment, 1999*. NCJ Report 184795, December 2000 (Washington, D.C.: Bureau of Justice Statistics, U.S. Department of Justice).

Although official, accurate counts are hard to come by, Amnesty International has estimated that in 1999, some 1,813 people were executed in 31 countries and that an additional 3,857 people were sentenced to death that year in 64 countries. It also reported the chilling figure that in 1999, 85% of all executions worldwide were performed in only five countries: China, Iran, Saudi Arabia, the Democratic Republic of the Congo—and the United States.

In sum, a minority of countries maintain the death penalty, and their number is growing smaller each year as the international trend appears to be toward abolition. Amnesty International has reported that in the past decade, more than 30 countries or territories have completely abolished the death penalty.[23] The drive for abolishing the death penalty is particularly strong in Europe. The Council of Europe has made the abolition of the death penalty a requirement for membership, and both the European Union and the United Nations Human Rights Commission have spoken out for a worldwide moratorium on the use of the death penalty.[24] It is rather ironic to say the least that the United States continues to rely so heavily on capital punishment when most democratic and advanced nations of the world have discarded it.

DEATH PENALTY JUSTIFICATIONS

Deterrence

One of the most frequently expressed reasons for supporting the death penalty is that it is believed to be a deterrent to serious crimes such as murder. The deterrence argument assumes that would-be murderers are rational actors, who contemplate the consequences of their actions and make decisions based on the costs and benefits of committing a crime. For example, a positive consequence of murder might be the permanent removal of an annoying or insulting person or of a business rival in the drug business. One of the negative consequences of committing murder would be that one could get caught, convicted, and punished. If the punishment for murder were light, would-be murderers would be more inclined to kill than if the punishment were heavy. The more severe the penalty, the deterrence argument goes, the less likely someone is to commit murder, because it has a greater cost. As the death penalty is the most severe sanction at the state's disposal, the fear of being executed is thought to be a steep enough penalty to discourage would-be killers from committing murder.

The deterrence argument, however, is actually more complicated than that. Because the question never compares the death penalty to *no* penalty for murder but rather the death penalty to long-term confinement in prison, the issue is actually one of *comparative* severity. That is, the question of deterrence should be, "Does the death penalty keep would-be murderers from committing their crime better than life imprisonment does?" To be a more effective punishment —in terms of a greater reduction in the number of murders committed—capital punishment must deter some people from committing murder who would not have been deterred had the possible punishment been only life imprisonment. Therefore, the deterrent argument for capital punishment actually relies on the assumption that a large number of people who would commit murder if the penalty were only life imprisonment would refrain from committing murder if they could possibly be executed.

A body of research has studied this issue empirically in a number of ways. Studies have

- examined the homicide rate in a particular state in the years before it abolished capital punishment and in the years after, to see if there is a difference;

- examined the homicide rate in a particular state in the years before it allowed capital punishment and in the years after the death penalty became law, to see if there is a difference;

- examined the homicide rates in two or more states that are comparable on other characteristics except the death penalty, to see if capital punishment states generally have lower homicide rates than life imprisonment states;

- used sophisticated statistical analyses to see if capital punishment deters more homicides than life imprisonment once other factors, such as population size, unemployment, and mean age of the population, have been taken into account.

When the issue is correctly framed as a matter of comparative deterrence, the collective weight of the evidence suggests that capital punishment is not a better deterrent than life imprisonment. After a comprehensive review of the literature, two prominent death penalty scholars concluded that "the available evidence remains 'clear and abundant' that, as practiced in the United States, capital punishment is not more effective than imprisonment in deterring murder."[25] In other words, the voluminous empirical evidence seems to show that if people are deterred from committing murder because they fear capital punishment, they will also be deterred by the fear of life imprisonment.

Incapacitation

A variation of the deterrence argument that speaks in favor of the death penalty is the incapacitation argument. This argument contends that capital punishment denies the executed murderer the opportunity to commit murder again and is the only sure way to protect the public, correctional officers, or other inmates from offenders who may kill again. At first glance, it is difficult to argue with this position. After all, executing someone does indeed deny them the opportunity to commit murder (or any other act) again. But as with deterrence, the incapacitation question is a comparative question: "Does capital punishment incapacitate murderers better than life imprisonment without parole?" Here again, it is inevitably true that capital punishment will incapacitate better than any alternative penalty, such as life imprisonment with no parole, simply because death precludes any further activity, including crime. With the death penalty, the probability that the executed offender will commit another crime is zero. With life imprisonment, however, there is always the possibility that the prisoner could either escape and kill someone in the community or kill a guard or inmate during his or her confinement.[26] The difficult question to answer is whether capital punishment incapacitates much better than life imprisonment.

Let us deal first with the issue of an imprisoned murderer escaping confinement and killing an innocent citizen while at large. There are no really good data on this question, because there is not a single documented case where a convicted first degree murderer serving a life sentence without parole has escaped and committed other crimes. The number of inmates serving parolable life sentences who have escaped from confinement and have committed other crimes is also extremely small. Two scholars, James Marquart and John Sorensen, have studied the behavior of condemned inmates who had their death sentences commuted to life imprisonment as a result of the previously mentioned *Furman* decision (more than 500 former death row inmates).[27] This is a good group to study because the inmates had been sentenced to death but then were returned to the regular prison population to serve their life sentences. The researchers did not find a single inmate from this group who had escaped confinement and committed new crimes. It would appear, therefore, that at least as far as protecting the public is concerned, life imprisonment is as effective at incapacitation as the death penalty.

But wouldn't convicted first degree murderers serving life without parole constitute a grave danger to correctional staff and other inmates, because they have really nothing to lose? The evidence indicates that they do not. In the same study of 558 death row inmates returned to the regular prison population following the *Furman* decision, Marquart and Sorensen found that six killings had been committed in prison by this group: four victims were other inmates, and two victims were correctional officers.[28] Considering the cumulative time period (558 inmates with an average time studied in the population of 15 years is 8,370 person-years), the probability of one of these offenders killing within the institution is .0007. That is, it was very unlikely that any one of these inmates who were sentenced to death would kill while behind bars. We must certainly admit that the probability of killing behind bars is not *exactly* zero, as it would have been had all these inmates been put to death. However, our point is that the marginal difference in incapacitation between capital punishment and life imprisonment is small. In fact, at least as far as these *Furman*-commuted inmates are concerned, 100 of them would have had to be executed in order to incapacitate one future killer.

Retribution

The third justification that is usually offered in support of capital punishment is retribution. The retributive argument is not utilitarian; that is, it does not argue that there will be a net benefit if first degree murderers are executed—in other words, that the death penalty will prevent murders against the public or against other inmates. The retributive position is a moral one, arguing that convicted murderers should be executed simply because they deserve to be. This position argues for a strict interpretation of the *lex talionis*—an eye for an eye. It asserts that justice requires that those who kill have their life taken from them. Note that no real empirical data can be brought to bear on the retributive position; you either believe in it or you don't.

We can, however, question the retribution argument on the grounds of moral consistency. Moreover, this argument may suggest punishments that we as a civilized society would find intolerable on other grounds. For example, if we take the retributive position that one who kills another forfeits the right to life and must be killed, then we must admit that this would require (1) that *only* murderers be sentenced to death and (2) that *all* convicted murderers be sentenced to death. The first component—that only those who take a life can have their life taken—is not too difficult to achieve, because most states only allow murderers to be eligible for the death penalty.[29] The second component—that all murderers be executed—is a little more difficult for supporters of retribution to deal with. The policy of executing all murderers is, first of all, inconsistent with existing U.S. constitutional law. The U.S. Supreme Court decided in *Woodson v. North Carolina* and *S. Roberts v. Louisiana* that mandatory capital statutes are unconstitutional because they fail to treat individuals according to their unique culpabilities. Second, a policy of executing all murderers ignores the commonsense fact that not every first degree murder is alike. Some murders are more aggravated than others (they involve additional felonies like rape or kidnapping, the victim was tortured before dying, the offender has a previous conviction of murder, more than one victim was murdered, and so on), and others are less aggravated than others (the offender was young, the offender was under the influence of drugs, alcohol, or emotional instability, the offender immediately turned him- or herself in, showed a great deal of remorse, and so forth). These critical differences among murders and murderers suggest that some but not all murderers may morally deserve to die.

Another problem with strict retribution that demands an eye for an eye is that it could lead to absurd, even uncivilized punishments if strictly enforced. For example, suppose we have an offender convicted of kidnapping a young woman and raping and torturing her before killing her. Would a strict eye-for-an-eye brand of retribution require that we also torture and rape this offender before executing him? Such a strict and literal brand of retribution would demand punishments that are at odds with a modern, humane, and civilized society. Moreover, the requirements of literal retribution cannot reasonably be met in cases of multiple murder. Would the only morally just punishment be to inflict pain and injury on these offenders to within an inch of their life, revive them, repeat the process for as many victims as they have killed, and then execute them?

Is it possible to take a retributive position and not require it to be literal? The answer is yes. *Proportional retribution* would only require that those who commit the most serious crimes be punished more than those who commit less serious crimes.[30] It would not require that we attempt to exactly pay back the transgressor or that the nature of the punishment reflect exactly or literally the harm done by the crime. However, it would likely also require that the penalties inflicted not trivialize the moral harm of the offense. Punishing first degree murderers with life imprisonment without parole would be consistent with proportional retribution. A very severe punishment would be visited upon a serious offense, but the penalty of life without parole would not be so minor as to trivialize the moral harm of a first degree murder.

Another way to examine the death penalty involves not looking at the underlying rationale for its use but rather at the ways in which it is applied. In many ways, the application of capital punishment in America is problematic.

PROBLEMS IN ADMINISTERING THE DEATH PENALTY

Many problems have arisen in the United States with the administration of the death penalty. Although most of these problems have plagued the administration of capital punishment since its early years, we will concentrate our examination on the more modern manifestations of these problems. These problems are (1) the cost of administering the death penalty, (2) the magnitude of racial discrimination in the capital punishment process, and (3) the danger of making errors in convicting or executing innocent people.

Cost

Proponents of the death penalty frequently claim that executing murderers is less expensive than having to support them in prison for life. Like many other issues about capital punishment that we have covered thus far, this issue is more complex than it first appears. It is undoubtedly true that it would be less expensive for a state to execute its convicted first degree murderers soon after a capital trial, but in this day and age it is simply not possible for states to execute convicted murderers soon after their trial.

Capital trials are not normal trials for many reasons, the most relevant of which concerns the fact that they are much more expensive to bring to a conclusion than a noncapital murder trial. For one thing, capital trials are *bifurcated*, which simply means that there are actually two trials in one. The first trial determines guilt or innocence, and if a defendant is found guilty of first degree murder, a second or penalty trial determines the punishment. Capital trials are also more expensive than noncapital trials because they typically involve intense legal wrangling, motion writing, investigation, and legal effort. In fact, at every point of the trial from beginning to end, a capital trial takes longer, involves more labor, and is more costly than a noncapital trial. For example, it has been reported that the number of pretrial motions in a capital case is more than two times greater than the number in a noncapital murder case.[31] These pretrial motions tend to be more complex, more heavily argued, and result in more delays and costs than in noncapital cases. There are special procedures for jury selection or *voir dire* in capital cases; jury selection is usually done individually, with sequestration, and more potential jurors are examined in greater detail than in noncapital cases. The costs of investigation are also substantially higher in a capital case. Such investigations must be undertaken for issues raised at both the guilt and the penalty phase of a capital trial. Both the prosecution and the defense hire investigation experts who examine every aspect of the crime, locate and interview witnesses, and ensure their appearance at trial. An adequate investigation requires extensive time and money for locating and interviewing the defendant's family, relatives, employers, and neighbors. For these and other reasons, investigations have been estimated to take three to five times longer in capital cases than in noncapital cases.[32]

Another reason why a capital trial is more expensive than a noncapital murder trial is that the appeals process in the former is extremely complex and extensive. Unlike noncapital cases, there is an automatic appeal to a state appeals court whenever a death sentence is imposed. Moreover, capital defendants can pursue both state and federal levels of appeal, along with at least one appeal to the U.S. Supreme Court. When a case is successfully appealed, it may result in the requirement that the state conduct a completely new trial, with all the expense that entails, or it may result in the state having to do the penalty phase over. If a conviction and death sentence is imposed again, the appeals process starts anew. Not surprisingly, because a defendant's life is at stake, appeals in capital cases involve numerous and complex issues that sometimes take years to resolve. Although the Supreme Court has in recent years tried to shorten the appeals process, it is not expected that there will be any dramatic effect on its length. In fact, since 1995, the average length of time from sentence to execution has only decreased by four months. On average, a ten-year period elapses between the imposition of the death penalty and the execution.

Critics of the appeals process in capital cases may be tempted to conclude that the obvious solution would be to drastically curtail appeals. However attractive this solution for cutting the costs of a capital case may appear, there is a very good reason to carefully review death sentences, namely the danger of executing innocent people. This risk is more than theoretical; since 1977, approximately 80 people have been released from death row because they were later found to be innocent.[33] Many of these individuals came within hours of being executed. Moreover, the possibility of a mistake in a capital case is not remote. A recent study found substantial errors in approximately two thirds of the death sentences imposed, and these errors were not mere legal technicalities but involved substantial transgressions, such as ineffective assistance of counsel, the withholding of evidence by police, and prosecutorial misconduct.[34] Here are a few examples:

- Kerry Max Cook has spent 18 years on death row for the 1977 murder of a Texas woman. Cook's conviction was based in large part on a jailhouse snitch who testified that Cook confessed to him about the killing. After Cook's first trial, this informant recanted his earlier testimony and admitted that in exchange for testifying against Cook, the prosecutor reduced his own murder charge to involuntary manslaughter and almost immediately released him from prison for time served. The prosecutor did not disclose any of these facts to Cook's original trial lawyer.[35]

- Oklahoma City prosecutor Robert Macy has put 53 defendants on death row. One of them was Clifford Henry Bowen, a 50-year-old professional poker player with a history of committing burglaries. Macy put Bowen on death row for the slaying of three men at an Oklahoma City motel at two o'clock in the morning. Bowen, however, had a good alibi. Twelve witnesses testified that he was at a rodeo 300 miles away in Tyler, Texas, until midnight on the night of the killing. The prosecution's case argued that Bowen may have taken a private plane from Tyler to Oklahoma City, even though there was no evidence to support such a theory, and the airstrip in Texas that Bowen supposedly used was both too small and abandoned. Furthermore, Macy had another suspect in the killing, who fit the description of eyewitnesses and against whom there was substantial evidence. Macy never notified Bowen's defense counsel that he had another suspect or solid evidence against that suspect. Bowen was convicted for the killings and sentenced to death. A federal appeals court, however, threw out the conviction five years later, castigating prosecutor Macy for withholding such crucial evidence.[36]

We could go on, but it should be clear by now that there is a very real danger in streamlining the capital appeals process too much. There is strong evidence that mistakes are made at the trial level and that innocent people are convicted far too often. If we as a society wish to maintain the death penalty, we must also be willing to assume the financial burden to ensure its proper administration. These costs are significant. Florida, for example, spends about $3.2 million for every execution, whereas Texas spends approximately $2.3 million and, in fact, spent more than $183 million on death penalty cases during one six-year period. From 1977 until 1996, the state of California executed five men for a grand total of more than $1 billion.[37]

The Role of Race

Race has always been part of the question of capital punishment in the United States. Under the Black Codes of the 1800s, African-Americans could be sentenced to death for offenses that were punishable at most by a prison term if committed by Whites. For example, an 1816 Georgia law provided for the imprisonment of Whites convicted of rape, whereas slaves and free Blacks could be—and were—put to death.[38] In addition to murder and rape, African-Americans were routinely sentenced to death and executed for the attempted rape of White women, for attempted murder, arson, and burglary, whereas Whites convicted of these crimes were punished far more leniently, or not at all if the victims were Black.[39]

Racial discrimination in the imposition of the death penalty continued after the Civil War. During the years from 1930 to 1968, there were 3,334 executions of defendants convicted of murder. One half of those executed were

Exhibit 8.4 Homicides Leading to Execution by Race of Offender and Victim since 1977

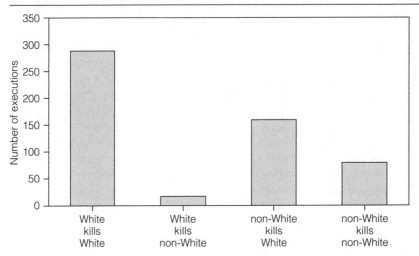

SOURCE: National Association for the Advancement of Colored People, *Death Row U.S.A.* (NAACP Legal Defense and Education Fund, 2000).

African-American, even though African-Americans constituted less than 20% of the population. There was even greater racial disparity among those executed for rape. Of the 455 executions for rape during this period, nearly 90% were African-Americans. In southern states, 400 rapists were executed; 398 (99.5%) of them were African-American.[40]

There is little evidence to indicate that the influence of race on the capital process has been eliminated under modern, procedurally reformed death statutes. Exhibit 8.4 shows the race of the victim–offender combinations for 588 of the executions that have taken place since 1977.[41] For ease of presentation, the victim's and the offender's race have been categorized as either White or non-White. Several clear patterns emerge here. First, a slightly higher proportion of White offenders have been executed than non-White offenders (56% of those executed were White, and 44% were non-White). Second, a substantially higher proportion of those executed had killed White victims. Of those executed since 1977, 82% were put to death for killing a White victim, compared to only 28% for killing a non-White victim. The disparity by the race of the victim is particularly dramatic. Offenders are far less likely to be put to death if they kill a non-White person. These initial disparities by race are only suggestive, however, because they may reflect relevant case characteristics. For example, perhaps killings involving White victims are more brutal and aggravated than those committed against non-White victims, thus producing the racial disparities we see in Exhibit 8.4. In order to examine this possibility, more detailed data are needed.

One of the most comprehensive examinations of the role of race in modern capital punishment systems was conducted by David Baldus and his colleagues. Their study examined more than 2,000 homicides that occurred in Georgia during the 1970s. After extensive analyses, they concluded that even taking into account the seriousness of the offense, the criminal history of the offender, and other relevant case characteristics, defendants charged with killing White victims were 4.3 times more likely to receive a death sentence than defendants charged with killing an African-American.[42] Baldus's data are consistent with the interpretation that White lives are more valuable in Georgia than the lives of African-Americans. Several other studies have found results that are consistent with Baldus's original findings. In fact, after a review of 28 such studies, the U.S. General Accounting Office concluded that they consistently showed a strong influence from the race of the victim.[43]

In spite of the consistent social science evidence that race affects the decision whether to sentence someone to death, the U.S. Supreme Court has not been receptive to the argument about discrimination in the application of the death penalty. The Baldus evidence was presented to the Supreme Court in *McCleskey v. Kemp*.[44] After examining the evidence, which showed a marked pattern of discrimination, the court rejected the argument, claiming that "at most, the Baldus study indicates a discrepancy that appears to correlate with race." Though dismissing the Baldus evidence in itself, the court did argue that statistical evidence of racial discrimination in capital sentences should be presented to state legislatures.

Errors

As we noted earlier, one of the problems with any capital punishment system is that it is operated by human beings and, therefore, is not error free. As yet, there is no documented case of an innocent person having been executed. The key word here, of course, is *documented*. However, there is ample evidence that defendants have been wrongly convicted of capital crimes, placed on death row, and in some cases have come within hours of being executed before the mistake was acknowledged. A recent study by Columbia University law professor James S. Liebman and two associates found that since 1970, there have been 80 documented cases of innocent persons being released from death row.[45] Since 1977, the state of Illinois has sent 11 men to the death chamber, but it has also released 13 innocent men from death row. This finding led Republican and pro−death penalty Illinois governor George Ryan to impose a moratorium on executions in the state. Illinois, however, is not alone in sending innocent people to death row because of poor lawyering, shoddy or corrupt police work, or prosecutorial misconduct. It is instructive to examine a few of these cases, not because they are extraordinary but because they are very common and characteristic of the capital punishment system as a whole.

In 1984, Kirk Bloodsworth was convicted and sentenced to death for the sexual assault and killing of nine-year-old Dawn Hamilton. There was no physical evidence linking Bloodsworth to the crime, and he was convicted primarily on the basis of the testimony of two children and an adult who claimed that Bloodsworth looked like a man whom they had seen with Dawn earlier in the day. Bloodsworth was granted a new trial by an appeals court because the prosecution had withheld evidence about another possible suspect in the crime from the defense. Although Bloodsworth was convicted again in this second trial, he continued to maintain his innocence. A new volunteer lawyer took Bloodsworth's case and discovered that the police did have physical evidence at the scene in sufficient quantity to allow DNA testing. The DNA tests showed that the sexual attacker of Dawn Hamilton could not have been Kirk Bloodsworth. A second batch of DNA tests completed by the FBI's crime laboratory confirmed Bloodsworth's innocence. After spending nine years in prison—two of them on Maryland's death row—Kirk Bloodsworth was finally released a free man.

Steve Manning, a former Chicago police officer, was convicted and sentenced to death in 1993 for the murder of James Pellegrino, a suburban Chicago trucking firm owner. His cell mate Joseph Dye testified at Manning's trial that Manning had admitted committing the execution-style killing during six hours of taped conversations between the two in the jail cell they shared. When the tapes were played in court, however, no confession was heard. Dye explained that the confession occurred in a two-second-long gap in the recording when the tape malfunctioned. There was no physical evidence connecting Manning to the murder, and Dye was no model witness; he had a criminal record that went back 15 years, and a federal prosecutor had once called him a pathological liar. In exchange for Dye's testimony, his prison sentence was cut by more than half, he and his girlfriend were placed in a witness protection program, and other criminal charges against him were dropped. Dye had also been used—and been known to lie—in other criminal cases. Manning's conviction was later reversed on other grounds.

In another case, law professor and death penalty lawyer Stephen Bright writes of a Talladega, Alabama, woman who was accused of murdering her physically abusive husband. Women who are convicted of killing their abusive husbands are rarely sentenced to death; however, this woman was—and her court-appointed lawyer may have been part of the reason. He was so drunk on the first day of the trial that it had to be delayed for a day—he was held in contempt and sent to jail. The trial resumed the next day. The lawyer never presented evidence from hospital records that documented the extensive abuse that the woman and her daughter endured at the hands of her husband. The lawyer did not bring an expert witness on domestic abuse to visit and interview the defendant until the evening before the expert testified. Not surprisingly, the woman was sentenced to death after a trial that lasted only a few days.[46]

The Bloodsworth and Manning cases and the case of the Talladega woman are only three of a growing number of examples showing that our capital punishment system is fraught with errors and injustice. Sometimes, the police conspire to frame innocent people by extracting confessions or simply by sloppy police work. Other times, prosecutors fail to inform defense counsel of critical and helpful information or even outright conceal and bury evidence that might support the defendant's innocence. More frequently, the defendant is poor and handicapped by a court-appointed lawyer or overworked public defender, both of whom have few resources to mount an adequate defense. Although there is no solid evidence that our system of capital punishment has executed an innocent person, there is ample evidence to indicate that it is broken.[47]

The aforementioned study by Liebman, Fagan, and West found many significant flaws in the death penalty system, describing it as "a system collapsing under the weight of its own mistakes." Specific findings included an error rate of 68% in capital cases nationwide during a 23-year period. Keep in mind that these were errors significant enough to reverse the legal decision. The authors of the study assert that so many mistakes were made that at least three judicial reviews were needed. Unfortunately, even multiple judicial reviews cannot guarantee an error-free process. Several of the most common reasons that prompted decision reversals included incompetent defense attorneys, who didn't find or didn't even try to find evidence vindicating their clients, and prosecutors who suppressed evidence supporting the innocence of the accused.[48] With problems such as these occurring as often as they do, it is easy to understand why many scholars believe the system is broken.

SUMMARY

In this chapter, we have talked about one specific form of killing that is legitimately perpetrated by the state—capital punishment. Capital punishment was at one time a very popular punishment. Historically, it was used by the vast majority of countries in the world for a wide variety of offenses. Today, however, the death penalty is becoming rare. Unlike all European countries, however, the United States has not abandoned it.

In the course of this chapter, we also discussed several problems in administering the death penalty. A system of criminal justice that includes the death penalty is probably much more expensive than one that has abolished it. Capital cases are expensive to run, from jury selection to presenting a case during the penalty phase. Furthermore, although there are attempts to shorten the appeals process, a complex of appeals is routinely undertaken in capital cases, and the evidence indicates that such a careful screening may be appropriate, given the significant possibility of errors in capital cases. We also examined the link between racial discrimination and capital punishment in the United States. Historically, capital punishment has been used disproportionately against racial minorities, and recent research strongly suggests that racial discrimination still exists, though perhaps in a more subtle form. Finally, we examined how innocent people have been erroneously convicted of murder or put on death row because of corrupt police and prosecutors or, more commonly, incompetent lawyers.

NOTES

1. Raymond Paternoster, *Capital Punishment in America* (Lexington, Ky.: Lexington Books, 1991), p. 285.

2. Amos O. Squire, *Sing Sing Doctor* (New York: Garden City, 1937).

3. Paternoster, *Capital Punishment in America.*

4. William J. Bowers, *Legal Homicide* (Boston: Northeastern University Press, 1984), p. 274. See also William J. Bowers and Glenn L. Pierce, "Arbitrariness and Discrimination under Post-Furman Capital Statutes," *Crime and Delinquency,* 26, 563–635 (1980); Derral Cheatwood, "Capital Punishment and the Deterrence of Violent Crime in Comparable Counties," *Criminal Justice Review,* 18, 991–1014 (1993).

5. Bowers, *Legal Homicide.*

6. Mark Costanzo, *Just Revenge: Costs and Consequences of the Death Penalty* (New York: St. Martin's Press, 1997).

7. Michael Meltsner, *Cruel and Unusual Punishment: The Supreme Court and Capital Punishment* (New York: Random House, 1987).

8. *Witherspoon v. Illinois,* 391 U.S. 510 (1968).

9. *Maxwell v. Bishop,* 398 F. 2d 138 (1968).

10. *Rudolph v. Alabama,* 375 U.S. 889 (1963); *Boykin v. Alabama,* 395 U.S. 238 (1969).

11. *McGautha v. California,* 402 U.S. 183 (1971). In a *single verdict trial,* the jury hears information about both the guilt or innocence of the defendant and the appropriate punishment. At the end of the trial, the jury deliberates at a single sitting to determine both guilt and punishment questions. The single verdict trial is different from a *bifurcated* trial. In the bifurcated capital trial, the jury first hears information solely about the question of guilt. At the end of the guilt trial or guilt phase, the jury deliberates about the guilt or innocence of the defendant. If the jury convicts the defendant of capital murder, the trial then advances to a second trial, the penalty phase. At this separate hearing, the jury hears information about the appropriate punishment in the case. After the penalty phase trial, the jury then deliberates again, this time solely about what penalty should be imposed. A *standardless* capital trial is one in which the jury is told very little about what it should consider in deciding whether the defendant should live or die. For example, a jury may be instructed that it cannot consider mercy or should not be moved by passion or prejudice, but within these parameters, the jury has complete discretion as to what factors they should consider and how much they should weight them in the life–death decision. Critics complain that such juries are given no guidance or standards to apply in making the penalty decision—that they are *standardless.* The lack of standards, critics argue, gives the jury too much sentencing discretion, and juries may let one defendant live and sentence another to die solely on the basis of whim or caprice.

12. *Furman v. Georgia,* 408 U.S. 238 (1972), pp. 309–310.

13. Paternoster, *Capital Punishment in America.*

14. The relevant cases are *Gregg v. Georgia,* 428 U.S. 153 (1976); *Jurek v. Texas,* 428 U.S. 262 (1976); *Proffitt v. Florida,* 428 U.S. 242 (1976); *S. Roberts v. Louisiana,* 428 U.S.325 (1976); and *Woodson v. North Carolina,* 428 U.S. 280 (1976).

15. The Supreme Court also seemed to imply in its 1976 decisions that constitutionally approved capital statutes would have to have some form of statewide review of each death sentence to ensure its correctness on the facts and to guarantee that it was not disproportionate to the penalty imposed on other, similar cases. In a subsequent decision, however, the U. S. Supreme Court was to hold that this last requirement, called *proportionality review,* was not required. See *Pulley v. Harris,* 465 U.S. 37 (1984).

16. *Woodson v. North Carolina,* 428 U. S. 280 (1976), p. 305.

17. Two other jurisdictions with capital punishment statutes are the U.S. Government and the U.S. Military. Abolitionist

jurisdictions include Alaska, the District of Columbia, Hawaii, Iowa, Maine, Massachusetts, Michigan, Minnesota, North Dakota, Rhode Island, Vermont, West Virginia, and Wisconsin. The only state that has a capital punishment statute but no death sentences imposed as of December 31, 1999, is New Hampshire. Death Penalty Information Center, *Death Row.* http://www.deathpenaltyinfo.org/ (retrieved April 10, 2001).

18. As you can see from Exhibit 8.3, some states allow two forms of execution. For example, the state of Delaware authorizes lethal injection as the method of carrying out the death penalty if the offense occurred after June 13, 1986, but the condemned may choose between lethal injection or hanging if the offense occurred before that date. The method of execution authorized by states has tended toward lethal injection and away from previous methods such as the firing squad, hanging, lethal gas, or the electric chair.

19. National Association for the Advancement of Colored People, *Death Row U.S.A.* (New York: NAACP Legal Defense and Education Fund, 2000).

20. Tracy L. Snell, *Capital Punishment, 1999. NCJ 184795.* (Washington, D.C.: Bureau of Justice Statistics, U.S. Department of Justice, 2000).

21. Michael L. Radelet and Marian J. Borg, "The Changing Nature of the Death Penalty Debates," *Annual Review of Sociology,* 26, 43–61 (2000).

22. *Amnesty International Report 1999* (London: Amnesty International, 1999). Information about the use of the death penalty in the United States and other countries can readily be obtained from the Amnesty International Web site: http://www.web.amnesty.org

23. Ibid.

24. Mary L. Dudziak, "Giving Capital Offense," *Civilization,* 7(Oct./Nov.), 50 (2000).

25. William C. Bailey and Ruth D. Peterson, "Murder, Capital Punishment, and Deterrence: A Review of the Literature," in *The Death Penalty in America,* ed. Hugo A. Bedau (New York: Oxford University Press, 1997).

26. Because the alternative sentence we are considering is life without parole, we preclude the possibility that the convicted murderer is serving a life sentence with the possibility of parole. With a parolable life sentence, the issue of the released murderer killing while on parole is a little more difficult to address. However, we would like to note that even when convicted first degree murderers are sentenced to life imprisonment with the possibility of parole, they must serve a long period of time before becoming eligible for parole. For example, in Texas, a convicted first degree murderer under a life sentence must serve 35 years before becoming eligible for parole; in the state of Kansas, the cutoff is 40 years. One consequence of this is that even if released, paroled murderers are old, well past their prime for committing violent crimes.

27. James W. Marquart and Jonathan Sorensen, "Institutional and Post-Release Behavior of *Furman*-Commuted Inmates in Texas," *Criminology,* 26, 677–693 (1988).

28. Marquart and Sorensen, "Institutional and Post-Release Behavior."

29. Some states permit the execution of those who, though not the actual killers, played a major role in a felony crime involving homicide and by their actions showed a reckless indifference to human life. See *Tison v. Arizona,* 481 U.S. 137 (1987).

30. See Stephen Nathanson, *An Eye for an Eye? The Immorality of Punishing by Death* (Totowa, N.J.: Rowman & Littlefield, 1987).

31. M. Garey, "The Cost of Taking a Life: Dollars and Sense of the Death Penalty," *University of California Law Review,* 8, 1221–1270 (1985); Robert L. Spangenberg and Elizabeth R. Walsh, "Capital Punishment or Life Imprisonment? Some Cost Considerations," *Loyola of Los Angeles Law Review,* 23, 47–58 (1989).

32. Garey, "The Cost of Taking a Life."

33. Radelet and Borg, "The Changing Nature of the Death Penalty Debates."

34. See Henry Weinstein, "Death Penalty Is Overturned in Most Cases," *Los Angeles Times,* June 12, 2000, p. A01.

35. *NACDL . . . and Justice for All.* (Washington, D.C.: National Association of Criminal Defense Lawyers, 2000).

36. Ken Armstrong, "'True Patriot' Not Quite a Shining Star," *Chicago Tribune,* January 10, 1999, p. 13.

37. For a thorough discussion, see Costanzo, *Just Revenge.*

38. Bowers, *Legal Homicide.*

39. Kenneth M. Stampp, *The Peculiar Institution: Slavery in the Ante-Bellum South* (New York: Vintage Books, 1956).

40. Timothy J. Flanagan and Kathleen Maguire, *Sourcebook of Criminal Justice Statistics, 1989* (Washington, D.C.: U.S. Department of Justice, Bureau of Justice Statistics, 1990), pp. 631–632.

41. Ten defendants who were executed for the multiple murders of different races were excluded from Exhibit 8.4. See NAACP, *Death Row U.S.A.*

42. David Baldus, George Woodworth, and Charles Pulaski, *Equal Justice and the Death Penalty.* (Boston: Northeastern University Press, 1990).

43. *Death Penalty Sentencing: Research Indicates Pattern of Racial Disparities* (Washington, D.C.: U.S. General Accounting Office, 1990). More recent research by Professor Baldus in Philadelphia has found that African-American defendants are more likely to be sentenced to death than White defendants. See David Baldus et al., "Racial Discrimination and the Death Penalty in the Post-Furman Era: An Empirical and Legal Overview with Recent Findings from Philadelphia," *Cornell Law Review,* 83, 1638–1670 (1998).

44. *McCleskey v. Kemp,* 481 U.S. 279 (1989).

45. James S. Liebman, Jeffrey Fagan, and Valerie West, *A Broken System: Error Rates in Capital Cases, 1973–1995.* http://justice.policy.net/jpreport/index.html (retrieved July 15, 2001).

46. Stephen B. Bright, "Counsel for the Poor: The Death Sentence Not for the Worst Crime but for the Worst Lawyer," *Yale Law Journal,* 103, 1835–1883 (1994).

47. Has at least one innocent person been put to death? Joseph O'Dell was executed in 1997 for the rape and murder of Helen Schartner in Virginia Beach, Virginia. O'Dell's conviction was based in part on testimony from a state forensic expert that blood found on O'Dell was "consistent" with the victim's. In 1990, more sophisticated DNA tests conclusively demonstrated that the blood found on O'Dell could not have come from Schartner. In 1997, O'Dell asked the state to perform new state-of-the-art DNA tests on the physical evidence it had. New methods, developed after O'Dell's original conviction, would have resolved the question whether O'Dell was the offender or not. The state refused the tests, and O'Dell was executed. After O'Dell's death, his attorney and the Roman Catholic Diocese of Richmond asked the court to release samples of the physical evidence, so that they could conduct the relevant DNA tests. The court and the state of Virginia refused and subsequently destroyed the evidence.

48. Liebman et al., *A Broken System.*

9

Where Do We
Go from Here?

Hidden Victims
and Social Policy

It is estimated that each homicide victim is survived by
an average of three loved ones for whom the violent
death produces a painful and traumatic grief.

DEBORAH SPUNGEN[1]

The structural strains and controls that influence the rate of homicide
are mediated . . . by public policies that protect people from economic
dislocations, strengthen social institutions, and promote norms of
collective obligation. The social production of homicide *can* be
tempered when people have the collective will to do so.

STEVEN MESSNER AND RICHARD ROSENFELD[2]

In closing this book, it is important to remember that murder is fundamentally
a human tragedy. It involves the destruction of human life and potential. Victims of homicide have their lives stolen from them, often in brutal and dramatic
ways that shock and move us. Thus far in this book, we have devoted considerable attention to the perpetrators and the victims of murder in this country.
However, the homicide event does not end with the death of the victim; instead, it affects many other individuals, especially the family and friends of the
victim, in a variety of ways. Just as a stone thrown into a pond sends ripples out

in all directions, so too does the impact of murder spread out beyond the people directly involved in the killing event. One death can influence a score of lives in significant ways for a long period of time. We begin this chapter with a discussion of the ways in which homicide affects the family members and loved ones left behind. We conclude this chapter by articulating the policy implications that have emerged from this book. Specifically, we underscore what we believe to be key actions needed in three policy areas: gun control, the death penalty, and America's war on poverty and inequality.

THE HIDDEN VICTIMS

The loss of a loved one is always painful, doubly so for the family members and friends of a homicide victim. The trauma for these survivors usually begins without any warning. Typically, a police officer—either in person or over a telephone—informs the unsuspecting family members that their son, their daughter, their father or mother has been murdered—quite possibly the worst news that they may ever hear. In a heartbeat, their lives are changed forever. In many cases, family members may not even be told directly about the murder. For example, after Tony Matthews was shot and killed while his car was broken down in Washington, D.C., his mother Wilhelmina Matthews received a message from the police to go to the seventh district station, where they were apparently "holding someone named Matthews." Then she received a second call to go to D.C. General Hospital because her son had been injured. When she arrived at the hospital, the doctor told her that her son was dead. Two detectives then arrived, expressed their sympathy, and told Wilhelmina they would get back to her. The police impounded Tony's car and kept his wallet, cell phone, pager, and gold chain with a cross—given to him by his aunt—as evidence. Twenty-two months passed before the police called Wilhelmina to say that the case had been closed administratively; they attributed the killing to a dead suspect and, therefore, solved the murder without an arrest.[3]

The trauma suffered by the victim's family and friends is often difficult to comprehend and results in a tremendous amount of physical and psychological damage. One mother whose son was murdered described the impact this way:

> As his mother, I've tried to find the words to tell you how his murder has impacted my life. There are no adequate words in the English language to describe the pain, anger, and despair that I've felt from his murder. When this woman took his life because of her jealousy and selfishness, my life was shattered. I've spent two years trying to put the pieces back together, but it can't be done, a big piece is missing. . . . It took my identity, it took my security, it took my innocence, it took my rest, it took my happiness, it took my peace, it took my ability to enjoy anything. His murder gave me . . . sleepless nights, nightmares, and night terrors. It gave me Post Traumatic Stress Disorder. It gave me depression and a struggle to simply

find a reason to survive each day. It gave me tears upon tears, pain upon pain. It covered my world in sadness, pain, and anger. It continues to destroy my health a little at a time. There is not one second of one day that I don't see his body, that I don't see his blood, that I don't live with the horror of finding my son dead in his own home. There is not one second that I don't long for him. He is the first thought in my mind when I wake and the last thought before sleep and all the thoughts through the day.[4]

The type of grief articulated by this mother is profound and long lasting. Her reactions are in many ways typical of those who lose a loved one due to some act of violence. They are clearly suffering from a form of *trauma,* which has been described as "any event outside the range of usual human experience. Traumatic experiences are markedly distressing to anyone and are usually experienced with intense fear, terror, and helplessness. The most common traumatic events involve either a serious threat to one's life or a threat to a person's physical being. A traumatic event may also involve a serious threat or harm to one's property, children, spouse, or other close relatives or friends."[5]

People who lose a loved one due to murder often suffer from dramatic emotional and psychological problems as well as physical ones. Initially, many experience feelings of fear, disbelief, and helplessness that can give way to anxiety, depression, numbness, increased irritability, and anger. They may have difficulties at work or with their friends and family because of problems in controlling their emotions or an inability to concentrate or think clearly. These problems are often compounded by sleeplessness, a heightened startle reflex, and a variety of other physical troubles.[6] These symptoms may last for years and can be triggered again many years later by other stressful or traumatic events.

Losing a loved one is always devastating, but having a loved one become a homicide victim compounds the grieving process in many ways. In addition to the shock of the sudden loss, the survivors must deal with a tremendous amount of anger that is often difficult to overcome, even if the homicide offender is convicted, sent to prison, or put to death. Because of the unique legal conditions under which their grief must take place, Deborah Spungen, who founded a group called Families of Murder Victims (FMV), has labeled survivors of homicide victims as *co-victims,* because they also suffer from the act of violence.[7] Following a murder, the co-victims represent the murder victim; the co-victims are the ones who deal with the medical examiner, the criminal justice system, and the media.

In cases of mass, spree, and serial murder, the term co-victim may be expanded to any group or community that is touched by the murder: a town, a school, or an office or workplace. In such cases, one of the difficult issues that co-victims must face is that their loved ones tend to get lost in the larger horror that has taken place; their identities often remain anonymous and simply attached to the larger disaster. For example, each of the 169 people who were killed at the federal building in Oklahoma City in 1995 will forever be remembered as "Oklahoma City bombing victims" rather than being connected to the tragedy individually. For someone who remembers and loves the unique qualities that every individual possessed, this anonymous victimhood can be quite painful.

Co-victims of homicide also include those who witness lethal violence in their neighborhoods. Researchers have found that more than two thirds of all school-age children in public housing projects have witnessed a shooting. What is the result? According to a survey of public housing residents performed by the U.S. Department of Housing and Urban Development, one in five residents reports feeling unsafe in his or her neighborhood, and children show symptoms of post-traumatic stress disorder similar to those seen in children exposed to war or other major disasters.[8]

When someone is murdered by a family member, the difficulties that affect co-victims are compounded. In addition to the trauma, grief, and difficult interactions with the criminal justice system, a variety of complicated family and legal issues must be taken care of, such as deciding the custody of surviving children or issues related to property. In fact, it is not uncommon for these issues to end up in both criminal and civil courts. The case of O. J. Simpson illustrates this well. Simpson was acquitted by a jury for the *murder* of his ex-wife Nicole Brown Simpson and her friend Ronald Goldman. After his criminal trial, however, a civil trial ruled that Simpson was responsible for the *wrongful deaths* of Nicole and Ronald.[9] Nicole's and Ronald's families were both awarded a financial sum to be paid by O. J. Simpson. To the families, the ruling in the civil case was not so much about the financial settlement as about accountability. What many people don't realize is that there was a third legal battle in family court, between Nicole's surviving parents and O. J. Simpson, for the custody of Nicole's and O. J.'s two children. The court battles went on for years after Nicole's murder and, although these legal battles are now over, the impact and trauma of this murder and the subsequent legal struggles will no doubt affect these families for many years to come.

Death Notification

Many co-victims of homicide say that the most traumatic event of their lives was when they were notified of their loved one's death. In fact, whatever co-victims remember or do not remember about the days immediately following the murder, they can usually recall with great clarity most of the details surrounding the time when they first learned of the murder. Therefore, proper notification procedures are very important. However, as the case of Tony Matthews illustrates, death notifications are sometimes ill-conceived and poorly delivered.

Only recently have trauma care providers become aware of the important role that the death notification process plays in co-victims' recovery. A poorly delivered notification of death can clearly "prolong survivors' grieving process and delay their recovery from the crime for years."[10] Although victim advocates are increasingly seeking death notification training, there is still an appalling lack of formal training for police, emergency room and medical personnel, and medical examiner's and coroner's office personnel. In most jurisdictions, death notification is provided by homicide detectives or other law enforcement

Exhibit 9.1 Guidelines for Death Notification to Survivors of Homicide Victims

1. Know the details surrounding the homicide victim's death before notification.
2. Have confirming evidence of the homicide victim's identity in the event of denial by the survivors.
3. Know as much as possible about the homicide victim's survivors before notification. Notify the appropriate closest survivor first.
4. Make notifications in person and in pairs. You can contact local volunteers who are specially trained in death notification through several agencies, including the National Organization for Victim Assistance. One person should take the lead in the notification while the other person should monitor the survivors for reactions dangerous to themselves or to others.
5. Do not bring personal articles of the homicide victim with you to the notification.
6. Conduct the notification in a private place after you and the survivors are seated.
7. Avoid engaging in small talk upon your arrival. Do not build up slowly to the reason for your visit and do not use any euphemisms for death such as "passed away," "we lost her/him," or "she/he expired." Be compassionately direct and un-ambiguous in giving notification to survivors. For example, "We've come to tell you something very terrible. Your daughter has been killed in a carjacking. I'm very sorry."
8. Ask survivors whether they would like you to contact a family member or friend.
9. Accept survivors' reactions, no matter how intense or stoic, in a nonjudgmental, empathetic manner. Be prepared for possible hostility toward you as a representa-tive of law enforcement and avoid responding defensively. Show empathy, but do not say "I understand," when clearly no one can.
10. Refer to the homicide victim by name out of respect to the victim and the survi-vors. Do not use terms like "the deceased" or "the victim."
11. Listen to the survivors and answer all of their questions. Explain to them that everyone grieves differently and encourage them to be understanding and sup-portive of one another.
12. Show respect for survivors' personal and religious or nonreligious understandings of death. Do not impose your personal beliefs about death on survivors by saying of the victim, for example, "She's in a better place now."
13. Before leaving the survivors, make sure that someone can stay with them and that they have contacts for support services.

SOURCE: Adapted from Office for Victims of Crime, *First Response to Victims of Crime* (Washington, D.C.: U.S. De-partment of Justice, 2000), pp. 15–17.

officers. To increase their awareness of these issues, the Office for Victims of Crime of the U.S. Department of Justice has recently outlined guidelines for the death notification process.[11] An abbreviated summary of these guidelines is displayed in Exhibit 9.1.

Although some of these guidelines may seem to make intuitive sense, keep in mind that most police officers have been trained *not* to show emotion when performing their professional duties, and only a very few are trained to deliver death notifications. For example, in one study of 50 homicide detectives, only 18% of the detectives had received some formal instruction or training in how to deliver a death notification. Not surprisingly, the majority of these detectives asserted that the experience of delivering a death notification was moderately to extremely stressful.[12]

Legal Rights for Co-Victims

When a homicide comes to the attention of the police, the adjudication process that occurs can take one of several paths. A case may or may not result in an arrest, an arrest may or may not result in a trial, and a guilty verdict may or may not result in incarceration. Throughout much of this process, the co-victims of the homicide remain essentially bystanders. In fact, the peripheral status of the co-victims is clearly indicated by the name typically given to a homicide case, *State of* _____ *v. John Smith* (the defendant). As this generic name illustrates, the state, not the victim's family, brings the case against the alleged murderer. In fact, the homicide victim's name does not even appear. So who represents the victim's family and loved ones, and what role do they play in the adjudication process? Historically, co-victims have had very few rights in this country. However, as a result of the efforts of victims' rights organizations and of many co-victims themselves, most states have now passed at least some form of victims' rights legislation.[13]

Victims' rights legislation varies widely across states, but most states include an enumeration of specific rights pertaining to crime victims and co-victims and a list of responsibilities of the criminal justice system. This legislation is often called the Victims' Bill of Rights, and Deborah Spungen notes eight general rights that are traditionally included:

- notification of, and the right to attend, court proceedings, including bail and parole hearings;
- eligibility for compensation and restitution;
- freedom from intimidation and harassment by the defendant;
- fair and dignified treatment;
- victim input at various stages of the criminal justice process;
- information about the release or escape of defendants;
- prompt return of victims' property; and
- notice of all the rights granted in the legislation.[14]

In addition to enacting victims' rights legislation, 32 states have also added crime victims' rights to their state constitutions. The crime victims' movement has also waged a campaign at the federal level to modify the U. S. Constitution. Among other things, the proposed amendment to the Constitution would endow victims of violent crime with the right to make statements during trial and parole hearings, grant them notification of trial proceedings, and give them the right to sue a perpetrator for damages. Victims' advocates contend that constitutional amendments at both the federal and the state levels are needed to increase the visibility of victims' rights and to give those rights a degree of permanence. Although the victims' rights amendment to the U.S. Constitution was introduced in Congress in 1996, it has still not been ratified by Congress at this writing. This is not surprising because, by design, the Constitution is difficult to amend; two-thirds majorities in the House and Senate are needed for the passage of amendments to the Constitution, in addition to ratification by three fourths of the 50 state legislatures.[15]

Crime Victim Compensation

In addition to statutes and state constitutional amendments mandating victims' rights, crime victim compensation programs also operate in all 50 states. These programs provide financial assistance to victims for crime-related out-of-pocket expenses. For homicides, this can include expenses for funerals, loss of support, and counseling for secondary victims. All state victim compensation programs are *payors of last resort,* covering losses not recouped from other sources such as public or private insurance, employee benefits, offender restitution, or civil judgments.

The Office for Victims of Crime (OVC) also makes formula grants available to all 50 states to support the provision of direct services to victims of crime, including homicide victims and their co-victims. For example, the Family Bereavement Center in Baltimore, Maryland, is one such program, funded by an OVC subgrant and administered by the state attorney's office. The center reaches out to every homicide victim's family by sending a letter encouraging them to call for services. Center staff provide liaison services with the police department, the medical examiner, and the state attorney's office. They offer crime scene cleanup services, court support and escort services, notification of case status and victims' rights, assistance in applying for victim compensation, and individual and group grief counseling sessions. They also sponsor educational and support activities, such as memorial services, weekend camps for adolescent and younger children who have lost family and friends to violence, and a quarterly newsletter.[16]

In sum, the families and loved ones of homicide victims suffer a tremendous amount of harm and trauma in the wake of a murder. Homicide does not just affect those directly involved in the murder event but dramatically affects the lives and well-being of many others. These co-victims also have unique concerns and needs that differ from those of other crime victims. In recent years, our society has made significant progress in meeting the needs of these co-victims. Clearly, however, the best strategy would be to prevent the harm and trauma from ever occurring in the first place. The most efficient way to mitigate the costs and consequences of murder in the United States would be to reduce murder rates. But how is this to be accomplished? This book has highlighted a variety of factors that are consistently identified in the research literature as being contributory elements to homicide. In the remainder of this chapter, we underscore pressing policy concerns in the areas of gun control, the war on poverty and inequality, and capital punishment.

IN GUNS WE TRUST

In chapter 7, we discussed the relationship between guns and lethal violence. Because the easy availability of guns in this country is inextricably related to the extremely high rates of lethal violence on our streets and in our homes, Franklin Zimring and Gordon Hawkins conclude that "the characteristic that most dominates the landscape of American lethal violence is the use of firearms in attacks, particularly the use of handguns."[17] Historically, the linkage between lethal violence and firearms has been sporadically and haphazardly addressed by a variety of legislative initiatives.

The regulations surrounding the purchase and use of guns are mandated by all levels of government—federal, state, and local—and as Philip Cook and Mark Moore point out, can be classified into three categories: (1) regulations designed to affect the supply and overall availability of guns, (2) regulations designed to influence who has these weapons, and (3) regulations designed to affect how guns are used by the people who have them.[18]

At the federal level, one of the most recent and well-known gun control measures, which was passed in 1994, is known informally as the Brady Bill. This law mandates that anyone seeking to purchase a firearm from federally licensed firearm dealers in the United States must wait five days after purchase before receiving the weapon. During this *waiting period,* local law enforcement officials conduct background checks to determine if the purchaser has a criminal record or is otherwise restricted from owning a firearm. Persons so restricted include those who

- are under indictment for or have been convicted of a crime punishable by imprisonment for more than one year;
- are fugitive from justice;
- are unlawful users of or are addicted to any controlled substance;
- have been adjudicated as mentally defective or committed to a mental institution;
- are illegal aliens or have been admitted to the United States under a non-immigrant visa;
- were discharged from the U.S. Armed Forces under dishonorable conditions;
- have renounced U.S. citizenship;
- are subject to a court order restraining them from harassing, stalking, or threatening an intimate partner or child;
- have been convicted in any court of a misdemeanor crime of domestic violence.

Furthermore, the Brady Bill makes it unlawful to sell a long gun to a person younger than 18 or any other type of firearm to a person less than 21 years of age. Many states have enacted similar or additional provisions to this federal legislation. For example, 24 states restrict persons who were adjudicated delinquent or who had committed serious offenses as juveniles, and 19 states restrict persons who are addicted to alcohol or have been convicted of alcohol-related offenses. It should be noted, however, that the Brady Bill applies only to firearm sales through licensed dealers and does not apply to gun shows, where thousands of firearms are purchased every year.

From the inception of the Brady Bill on March 1, 1994, to December 31, 2001, nearly 30 million applications for firearm sales have been subject to background checks, and about 689,000 of these applications have been rejected. In 2000 alone, 2% (153,000) of the approximately 7,699,000 applications were rejected. The majority of these rejections were because the applicant had a felony indictment or conviction (57.6%), and another 12.2% of applicants were domestic violence offenders.[19] These rejections provide clear evidence that the Brady Bill has been at least partially successful in its mission. Despite the efficacy of gun control legislation, however, policies regulating the gun industry are ultimately written and voted on by politicians. Unfortunately, such policies are not always informed by empirical facts.

Much of the political power in Congress is controlled by lobbying groups. In the world of lobbyists, no other group is as powerful or as effective in its efforts as the National Rifle Association (NRA). In fact, in *Fortune* magazine's Power 25 survey of lobbying groups, the NRA recently replaced the American Association of Retired Persons (AARP) as the number one group with clout on Capitol Hill. How do lobbying groups parlay power? In a word, money. Evidence of this is presented in Exhibit 9.2, which displays the amount of money received from the NRA by United States senators and their respective votes on the Brady Bill. Those who voted against the Brady Bill are displayed in bold italics. It does not take a statistician to determine that the senators who received money from the NRA were less likely to vote for the Brady Bill than those who did not receive NRA money.

After the passage of the Brady Bill, the NRA poured millions of dollars into federal and state elections to remove senators who voted for the Brady Bill and other gun control legislation. In fact, before the 2000 elections, the NRA launched its largest political campaign ever, spending nearly $20 million, including $1.6 million in support of President Bush's campaign. *Fortune*'s Jeffrey Birnbaum believes that one of the reasons for the NRA's rise to his magazine's number one spot was because it "held gun control legislation at bay" by getting its people elected to Congress and helping to defeat Vice President Al Gore.[20]

Since the 2000 elections and the NRA's multimillion-dollar campaign effort, the political climate regarding gun control legislation has changed dramatically. For example, in the aftermath of the 1999 Columbine school massacre, talk of gun control could be heard throughout the halls of Congress. In fact, the Senate quickly passed a bill that would have extended the Brady Bill background checks to purchasers at gun shows, and the House narrowly defeated the same bill. However, the reaction to one of the latest school shootings in a San Diego suburb in March of 2001 was very different. Although it was not surprising that President Bush made no mention of gun control in his remarks following the San Diego school shooting, references to gun control legislation were also no-

Exhibit 9.2 U.S. Senators' Votes on the Brady Bill and Previous Contributions Received by Each Senator from the National Rifle Association

Senator	Contribu-tions ($)	Senator	Contribu-tions ($)
Paul Coverdell (R-Ga.)	95,806	Thad Cochran (R-Miss.)	4950
Alfonse M. D'Amato (R-N.Y.)	20,486	Robert J. Dole (R-Kan.)	4950
Dan Coats (R-Ind.)	19,800	Pete V. Domenici (R-N.M.)	4950
Arlen Specter (R-Pa.)	18,072	Robert C. Byrd (D-W.Va.)	4950
Lauch Faircloth (R-N.C.)	17,973	Dennis DeConcini (D-Ariz.)	4950
Jesse Helms (R-N.C.)	17,957	Richard G. Lugar (R-Ind.)	4950
Christopher S. Bond (R-Mo.)	14,850	William V. Roth Jr. (R-Del.)	4950
Max Baucus (D-Mont.)	14,639	William S. Cohen (R-Maine)	4950
Larry Pressler (R-S.D.)	14,400	John C. Danforth (R-Mo.)	4500
Kay Bailey Hutchinson (R-Tex.)	11,509	Byron L. Dorgan (D-N.D.)	4450
Larry E. Craig (R-Idaho)	11,286	Mitch McConnell (R-Ky.)	3085
Robert C. Smith (R-N.H.)	11,000	Mark O. Hatfield (R-Ore.)	3000
Slade Gorton (R-Wash.)	10,900	Bob Packwood (R-Ore.)	2000
Howell T. Heflin (D-Ala.)	10,244	Wendell H. Ford (D-Ky.)	1568
Richard C. Shelby (D-Ala.)	10,226	Conrad Burns (R-Mont.)	1000
Ted Stevens (R-Alaska)	10,197	Bob Kerrey (D-Neb.)	1000
Robert F. Bennett (R-Utah)	9900	John D. Rockefeller IV (D-W.Va.)	1000
John Breaux (D-La.)	9900	John W. Warner (R-Va.)	1000
Dirk Kempthorne (R-Idaho)	9900	Hank Brown (R-Colo.)	0
Phil Gramm (R-Tex.)	9900	Patrick J. Leahy (D-Vt.)	0
Charles E. Grassley (R-Iowa)	9900	Alan K. Simpson (R-Wyo.)	0
Ernest Fl. Hollings (D-S.C.)	9900	Daniel K. Akaka (D-Hawaii)	0
John McCain (R-Ariz.)	9900	Joseph R. Biden Jr. (D-Del.)	0
Frank Murkowski (R-Alaska)	9900	David L. Boren (D-Okla.)	0
Don Nickles (R-Okla.)	9900	Barbara Boxer (D-Calif.)	0
James Exon (D-Neb.)	9900	Bill Bradley (D-N.J.)	0
Strom Thurmond (R-S.C.)	9900	Dale Bumpers (D-Ark.)	0
J. Bennett Johnston (D-La.)	9508	John H. Chafee (R-R.I.)	0
Harry M. Reid (D-Nev.)	9450	Christopher J. Dodd (D-Conn.)	0
Kent Conrad (D-N.D.)	9450	Russell Feingold (D-Wis.)	0
Malcolm Wallop (R-Wyo.)	8764	Dianne Feinstein (D-Calif.)	0
Orrin G. Hatch (R-Utah)	7950	John Glenn (D-Ohio)	0
Connie Mack (R-Fla.)	6500	Bob Graham (D-Fla.)	0
Trent Lott (R-Miss.)	6000	Tom Harkin (D-Iowa)	0
Judd Gregg (R-N.H.)	5950	Daniel K. Inouye (D-Hawaii)	0
Jeff Bingaman (D-N.M.)	5950	James M. Jeffords (R-Vt.)	0
Thomas A. Daschle (D-S.D.)	5950	Nancy Landon Kassebaum (R-Kan.)	0
Dave Durenberger (R-Minn.)	5900	Edward M. Kennedy (D-Mass.)	0
Jim Sasser (D-Tenn.)	5450	John F. Kerry (D-Mass.)	0
Richard H. Bryan (D-Nev.)	4950	Herb Kohl (D-Wis.)	0
Ben Nighthorse Campbell (D-Colo.)	4950		

Exhibit 9.2 (*continued*)

Senator	Contribu- tions ($)	Senator	Contribu- tions ($)
Frank R. Lautenberg (D-N.J.)	0	Patty Murray (D-Wash.)	0
Carl M. Levin (D-Mich.)	0	Sam Nunn (D-Ga.)	0
Joseph I. Lieberman (D-Conn.)	0	Claiborne Pell (D-R.I.)	0
Harlan Mathews (D-Tenn.)	0	David Pryor (D-Ark.)	0
Howard M. Metzenbaum (D-Ohio)	0	Donald W. Riegle Jr. (D-Mich.)	0
		Charles S. Robb (D-Va.)	0
Barbara A. Mikulski (D-Md.)	0	Paul S. Sarbanes (D-Md.)	0
George J. Mitchell (D-Maine)	0	Paul Simon (D-Ill.)	0
Carol Moseley-Brawn (D-Ill.)	0	Paul Wellstone (D-Minn.)	0
Daniel Patrick Moynihan (D-N.Y.)	0	Harris Wofford (D-Pa.)	0

Key: **Voted against Brady Bill;** *Abstained;* Voted in Favor of Brady Bill.

SOURCE: Adapted from "NRA Money and Handgun Voting," *Washington Post*, December 8, 1993, p. A21.

ticeably absent from the statements of former sponsors of gun control legislation. For example, Richard Gephardt (D-Mo.) called for more resources to combat violence in schools and urged teachers and parents to look for "warning signs that may be a precursor to violence among youngsters." He did not mention gun control.[21]

In light of the new political climate in Washington, D.C., it is likely that no new gun control legislation will be enacted by Congress in the near future. Nevertheless, based on what we know about former and current gun control legislation, Philip Cook and Mark Moore have outlined several steps that should be taken at the federal level, including

- raising the tax on guns and ammunition to make the cost of owning guns more accurately reflect the social costs and benefits of having them;
- requiring all gun transfers to pass through federally licensed dealers, with the same screening and paperwork provisions as if the gun were being sold by the dealer;
- increasing criminal enforcement efforts against gunrunning operations;
- enhancing the quality and completeness of state and federal criminal records files and facilitating access by law enforcement agencies to these files;
- mandating that new guns meet minimum safety requirements.

Cook and Moore see the greatest opportunities for reducing gun violence at the local level, however. In particular, they contend that local efforts should include reducing youth access to and use of all types of weapons through innovative policies and programs. One such program is the *Boston Gun Project*.[22] The Boston Gun Project is an interagency working group, including members from such organizations as the Boston Police Department; the Bureau of Alcohol, Tobacco, and Firearms; the U.S. Attorney for the Commonwealth of

Massachusetts; the Massachusetts Department of Parole; the Boston school police; and a research team from Harvard University. The goal of the project is to prevent violence in Boston's inner-city neighborhoods through heightened surveillance, rapid identification of violence and violent groups, and swift sanctions (such as arrest and conviction). The basic idea of this deterrence strategy is to communicate to at-risk youth that there is "a new game in town where violence is concerned; that authorities intend to respond to violence in a rapid, powerful, concerted, and predictable fashion; that all the authorities represented on the working group are sharing information and intelligence regularly; that violence will bring the imposition of a wide variety of sanctions; and that various kinds of help are available for those who wish it."[23] A second goal of the Boston Gun Project is to disrupt the illicit market that provides guns to area youth by stepping up surveillance and investigations of illegal weapons possessions. Although an official evaluation of the Boston Gun Project has yet to be published, the fact that Boston's youth homicide rates have fallen since the project's inception is promising. Moreover, it remains one of the most comprehensive and innovative strategies for decreasing the high rates of violence and violent death faced by the most vulnerable groups in our society.

Another strategy used by some local jurisdictions has been to implement policies that aggressively prosecute felons caught with illegal guns to the fullest extent of the laws on the books. *Project Exile* in Richmond, Virginia, is an example of such a program. Under federal law, it is illegal for any person with a prior felony conviction to possess a gun. Violation of this law is punishable by 10 years in federal prison with no possibility of parole. The goal of Project Exile is to provide an expedited prosecution effort of such "felon in possession" cases. For example, the project has fully integrated and coordinated local police, state police, federal investigators, and local and federal prosecutors to promptly arrest, incarcerate, detain without bond, prosecute, and sentence an armed offender. The expedited reporting system has decreased the processing time of these cases from several months to only a few days. Project Exile is intended to reduce violence through both specific and general deterrence. In addition to sending dangerous violent criminals to prison for longer terms, Project Exile will communicate to would-be offenders that committing a crime with a gun will automatically and swiftly get them time in state or federal prison. This communication has been facilitated not only by word on the street, but also by strong advertising campaigns via billboards and television commercials. It is important to note that there have been no scientific evaluations of Project Exile. However, since the program's inception, Richmond's homicide rate has significantly declined, and because of Richmond's apparent success, Congress has funded the replication of Project Exile in several other cities.[24]

In sum, gun control issues will continue to be contentious, primarily because the debate revolves around deeply rooted values, not simply empirical facts. As Cook and Moore conclude, "even a definitive empirical demonstration that a gun control measure would save lives will not persuade someone who believes that any infringement on the individual right to bear arms is tantamount to opening the door to tyranny."[25] However, as the Boston Gun Project and Project Exile have demonstrated, many innovative projects appear to show great promise in reducing lethal violence without compromising the value systems of those on either side of the gun control debate.

POVERTY AND INEQUALITY

Historically and contemporaneously, poverty has been an ever-present correlate of murder. Cassiodorus,[26] a Roman senator, writer, and commentator noted long ago that "poverty is the mother of crime," and his observation is no less true for modern America than it was for ancient Rome. More recently, a presidential commission investigating the roots of crime asserted that "crime flourishes where the conditions of life are the worst."[27] It is no accident that murder in the United States tends to be concentrated in the ranks of the urban poor, who are also usually minority group members. Material deprivation and the racial and ethnic discrimination that often accompanies it help breed a variety of social problems, including violence. James Gilligan, who has worked with violent felons for many years, echoes this reality when he writes, "You cannot work for one day with the violent people who fill our prisons and mental hospitals for the criminally insane without being forcibly and constantly reminded of the extreme poverty and discrimination that characterizes their lives."[28] Nevertheless, the linkage between poverty and violence has not gone unchallenged.

In recent years, it has become fashionable in some circles to minimize or discount the link between poverty and homicide. Discounting the role that poverty and structural inequalities play, a variety of writers have suggested that the causes of criminality and violence can instead be found in individual character defects or moral failings.[29] For them, violence is not a reaction to or a byproduct of deprivation rather, it is brought about by some failing or weakness in a person's makeup. Some see it as a failure on the part of the family, whereas others hold that it is a moral failing on the part of those who engage in violence and criminality. But then why do poor minority groups suffer from such perennially high rates of lethal violence? Can we assume that the problem is linked to a cultural or personality deficiency among certain minority groups? Do some populations harbor aggressive traits? If this were true, we would expect these groups to have higher rates of violence no matter what their economic status. But this is not the case; rates of violence decrease dramatically when we examine populations from the same minority groups with higher standards of living. Poverty increases the risk of violence and criminality across all races and ethnicities.[30] It is to the destructive effects of poverty that we must look if we are to understand and diminish the rates of lethal violence in the United States.

Although poverty does not directly cause murder, it does produce certain conditions of life that make it more likely. Individuals living in poverty may be tempted to engage in high-risk activities such as drug dealing in order to gain the resources they desire, whereas others may lash out violently from their frustration, anger, and resentment. Elijah Anderson summarizes this reality quite eloquently: "The inclination to violence springs from the circumstances of life among the ghetto poor—the lack of jobs that pay a living wage, limited basic public services (police response in emergencies, building maintenance, trash pickup, lighting, and other services that middle-class neighborhoods take for granted), the stigma of race, the fallout from rampant drug use and drug trafficking, and the resulting alienation and absence of hope for the future. Simply living in such an environment places young people at special risk of falling victim to aggressive behavior."[31]

As Anderson points out, the linkage between violence and poverty is not simple, nor is it direct. Rather, poverty helps create a climate and an environment in which individuals are more likely to make choices or be in situations that increase the risk of violence and killing. Research has indicated that high-risk behavior among adolescents, for example, is affected by incentives and opportunities as well as costs.[32] In other words, violence and other high-risk activities are more likely when an individual has nothing to lose or perceives no gain in refraining from them. Similarly, William Julius Wilson and others have found that communities with high unemployment rates and scarce job opportunities also have higher rates of homicide.[33] Individuals who do not have access to jobs or other opportunities for material success may choose to engage in other behaviors, such as drug dealing, to acquire the economic capital they seek.

Poverty also places a great deal of stress on the family, and in this sense the critics of the poverty argument are correct in stressing the breakdown of the family as a contributor to violence. The family is indeed important in limiting the likelihood that an individual will rely on violence, but we cannot forget that poverty takes a tremendous toll on this primary group. Families living in poverty are more likely to divorce or to have a parent missing because of imprisonment, addiction, or abandonment. Divorced and single-parent families, especially those headed by a woman, are significantly more likely to experience poverty.[34] Poor families tend to have higher rates of family violence, which not only contribute to higher rates of homicide but also assist in perpetuating the cycle of violence.[35] Of this kind of violence, Anderson writes, "The seeming intractability of their situation, caused in large part by the lack of well-paying jobs and the persistence of racial discrimination, has engendered deep-seated bitterness and anger in many of the most desperate and poorest Blacks, especially young people. The need both to exercise a measure of control and to lash out at somebody is often reflected in the adults' relations with their children. At the very least, the frustrations associated with persistent poverty shorten the fuse in such people, contributing to a lack of patience with anyone—child or adult—who irritates them."[36] We can also point out that those living in poverty have less education and fewer tools and skills to deal with life's problems and stressors, which also contributes to violent solutions or responses. From both community-level and individual-level data, it can be seen that poverty is closely tied to rates of lethal violence in this country. But what can be done? M. Greene suggests the following nine strategies for effectively reducing rates of violence:

- Street outreach and referral. Programs need to actively recruit young people on the streets and encourage their friends and relatives to come to the program.

- Needs and interest assessment. Programs need to develop an individual plan to meet the needs of the youth.

- A supportive, personal relationship with an adult. The adolescent needs at least one successful relationship with an adult.

- Role models. Young people need exposure to adults they can identify with.

- Peer group discussions. Programs need to teach young people how to peacefully resolve interpersonal conflicts.

- Family interventions. Home-based counseling needs to be provided.

- Neighborhood projects. Programs need to draw on the resourcefulness of young people for developing community programs.

- Education and job preparedness training. Programs need to teach youth skills they will use in the working world.

- Program evaluation. Programs need to develop feedback mechanisms in order to assess their own success.[37]

However important they are in the short term, these strategies do not address the fundamental sources of violence that arise out of poverty. Ultimately, we must focus on the ways in which income inequality is created and fostered. But this is not an easy task. Philippe Bourgois puts it well when he asserts, "Solutions to inner-city poverty and substance abuse framed in terms of public policy often appear naive or hopelessly idealistic. Given the dimensions of structural oppression in the United States, it is atheoretical to expect isolated policy initiatives, or even short-term political reforms, to remedy the plight of the poor in U.S. urban centers in the short or medium term. Racism and class segregation in the United States are shaped in too complex a mesh of political–economic structural forces, historical legacies, cultural imperatives, and individual actions to be susceptible to simple solutions."[38] Programs to strengthen the family and to provide educational and job opportunities may go a long way in reducing the persistent problem of lethal violence among our impoverished citizens. However, if we are to truly make our society a safer and more just place, we need to more closely examine the ways in which violence is fostered by the blatant hypocrisy posed by persistent deprivation for some in the midst of extreme wealth and opulence enjoyed by others.

RECENT DEVELOPMENTS
IN CAPITAL PUNISHMENT

In this last section, we want to highlight a few recent legal and legislative developments regarding the administration of the death penalty in several states. These developments include:

- Evidence is accumulating that innocent people are in danger of being executed because of fundamental flaws in their state trials.

- Several states have implemented a moratorium on executions.
- State and federal lawmakers have begun introducing legislation to ensure greater procedural protection for capital defendants.
- Public support for capital punishment, which was at an all-time high in the early 1990s, is now substantially declining.

Recall that in 1972, the U. S. Supreme Court struck down existing state death penalty statutes as unconstitutional.[39] The *Furman* case formalized a moratorium on state and federal executions that had been in place since 1967. However, the states did not abandon the death penalty in response to the *Furman* decision; rather, they attempted to remedy the identified defects in their statutes through various procedural reforms (bifurcated capital trials, statutory aggravating or mitigating circumstances, automatic appeal). After reviewing these reforms, the Supreme Court ended the *de facto* moratorium on executions in 1976.[40] The court claimed that these procedurally reformed state death penalty statutes would ensure that the death penalty was fundamentally fair, because there would be a "meaningful basis to distinguish those who live and those who will die."

Evidence in recent years, however, has raised some grave doubts about the effectiveness of these procedural reforms. As noted in chapter 8, one of the most comprehensive studies of the modern system of capital punishment was published in the *Columbia University Law Review* by James Liebman.[41] This study examined every completed death penalty appeal over the period from 1972 to 1995 and found that an appeals court judged an error at trial serious enough to warrant the reversal of either the conviction or the penalty in 68% of the cases. In other words, a reviewing court found an error so serious as to call into question the defendant's guilt or death sentence in almost seven out of ten cases! Professor Liebman also examined a sample of capital cases that were retried and reported that in these new trials, 82% of the defendants were given a sentence other than death (that is, the death penalty was rejected for these cases), and in 7%, the defendant was acquitted.

Other recent incidents have alarmed even death penalty proponents. For example, in January of 2000, Governor George Ryan, the Republican, conservative, and pro–death penalty governor of the state of Illinois, announced that there would be a moratorium on all executions in the state until he could be sure—with moral certainty—that no innocent man or woman was facing a lethal injection. Governor Ryan stated, "We have now freed more people than we have put to death under our system—13 people have been exonerated and 12 have been put to death. There is a flaw in the system, without question, and it needs to be studied."[42] The moratorium will last until a state-sponsored investigation into the death penalty process is completed. Similar studies have been undertaken in Arizona, Maryland, North Carolina, Indiana, and Nebraska. Nationwide, nearly 100 people on death row awaiting execution have been freed after detailed investigations—usually by some outside interest—discovered that they were actually innocent of the crimes for which they had been convicted and sentenced to death. Together, these innocent people have spent more than 1,000 years in prison.

Investigations in Texas, the most active death penalty state in the nation, have revealed that then-Governor George Bush's faith in the system may also have been misplaced.[43] A study conducted by reporters for the *Chicago Tribune* investigated all 131 executions during Bush's tenure as governor of the state.[44] They found numerous instances of gross professional incompetence by appointed counsel and other trial irregularities that would lead one to question the fairness of the trial. For example, even though their client's life was at stake, the defense attorneys in 40 of these 131 cases presented either no witnesses or only one witness during the crucial penalty phase that determined their defendant's fate. In 43 cases (33%), a defendant had an appointed lawyer who was later disbarred, suspended, or professionally reprimanded. In 29 cases, the prosecution presented testimony from a psychiatrist who, without personally examining the defendant, predicted with a high degree of certainty that the defendant would likely commit violent crimes in the future. This kind of hypothetical testimony that predicts future dangerousness has been condemned as unreliable by the American Psychiatric Association. Testimony in other Texas capital cases has come from a forensic scientist who was temporarily released from a mental institution in order to provide testimony for the prosecution, from a psychiatrist—nicknamed "Dr. Death" because of his frequent role as expert witness for the prosecution in predicting the future dangerousness of capital defendants—who was expelled from the American Psychiatric Association, and from a forensic pathologist who has admitted faking autopsies.

Another study of the Texas death penalty system was undertaken by the Texas Defender Service, a statewide non-profit organization concerned with improving the quality of legal representation in the state. Texas, like several other states, has no statewide public defender system; indigent capital defendants generally have counsel appointed for them by elected judges. Not surprisingly, then, considerations other than professional competence determine the appointment of counsel in many capital cases. Among the more egregious findings of the study were the following: (1) appointed counsel were almost always underfunded, both in terms of direct payment for work on the case and in terms of support services such as funding for expert witnesses and investigation; (2) appointed counsel were more likely to have been professionally sanctioned than other lawyers in the state; and (3) all too often, appointed counsel mounted a measly defense or no defense at all.[45] Some examples:

- Joe Lee Guy was the lookout in a botched robbery of a convenience store in which Guy's co-defendants killed the store owner. The two co-defendants—including the actual triggerman—received life sentences, whereas Guy was sentenced to death. Guy was represented by appointed counsel Richard Wardroup, who at the time had already been disciplined twice by the state bar and was battling drug and alcohol addiction. Testimony at another disciplinary hearing after Guy's trial indicated that Wardroup used cocaine during Guy's trial and was frequently drunk.

- George McFarland was represented by appointed counsel John Benn at his 1992 capital trial. Benn admitted spending only four hours preparing for McFarland's trial, did not examine the crime scene, interviewed no witnesses, prepared no motions, and only visited McFarland twice. Moreover, Benn spent much of the trial sleeping. When asked during one recess if, in fact, he had fallen asleep during the trial, Benn replied, "It's boring." Remarkably, in reviewing the case, the Texas Court of Criminal Appeals noted that Benn's sleeping in court may have been sound trial strategy, designed to garner sympathy from the jury!

- Calvin Jerold Burdine was represented by attorney Joe Frank Cannon, who had an established reputation both for speeding up the trials of his clients and for nodding off while in court. Cannon's sleeping during Burdine's trial was so pervasive that it was the subject of discussion among the jurors, and Cannon was noted to have fallen asleep from five to ten times during the trial. Perhaps a sleeping Cannon was Burdine's best chance, because the awake Cannon was not much help. Cannon failed to investigate the case or to present any mitigating evidence on behalf of Burdine and failed to object when the prosecutor argued to the jury that sentencing the gay Burdine to life in prison "isn't a very bad punishment for a homosexual."

In sum, many believe that the procedures for state death penalty statutes are not any more effective now in separating those deserving death from those who do not than were pre-*Furman* statutes. Suspected capital defendants—generally all poor—are given poor lawyers, have trials of suspect quality, and are sent to death row with some degree of regularity, with only luck determining who eventually gets exonerated and who is put to death.

Public Support for the Death Penalty

In the not-too-recent past, a substantial majority of the American public expressed approval of the death penalty for those convicted of murder. In fact, in a Gallup poll taken in September of 1994, 80% of respondents said that they were in favor of the death penalty for murderers. This was one of the highest percentages of support for capital punishment since the Gallup organization began asking that question in 1937. However, because of the recent revelations about the way the death penalty has been operating, support for the death penalty has been falling. Polls now suggest that doubts are quickly replacing public confidence in the way that capital defendants are treated by the legal system.

In a Gallup poll taken in May of 2001, only 65% of the respondents stated that they were in favor of the death penalty for those convicted of murder. This is down from February of 1999, when 71% expressed approval, and is the lowest level of support found for capital punishment in more than twenty years (since March of 1978). Further indication that support for the death penalty among the American public is soft is revealed in the fact that in the May 2001 Gallup poll, it was found that only a bare majority of those surveyed stated that they approved of the death penalty for murder (52%) compared with life imprisonment (43%). In addition to this soft support, other recent Gallup polls have suggested that many Americans are now questioning the fairness of the death penalty system. When asked if they would favor a moratorium on executions in all other states until it could be determined that the death penalty was being administered fairly and accurately, a majority (53%) replied in the affirmative; 41% of those surveyed thought that the death penalty in the United States was being unfairly applied, 80% thought that an innocent person had been executed in the past five years, and 65% thought that a poor person was more likely than a more affluent one to receive the death penalty for the same crime.[46]

Thus, it appears that recent revelations about the exoneration of innocent persons and their release from death row and about the breakdown in the administration of capital punishment have begun to take a toll on public support. Since reaching its peak in the mid-1990s, public support for the death penalty has fallen substantially and has been replaced by suspicions about the fairness and necessity of capital punishment in America.

Legislative and Other Developments

In response to the public's skepticism regarding the death penalty, a number of developments have taken place. First, we have already alluded to the fact that at least one state (Illinois) has a moratorium on executions pending study of the state's capital punishment system, and several other states have *de facto* moratoriums until studies in their states have been completed. There is a sense that the system of capital punishment is perilously close to breaking down and must be fixed (if it can) before executions are resumed.

In May of 2000, a national organization called The Constitution Project, composed of liberals and conservatives, supporters and opponents of the death penalty, and Republicans and Democrats alike, was organized to investigate the administration of capital punishment in the United States and to make policy recommendations. The project's death penalty initiative, known as the National Committee to Prevent Wrongful Executions, announced that the risk of wrongful conviction and the execution of innocents was too high to be tolerable and pledged to investigate the current state of affairs. The committee includes Beth Wilkinson, who prosecuted the Oklahoma City bombing case; Mario Cuomo, former governor of New York; and William Sessions, former director of the Federal Bureau of Investigation. In its July 2001 report, *Mandatory Justice,* the committee announced eighteen proposed reforms to the death penalty, including the provision of competent counsel for indigent defendants; the provision of adequate funding for lawyers and expert and investigative services; the abolition of the death penalty for mentally retarded people, for offenders under the age of eighteen at the time of the offense, and for those who neither killed nor intended to kill during the commission of a felony; the performance of studies to ensure the racial fairness of the death penalty; the expanded use of life imprisonment without parole; and the requirement that capital juries be informed of that sentencing possibility.

Finally, reflecting the growing concern about the fairness of the death penalty, in February of 2000, Senator Patrick Leahy of Vermont introduced in the U.S. Congress the Innocence Protection Act. Among other things, the purpose of this act is to allow for DNA testing for all inmates and for the improvement of legal representation for those accused of a capital crime. Although this bill has bipartisan support, the Senate has not formally voted on it as of this writing.

SUMMARY

To understand and respond effectively to lethal violence in our country, we must assemble knowledge from many disciplines, including sociology, psychology, and the medical and legal fields. The high rates of murder that our society endures annually affect us all. Even those of us who have never been personally touched by lethal violence are aware of the widespread presence of this violence in our communities. The ever-present fear that we or someone we love may be killed is but another form of psychic violence that we must all endure.

Because of the heterogeneous nature of murder in this county, the efforts at reducing it must also take many forms. Different policies are needed to target different vulnerable groups. For example, the policies aimed at preventing and mitigating the consequences of homicides that occur in the family may not be the same as the policies intended to decrease incidents of youth murder. Promising solutions and strategies do already exist for many types of murder. We must, however, have the will to implement them. As James Mercy and Rodney Hammond conclude, "if we effectively use our knowledge to strategically allocate our resources among health care, education, and research programs, there is considerable reason to believe that we can reduce significantly the prevalence of homicide and assaultive violence in this society."[47]

NOTES

1. Deborah Spungen, *Homicide: The Hidden Victims. A Guide for Professionals* (Thousand Oaks, Calif.: Sage, 1998).

2. Steven F. Messner and Richard Rosenfeld, "Social Structure and Homicide: Theory and Research," in *Homicide: A Sourcebook of Social Research,* ed. M. Dwayne Smith and Margaret A. Zahn (Thousand Oaks, Calif.: Sage, 1999).

3. Cheryl W. Thompson, "D.C. Police Often Close Cases without Arrests," *Washington Post,* December 4, 2000, p. A01.

4. Karen Drummond McCombs, *Victim Impact Statement.* http://www.murder victims.com/Impact/McCombsImpact .htm (retrieved October 1, 2001).

5. Carole Conner McKelvey and Conrad Boeding, *Children of Rage: Preventing Youth Violence after Columbine* (Lakewood, Colo.: Passages Press, 2000), p. 214.

6. See, for example, Eve B. Carlson and Joseph Ruzek, *Effect of Traumatic Experiences.* http://www.ncptsd.org/facts/ general/fs_effects.html (retrieved October 2, 2001).

7. Spungen, *Homicide: The Hidden Victims.*

8. *In the Crossfire: The Impact of Gun Violence on Public Housing Communities* (Wash-

ington, D.C.: U.S. Department of Housing and Urban Development, 2000).

9. The burden of proof in a civil case is much lower than in a criminal case. In a criminal action, the prosecutor seeks proof *beyond a reasonable doubt* that the defendant is guilty of a degree of murder; the only issue in a wrongful death suit is whether it has been shown *by a preponderance of the evidence* that the defendant has caused the victim's death and is legally responsible to pay the damages. The difference is often expressed in terms of percentages. Whereas in a criminal trial we are looking for approximately 90% proof, in a civil case the burden is only 51%.

10. Office For Victims of Crime, *First Response to Victims of Crime: A Handbook for Law Enforcement Officers on How to Approach and Help Elderly Victims, Victims of Sexual Assault, Child Victims, Victims of Domestic Violence, Survivors of Homicide Victims* (Washington, D.C.: U.S. Department of Justice, 2000), p. 15.

11. Office for Victims of Crime, *First Response to Victims of Crime.*

12. S. Eth, D. A. Baron, and R. S. Pynoos, "Death Notification," *Bulletin of the American Academy of Psychiatry and the Law,* 15, 275–281 (1987).

13. Spungen, *Homicide: The Hidden Victims.*

14. Spungen, *Homicide: The Hidden Victims,* p. 205.

15. CNN.com, *Senate Fails to Take Action on Victims' Rights, Marriage Penalty Legislation.* http://www.cnn.com/2000/ALLPOLITICS/stories/04/27/victims.rights (retrieved April 27, 2001).

16. Judith Bonderman, *Working with Victims of Gun Violence* (Washington, D.C.: Office for Victims of Crime, U.S. Department of Justice, 2001).

17. Franklin E. Zimring and Gordon Hawkins, *Crime Is Not the Problem: Lethal Violence in America,* ed. Michael Tonry and Norval Morris, *Studies in Crime and Public Policy* (New York: Oxford University Press, 1997).

18. Philip J. Cook and Mark H. Moore, "Guns, Gun Control, and Homicide: A Review of Research and Public Policy," in

Homicide: A Sourcebook of Social Research, ed. M. Dwayne Smith and Margaret A. Zahn (Thousand Oaks, Calif.: Sage, 1999).

19. Michael Bowling et al., *Background Checks for Firearm Transfers, 2000* (Washington, D.C.: Bureau of Justice Statistics, U.S. Department of Justice, 2001).

20. Juliet Eilperin, "A Pivotal Election Finds NRA's Wallet Open," *Washington Post,* November 1, 2000, p. A16.

21. John Lancaster, "Hill Reaction Muted on Latest Shooting: Lawmakers Largely Silent on Gun Control," *Washington Post,* March 7, 2001, p. A10.

22. Cook and Moore cite the success of the Boston Gun Project, which was designed to curb the city's epidemic of youth gun violence. For an evaluation of this project, see David M. Kennedy, Anne M. Piehl, and Anthony A. Braga, "Youth Violence in Boston: Gun Markets, Serious Youth Offenders, and a Use-Reduction Strategy," *Law and Contemporary Problems,* 59, 147–196 (2000).

23. Kennedy et al., "Youth Violence in Boston," p. 167.

24. See H11058 of the Congressional Record, October 19, 1998, U.S. House of Representatives.

25. Cook and Moore, "Guns, Gun Control, and Homicide," p. 277.

26. His full name was Flavius Magnus Aurelius Cassiodorus, and he lived from about 485 until about 585.

27. Quoted in Elliott Currie, *Crime and Punishment in America: Why the Solutions to America's Most Stubborn Social Crisis Have Not Worked—and What Will* (New York: Metropolitan Books, 1998).

28. James Gilligan, *Violence: Our Deadly Epidemic and Its Causes* (New York: Grosset/Putnam, 1996), p. 191.

29. See, for example, William J. Bennett Jr., John J. DiIulio, and James P. Walters, *Body Count: Moral Poverty . . . And How to Win America's War against Crime and Drugs* (New York: Simon & Schuster, 1996); James Q. Wilson, *Crime and Human Nature* (New York: Free Press, 1998).

30. For a full discussion of these issues, see Currie, *Crime and Punishment in America;* Gilligan, *Violence: Our Deadly Epidemic.*

31. Elijah Anderson, *Code of the Street: Decency, Violence, and the Moral Life of the Inner City* (New York: W. W. Norton, 1999), p. 32.

32. Jonathon Gruber, *Risky Behavior among Youth: An Economic Analysis* (Chicago: University of Chicago Press, 2001).

33. William Julius Wilson, *The Truly Disadvantaged: The Inner City, the Underclass, and Public Policy* (Chicago: University of Chicago Press, 1987).

34. Naomi Lopez, *The State of Children: What Parents Should Know About Government's Efforts to Assist Children* (San Francisco: Pacific Research Institute for Public Policy, 1998).

35. G. Wolfner and Richard J. Gelles, "A Profile of Violence toward Children: A National Study," *Child Abuse and Neglect,* 17(2), 197–212 (1993).

36. Anderson, *Code of the Street,* p. 46.

37. M. Greene, "Chronic Exposure to Violence and Poverty: Interventions That Work for Youth," *Crime and Delinquency,* 39, 106–124 (1993).

38. Philippe Bourgois, *In Search of Respect: Selling Crack in El Barrio* (Cambridge, U.K.: Cambridge University Press, 1996).

39. *Furman v. Georgia,* 408 U.S. 238 (1972).

40. *Gregg v. Georgia,* 428 U.S. 153 (1976); *Jurek v. Texas,* 428 U.S. 262 (1976); *Proffitt v. Florida,* 428 U.S. 242 (1976); *S. Roberts v. Louisiana,* 428 U.S.325 (1976); *Woodson v. North Carolina,* 428 U. S. 280 (1976).

41. James S. Liebman, *A Broken System: Error Rates in Capital Cases, 1973–1995.* http://justice.policy.net/jpreport/index.html (retrieved July 15, 2001).

42. CNN.com, *Illinois Suspends Death Penalty: Governor Calls for Review of Flawed System.* http://www.cnn.com/2000/US/01/31/illinois.executions.02/index.html (retrieved January 31, 2001).

43. Since the moratorium on executions was lifted in 1977, Texas has executed about one third of the total number of convicts put to death in the country.

44. Steve Mills, Ken Armstrong, and Douglas Holt, "G. W. Bush Has Executed 131 Inmates—Many with Seriously Flawed Trials," *Chicago Tribune,* June 11, 2000, p. A01.

45. Texas Defender Service, *A State of Denial: Texas Justice and the Death Penalty.* (Houston: Texas Defender Service, 2001).

46. Gallup Organization, *Gallup Poll Topics: A–Z.* http://www.gallup.com (retrieved February 22, 2001).

47. James A. Mercy and W. Rodney Hammond, "Combining Action and Analysis to Prevent Homicide," in *Homicide: A Sourcebook of Social Research,* ed. M. Dwayne Smith and Margaret A. Zahn (Thousand Oaks, Calif.: Sage, 1999).

Index